Fourth Edition

FRENCH IS FUN

BOOK 1

Lively Lessons for Beginners

Gail Stein
Former Teacher
Foreign Language Department
New York City Schools

Heywood Wald, Ph.D.
Former Assistant Principal
Foreign Language Department
Martin Van Buren High School
New York City

AMSCO

AMSCO SCHOOL PUBLICATIONS, INC.
315 Hudson Street, New York, N.Y. 10013

Text design by Northeastern Graphic, Inc.

Cover design by Lisa Delgado

Cover art © Images.com/Corbis

Illustrations by Edward Malsberg / Noel Malsberg

Additional illustrations and maps by Hadel Studio

Electronic composition by Northeastern Graphic, Inc.

Please visit our Web site at: *www.amscopub.com*

When ordering this book, please specify:
either **R 690 P** *or* FRENCH IS FUN, BOOK 1, 4th Edition

ISBN: 978-1-56765-342-7

Printed in the United States of America

6 7 8 9   15 14 13 12

Preface

FRENCH IS FUN, BOOK 1 offers an introductory program that makes language acquisition a natural, personalized, enjoyable, and rewarding experience. The book provides all the elements for a one-year course. It incorporates and reflects the National Standards for Foreign Language Learning in the 21st century: Communication, Cultures, Connections, Comparisons, and Communities.

FRENCH IS FUN, BOOK 1 is designed to help students attain an acceptable level of proficiency in four basic skills—listening, speaking, reading, and writing—developed through simple materials in visually focused topical contexts that students can easily relate to their own experiences. Students are asked easy-to-answer questions that require them to speak about their daily lives, express their opinions, and supply real information.

The **FOURTH EDITION**, while retaining the proven organization and successful program of previous editions, has been strengthened in several ways:

1. All lesson materials are built on a clearly focused content topic.
2. Each lesson follows a consistent program sequence with a deductive learning approach.
3. Many exercises are presented in a communicative framework, with greater emphasis on personalized communication.
4. Each lesson contains listening activities focusing on students' comprehension of lexical and structural items.
5. Situational paired conversations are included in every lesson.
6. Updated *Page culturelle* sections follow each lesson and include comprehension questions.
7. A new Internet section, *La Chasse au trésor*, encourages students to do independent research based on the cultural theme of the lesson.
8. Each lesson includes alternative assessment activities.
9. Realia is used to measure student comprehension of the elements of every lesson.
10. A pronunciation section with the basic sounds of French is included to aid speaking proficiency.
11. Topical vocabulary at the end of each chapter helps students recapitulate new words acquired in the lesson.
12. Section icons make lessons easier to follow.
13. An updated separate CAHIER D'EXERCICES provides additional written practice.
14. A new Glossary of Grammatical Terms defines the basic parts of speech and grammatical terms.
15. An updated audio program to supplement the FOURTH EDITION is available separately.

FRENCH IS FUN, BOOK 1 consists of six parts. Each part contains four lessons followed by a **Révision**, in which structure is recapitulated and practiced through various *activités*. These include games and puzzles as well as more conventional exercises.

Each lesson includes a step-by-step sequence of elements designed to make the materials immediately accessible, as well as give students the feeling that they can have fun learning and practicing their French.

Vocabulary

Each lesson begins with topically related sets of drawings that convey the meanings of new words
in French without recourse to English. This device enables students to make a direct and vivid
association between the French terms and their meanings. Many of the *activités* also use pictures
to practice French words and expressions.

The lesson vocabulary, together with useful words and expressions, is glossed at the end of each
lesson.

To facilitate comprehension, the book uses cognates of English words wherever suitable, especially in the first lesson. Beginning a course in this way shows the students that French is not so
"foreign" after all, and helps them overcome any fears they may have about the difficulty of learning a foreign language.

Structures

FRENCH IS FUN, BOOK 1 uses a simple, straightforward, guided, deductive presentation of new
structural elements. These elements are introduced in small learning components—one at a
time—and are directly followed by appropriate *activités*, many of them visually cued, personalized, and communicative. Students thus gain a feeling of accomplishment and success by making their own discoveries and formulating their own conclusions.

Reading

Each lesson (after the first) contains a short, entertaining narrative or playlet that features new
structural elements and vocabulary, and reinforces previously learned grammar and expressions.
These passages deal with topics that are related to the everyday experiences of today's students.
Cognates and near-cognates are used extensively.

Conversation

To encourage students to use French for communication and self-expression, each lesson includes *Parlons français*, conversational activities that serve as springboards for additional personalized conversations. Real-life situations pertinent to the subject material of the chapter are
provided to encourage communicative learning through group work. Speaking skills will gradu-
ally improve as students become more proficient in French.

Each lesson also includes a *Conversation*—sometimes practical, sometimes humorous. All conversations are illustrated in cartoon-strip fashion to provide a sense of realism. Conversations are generally followed by dialog exercises, with students filling empty "balloons" with appropriate bits of
dialog. These activities provide the students with even more oral practice.

Alternative Assessment

Each chapter provides the teacher and students with additional exercises in *À vous*, which allow
for alternative assessment of the students' abilities. The multiple intelligences are incorporated
in many chapters through activities such as making charts and posters, playing and creating

games, drawing, and writing. The activities can be used as in-class extensions to the lessons or assigned as homework. Group work is often involved.

Realia

Authentic materials are presented in *C'est authentique!* to provide further communicative practice. Students will be able to judge their language progress through these exercises, which demonstrate the use of French in today's real world.

Culture

Each lesson is followed by a *Page culturelle*. These twenty-four readings, most of them illustrated, offer students picturesque views and insights into well-known and not so well known aspects of French culture.

Internet Activity

Each lesson ends with an Internet activity, *La Chasse au trésor*. These exercises allow students to gain further insight into different aspects of the culture of France and of francophone countries.

The Cognate Connection

Since more than half of all English words are derived from Latin, there is an important relationship between French and English vocabulary. Exercises in derivations are designed to improve the student's command of both French and English.

Glossary of Grammatical Terms

New to the FOURTH EDITION, the glossary provides simple, clear-cut definitions of the basic parts of speech and important grammatical terms.

Cahier d'exercices

FRENCH IS FUN, BOOK 1 has a companion workbook, CAHIER D'EXERCICES, which features additional writing practice and stimulating puzzles to supplement the textbook exercises. (R 6900 W)

Teacher's Manual and Key

A separate *Teacher's Manual and Key* provides suggestions for teaching all elements in the book, additional oral practice materials, teacher scripts for listening comprehension exercises, quizzes and unit tests, two achievement tests, and a complete Key to all exercises, puzzles, quizzes, and unit tests. (R 6900 TCD)

G. S.
H. W.

Contents

TROISIÈME PARTIE

QUATRIÈME PARTIE

CINQUIÈME PARTIE

1

première
partie

Le français et l'anglais

Words that are Similar in French and English;
Saying "The" in French; Making Things Plural

French is spoken by more than one hundred million people as their mother tongue, and by so many other people, that it ranks with English as a second language of communication throughout the world. Can you name some of the countries where French is spoken? Where are they? Look at the map on pages 15 and 16.

You'll have fun learning French and it will probably be easier than you think. Do you know why? Well, there are lots of words that are identical in both French and English. They may be pronounced differently, but they are spelled the same way and have exactly the same meaning. Also, there are many words that have a slightly different spelling (often just one letter) but can be recognized instantly by anyone who speaks English.

Let's look at some of them and pronounce them the French way. Your teacher will show you how.

 Words that are exactly the same in English and French:

blond	la blouse	le bureau	l'accident
cruel	la boutique	le chef	l'animal
excellent	la photo	le fruit	l'automobile
horrible	la phrase	le menu	
immense	la question	le pull-over	
important	la radio	le restaurant	
intelligent	la table	le sandwich	
sociable		le sport	
		le train	

 Here are some French words that look almost like English words. Repeat them aloud after your teacher.

confortable	la bicyclette	le criminel	l'acteur
moderne	la carotte	le docteur	l'anniversaire
ordinaire	la classe	le jardin	l'appartement
populaire	la danse	le monstre	l'artiste

3

riche	la **famille**	le **moteur**	l'**enfant**
stupide	la **guitare**	le **parc**	l'**exercice**
superbe	la **maman**	le **professeur**	
	la **musique**	le **programme**	
admirer	la **personne**	le **tigre**	
adorer	la **soupe**	le **vocabulaire**	
chanter			
danser			

Some words in French have accent marks. Accents may affect the pronunciation of a letter or the meaning of a word. Learn to recognize these accent marks:

accent aigu	(on the letter **é**)
accent grave	(on the letters **à**, **è** or **ù**)
accent circonflexe	(on the letters **â**, **ê**, **î**, **ô** or **û**)

Learn also to recognize two other marks that affect pronunciation:

cédille	(under the letter **ç**)
tréma	(on the letters **ë**, **ï**)

Be careful about placing all accent marks properly. Here are some French words that have exactly the same or almost the same spelling as English words, but also have accents:

américain	la **cathédrale**	le **bébé**	l'**éléphant**
délicieux	la **leçon**	le **café**	l'**hôpital**
différent	la **télévision**	le **président**	l'**hôtel**
élégant		le **téléphone**	l'**océan**
grillé		le **théâtre**	
intéressant	**préparer**		
nécessaire			
sincère			

Of course, there are many French words that are quite different from the English. You must memorize these words. You will probably be able to learn many of them easily by connecting them with some related English word. For example: **le poulet** (*chicken*) is related to *poultry*; **le vendeur** (*salesperson*) is related to *vendor*, a person who sells; **l'arbre** (*tree*) is related to *arbor*.

Here are some new words to add to your French vocabulary:

le cinéma

le CD

le journal

la maison

la poule

le vendeur

la femme

l'homme

la fille

le garçon

la mère/le bébé

le père

l'école

l'ami

le stylo

 Well, so much for vocabulary. Let's learn a little French grammar. Did you notice the words **le, la, l'** before all of the nouns? These three words are the French words for *the*. That's right. French has three words for *the* in the singular, **le, la,** and **l'**. The reason is that all French nouns, unlike English nouns, have GENDER. Nouns are either MASCULINE (*m*) or FEMININE (*f*).

Le is used before masculine singular nouns that start with a consonant.

La is used before feminine singular nouns that start with a consonant.

L' is used before all singular nouns that start with a vowel or with silent **h**.

Le, la, l' mean *the*. They are definite articles and refer to a specific singular noun.

How do you tell which words are masculine and which are feminine? For some words, it's easy. Obviously, **maman, mère, fille,** and **femme** are feminine, while **père, garçon,** and **homme** are masculine. But why is **programme** masculine and **maison** feminine? There really is no logical reason. So, the only way to learn French nouns is with the word for *the*. You don't memorize **tigre** but *le tigre*, not **musique** but *la musique*, and so on.

Activités

A. Listen to your friends' opinions and check whether they are positive or negative. You will hear the word **est** in each sentence. **Est** means *is*.

	+	−		+	−
1.	____	____	4.	____	____
2.	____	____	5.	____	____
3.	____	____	6.	____	____

B. What are your friends describing? Place a check mark under the correct category.

1.	____	____	____
2.	____	____	____
3.	____	____	____
4.	____	____	____
5.	____	____	____
6.	____	____	____

C. Listen to your teacher read the professions of five people. Match the person with his/her work place.

1.	M. Dupont	____	a.	le restaurant
2.	Angèle Legrand	____	b.	le théâtre
3.	Mme Restaud	____	c.	le bureau
4.	Georges Pierrot	____	d.	l'hôpital
5.	Jean-Claude Dominique	____	e.	l'école

D. Work with a partner. Take turns. Give your opinion by completing each sentence with one or more of the adjectives listed below. Then write your answers in complete sentences.

confortable	cruel	intéressant	immense
riche	important	horrible	élégant

1. Le professeur est _____ .

2. Le train est _____ .

3. L'acteur est _____ .

4. Le parc est _____ .

5. Le tigre est _____ .

6. Le président est _____ .

7. L'hôtel est _____ .

8. L'artiste est _____ .

E. Work with a partner. Using the words given below, ask each other to describe yourself. Follow the model.

populaire	sociable	moderne
intelligent	sincère	superbe

EXAMPLE: You: **Comment es-tu?** *(What are you like?)*
                Partner: **Je suis sociable.** *(I am friendly.)*

F. Now let's see if you can figure out the meanings of these ten sentences. Repeat them aloud after your teacher.

1. **Le professeur est intéressant.**

2. **Le menu est excellent.**

3. **Le sandwich est grillé.**

4. **La famille est riche.**

5. Le garçon est sociable.

6. L'artiste est populaire.

7. L'acteur est élégant.

8. L'appartement est confortable.

9. L'éléphant est immense.

10. L'hôtel est superbe.

G. You have decided to clean your room. Label the objects you have to pick up.

| la guitare | le journal | le stylo |
| le téléphone | le pull-over | la photo |

1. _____

2. _____

3. _____   4. _____

5. _____   6. _____

H. Here are some places you could visit today. Label the pictures and make sure to use **le, la,** or **l'.**

1. _____   2. _____   3. _____

4. _____   5. _____   6. _____

7. _____   8. _____

I. Here are some things you see as you walk along the street. Use **le, la,** or **l'** to identify what you observe.

1. _____ parc   5. _____ homme   8. _____ personne
2. _____ automobile   6. _____ restaurant   9. _____ boutique
3. _____ table   7. _____ cinéma   10. _____ enfant
4. _____ jardin

 When we speak about more than one person or thing, we must use the PLURAL. How do we change nouns from the singular to the plural in French? Let's see if you can figure out the easy rules. Look carefully:

I	II
le fruit	les fruits
le restaurant	les restaurants
le docteur	les docteurs
la photo	les photos
la fille	les filles
la famille	les familles
l'acteur	les acteurs
l'enfant	les enfants
l'hôtel	les hôtels

Now compare the two groups of nouns. Which letter did we add to the nouns in Group II? _____ If you wrote the letter **s**, you are correct. Here's the first rule:

For most French nouns, just add the letter **s** to the singular form of a noun to make it plural.

Now let's look at one exception to this rule:

le fils (*the son*)   **les fils** (*the sons*)

How do you make a French noun plural if it already ends in **s**?

_____

Now underline all the words in Group I that mean *the*. Look carefully at Group II, do the same, and fill in the rest of the rule:

The plural form of **le** is _____ .
The plural form of **la** is _____ .
The plural form of **l'** is _____ .
les means _____ . It is a definite
article and refers to a specific plural noun.

7 Some nouns do not add **s** to form their plurals. Look at these exceptions:

le bureau   les bureau*x*
l'animal   les anim*aux*
l'hôpital   les hôpit*aux*
le journal   les journ*aux*

Most nouns ending in **-eau** add _____ to form the plural.
Most nouns ending in **-al** change **-al** to _____ in the plural.

8 Remember, there are four words for *the* in French: **le, la, l', les.**

When do you use **le?** _____

             la? _____

             l'? _____

            les? _____

Activités

J. Here are some things you may see every day. Label them by using the correct word for *the* in French.

1. _____ famille
2. _____ maison
3. _____ océan
4. _____ sandwich

5. _____ bureaux
6. _____ restaurant
7. _____ journal
8. _____ professeurs

9. _____ enfants
10. _____ fille
11. _____ classe
12. _____ animaux

K. You are comparing many things. Express that you are looking at more than one of them by using the plural.

EXAMPLE: (Je regarde) l'enfant   **les enfants**

1. l'artiste _____
2. le cinéma _____

3. la question _____
4. le parc _____

5. l'hôtel _____   8. le journal _____

6. l'exercice _____   9. le bureau _____

7. le fils _____   10. la photo _____

CONVERSATION

Vocabulaire

bonjour hello
Comment t'appelles-tu?
   What's your name?
Je m'appelle My name is

Comment ça va?
   How are you?
très bien very well
merci thanks

et toi and you
à bientôt see you soon
à demain till tomorrow
au revoir good-bye

Parlons français

Work with a partner. Using the conversation that you just read, introduce yourselves, ask each other how you are, and then say good-bye.

EXAMPLE: You: **Bonjour. Comment ça va?**
            Partner: **Bien, merci. Comment t'appelles-tu?**

Salutations! *(Greetings!)*

Here are some pictures of people talking to each other. Can you figure out what they are saying?

Bonjour, Catherine.
Bonjour, Michel.

Salut, Philippe!
Salut! Ça va?

Lise! Comment vas-tu?
Très bien, Danielle. Et toi?

Je m'appelle Claire.
Enchanté, Mademoiselle!

Comment t'appelles-tu?
Je m'appelle Pierre.

Comment s'appelle le garçon?
Il s'appelle Jacques.

Bonsoir, Monsieur.
Bonsoir, Madame.

Merci beaucoup.
De rien.

Au revoir, Solange.
À demain, Sylvie.

Prononciation

Some accents or other marks make a difference in how you pronounce a letter.

- An accent aigu ´ is seen only on the letter **e**. **é** has the sound *ay* as in *Ray*. **é** sometimes replaces an **s** that was used in old French.

   épice *spice*   **éponge** *sponge*   **état** *state*   **étrange** *strange*

- An accent grave ` may be used on **a, e,** or **u** in the word **où.** It doesn't change the sound of the **a** or **u.** An **è,** however, has the sound *eh* as the **e** in *get.*

élève   Hélène   célèbre   sévère   préfère   répète

- An accent circonflexe ^ may be used on all vowels. It sometimes indicates a long vowel. It may replace an **s** that was used in old French.

forêt *forest*   **île** *island*   **hôpital** *hospital*   **coûter** *to cost*

- A cédille ¸ is used only on a **c** (**ç**) before **a, o,** and **u** to create a soft **s** sound.

ça   garçon   commençons   leçon   déçu   reçu

- A tréma ¨ may be used on the second of two vowels that are next to each other. The tréma tells you to pronounce each vowel separately.

Noël   Haïti   Loïc   Israël

Page culturelle

La francophonie *(French-speaking world)*

Why learn French? The answer is simple. Look at the maps and you will see why French is a language that can be used throughout the world. Did you know that two hundred million people speak French every day? French is spoken not only in France but also on all seven continents and in over fifty countries where it is the first, second, or third language. Twenty-eight countries use French as their official language and French is an official working language of the United Nations, UNESCO, NATO, the International Red Cross, and other international organizations.

FRANCE AND HER NEIGHBORS. Of course French is spoken in France, but it is also the major language of several of its European neighbors: Belgium, Luxembourg, Switzerland, Monaco, Corsica (a mountainous Mediterranean island that is part of France), and Andorra (a small country that borders Spain and France).

NORTH AMERICA. According to U.S. census figures from the year 2000, French is spoken by 1.6 million Americans over the age of five at home. During the seventeenth century, French settlers lived in Acadie in eastern Canada. In 1755, when the British took possession of that territory, the Acadians left and went on to colonize Louisiana. Today, many of the traditions and customs of their ancestors are practiced by Cajuns, descendants of French-speaking Acadian settlers.

In Canada, about one third of the population speaks French. Many descendants of French colonists live in Quebec, where French has been the official language since 1977. According to the 2006 Census, 95% of Quebec's inhabitants speak French as

LA LANGUE FRANÇAISE DANS LE MONDE

their first, second, or third language. These people maintain and promote their language, traditions, and cultural identity. For that reason, French influence can be observed everywhere throughout the province. After Paris, Montréal is the second-largest French-speaking city in the world.

Saint-Pierre-et-Miquelon is a French territorial collectivity.

THE CARIBBEAN and SOUTH AMERICA. In the Greater Antilles, the French-speaking population of Haiti shares the island of Hispañola with the Spanish-speaking Dominican Republic. Although Haiti is totally independent from France, French is the official language and French influence plays an important role in Haitian life. In Haiti, most people speak Creole, a French dialect influenced by African elements.

Martinique and Guadeloupe, overseas subdivisions of France, are known as Départements d'Outre-Mer (D.O.M.). The people living there are French citizens and have the same rights, privileges, laws, government, system of education, and responsibilities as

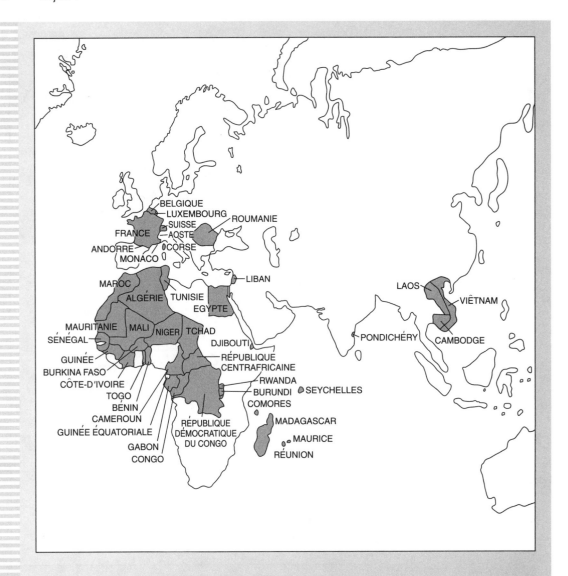

French citizens in France. Some small islands near Guadeloupe (Les Saintes, Marie Galante, La Désirade, St. Barthélemy, and St. Martin) belong to the same administrative subdivision.

Did you know that French is spoken in South America in just one country? In French Guiana, an overseas French subdivision, French is the official language and the residents are French citizens.

IN AFRICA, the island of Réunion is an overseas department of France, and Mayotte is a French territorial collectivity administered by France. In many of the former African colonies that are now independent, French is still the official language. These countries have kept close cultural and economic ties with France. French is often used as a common language between varied ethnic groups. The French government provides these nations with financial and technical assistance. Algeria, Morocco, and Tunisia belong to a region called the Mahgreb (the setting sun). Arabic is the official language of these countries, but the people continue to use French and have institutions and school systems that are based on those originally established by the French. French is spoken in 19 other countries in Africa, including Senegal and the Ivory Coast.

THE FAR AND MIDDLE EAST. In Indochina, French culture still exists in Vietnam, Laos, and Cambodia, even though these countries are independent from France. In the Middle East, French is spoken by many people in Lebanon and Egypt.

Tahiti and New Caledonia, islands in the Pacific Ocean, are overseas territories of France. The people of these islands maintain close ties with France, but have no voice in French politics.

Rappel

Complete the sentences.

1. In the United States, French is spoken in _____ .

2. _____ is a neighboring country to the U.S. where French is spoken.

3. Three European countries where French is spoken are: _____ , _____ , and _____ .

4. If you want to take a vacation on a French-speaking island you might go to _____ .

5. French is spoken on _____ continents.

À vous

1. Write a T.V. or radio commercial advertising a trip to a French-speaking country.

2. Create a collage of places to visit in different French-speaking countries.

3. Make a travel poster encouraging tourists to visit the French-speaking country of your choice.

La Chasse au trésor

http:

Using your best Internet search skills, find the answers to the following questions:

1. Who are the President and Prime Minister of France?
2. Where is French spoken in Canada?
3. What tourist attractions can you see in Haiti?
4. What is the capital of Senegal?

5. Which famous 18th century French ruler married a woman who was born in Martinique? What was her name?

6. What is the *Organisation internationale de la Francophonie*? When was it created and how many countries are members?

C'est authentique!

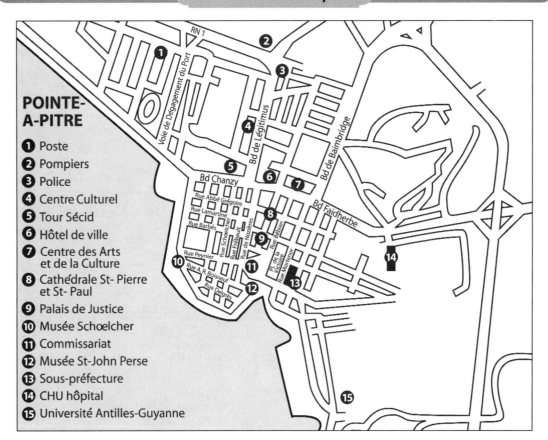

POINTE-A-PITRE

❶ Poste
❷ Pompiers
❸ Police
❹ Centre Culturel
❺ Tour Sécid
❻ Hôtel de ville
❼ Centre des Arts et de la Culture
❽ Cathédrale St- Pierre et St- Paul
❾ Palais de Justice
❿ Musée Schoelcher
⓫ Commissariat
⓬ Musée St-John Perse
⓭ Sous-préfecture
⓮ CHU hôpital
⓯ Université Antilles-Guyanne

Imagine that you took a trip to Pointe-à-Pitre, the capital of Guadeloupe, an island in the Caribbean Sea. Look at the map and write the number(s) of where you would go if

a. you became ill.   _____

b. you wanted to visit a museum.   _____

c. you wanted to learn more about culture.   _____

d. you wanted to see a church.   _____

e. you wanted to tour the university.   _____

MOTS NÉCESSAIRES

NOUNS

la bicyclette bicycle
la famille family
la femme woman
la fille girl, daughter
la leçon lesson
la maison house
la mère mother

l'acteur *m.* actor
l'ami *m.* friend
l'école *f.* school
l'éléphant *m.* elephant
l'homme *m.* man

le bébé baby
le cinéma movies
le docteur doctor
le fils son
le garçon boy

le jardin garden
le journal newspaper, journal
le père father
le professeur teacher
le vendeur salesman

ADJECTIVES

délicieux delicious
grillé grilled
intéressant interesting

EXPRESSIONS

à bientôt see you soon
à demain until tomorrow
au revoir good-bye
Ça va? How are you?
Comment t'appelles-tu?
   What's your name?
Je m'appelle My name is
pas mal not bad

ARTICLES

ce *m.* this, that
l' *m.* or *f.* the
la *f.* the
le *m.* the
les *m./f. pl.* the

IMPORTANT WORDS

bien well
bonjour hello
comment how
est (**être** to be) is
et and
merci thank you
salut! *hi!*
toi you
très very

La classe et l'école

Saying "A" and "Some."

 Vocabulaire–La salle de classe

Say the following words aloud after your teacher.

le professeur

le professeur

l'élève / l'étudiant

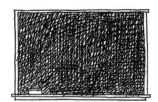

l'élève / l'étudiante

la leçon

le tableau (noir)

le drapeau

le bureau

la fenêtre

la porte

la note

les devoirs

Activité

A. It's your first day in the new school year. Identify what you see in the classroom by writing the letter next to the correct number. Listen to your teacher.

a.

b.

c.

d.

e.

f.

1. _____   2. _____   3. _____

4. _____   5. _____   6. _____

 Here are some more words for you to say aloud.

Le matériel scolaire
Qu'est ce que c'est? *What is it?* **C'est . . .** *it's*

le classeur

le papier
la feuille de papier

le crayon

la craie
le bâton de craie

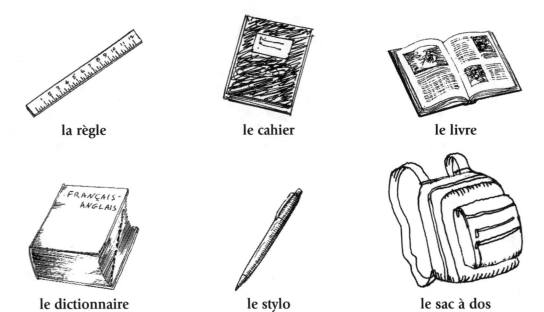

la règle   le cahier   le livre

le dictionnaire   le stylo   le sac à dos

Activités

B. Work with a partner. Practice asking for the names of school supplies and giving the answers.

EXAMPLE: You: **Qu'est-ce que c'est?** (*show notebook*).
Partner: **C'est le cahier. Qu'est ce que c'est?** (*show ruler*).

C. Identify the contents of Bernard's bookbag.

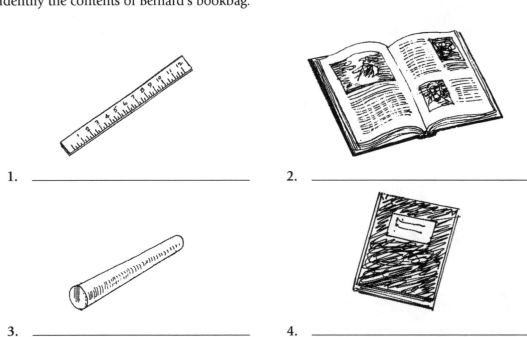

1. _____   2. _____

3. _____   4. _____

5. _____   6. _____

7. _____   8. _____

D. Dominique is studying for his first French test. Help him correctly group the vocabulary words.

élève	bureaux	professeurs	porte
élèves	cahier	tableau	stylo
note	école	livre	fenêtre
leçon	règle	dictionnaire	crayons

LE   LA   L'   LES

_____   _____   _____   _____

_____   _____   _____   _____

_____   _____   _____   _____

_____   _____   _____   _____

_____   _____   _____   _____

3 What are you studying in school this term? See if you can identify the subjects.

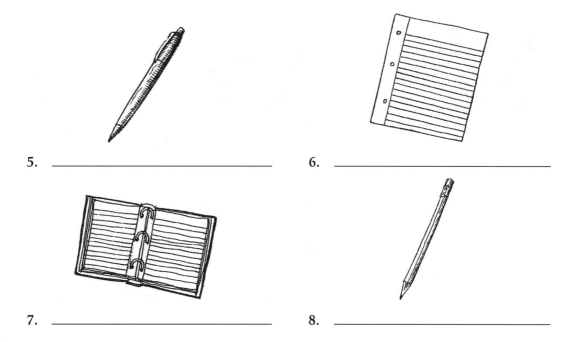

les sciences *f.*   les mathématiques *f.*   le français

l'anglais *m.*

l'histoire *f.*

l'éducation physique *f.*

l'informatique *f.*

l'art *m.*

la musique

Activités

E. Your friend is reading a list of subjects he's taking. Match them with the clues below.

a.  _____

b.  _____

c.  _____

d.  _____

e. 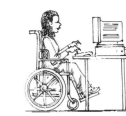 _____

f. 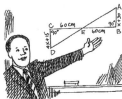 _____

g.  _____

h. 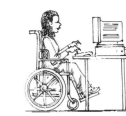 _____

F. Write a list of the subjects you have this term.

J'ai (*I have*)

_____   _____

_____   _____

G. Express how you feel about your classes.

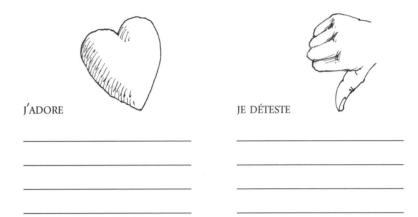

J'ADORE   JE DÉTESTE

_____   _____

_____   _____

_____   _____

_____   _____

 Au travail! *(Let's work!)*

Read these classroom commands after your teacher.

Écrivez!	Write!
Écoutez!	Listen!
Lisez!	Read!
Répétez!	Repeat!
Levez-vous!	Stand up!
Asseyez-vous!	Sit!
Levez la main!	Raise your hand!
Répondez à la question!	Answer the question!
Allez au tableau!	Go to the board!
Complétez la phrase!	Complete the sentence!
Corrigez l'exercice!	Correct the exercise!
Prenez une feuille de papier!	Take a piece of paper!
Ouvrez le livre!	Open the book!
Fermez le livre!	Close the book!
Faites attention!	Pay attention!
Parlez plus fort!	Speak louder!
Étudiez le vocabulaire!	Study the vocabulary!

Activités

H. Listen to each command M. Carnet gives his class. Put the number of the command under the corresponding picture.

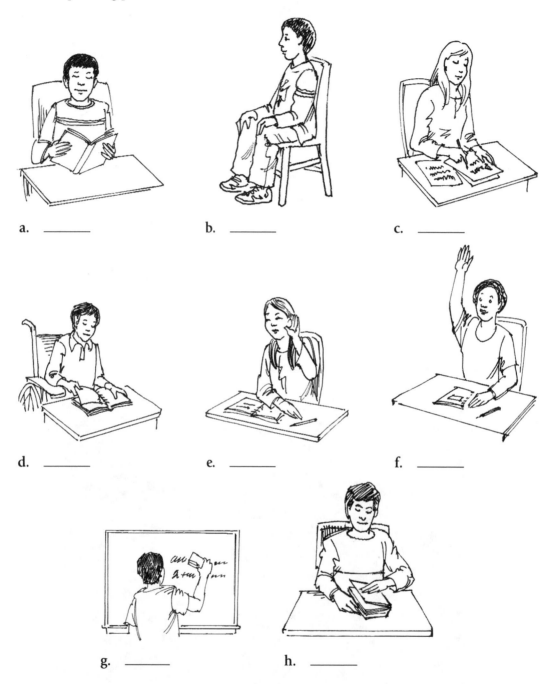

a. _____   b. _____   c. _____

d. _____   e. _____   f. _____

g. _____   h. _____

I. Work with a partner. Take turns playing the role of the teacher and the student. Tell each other what to do in the classroom and act out the commands.

EXAMPLE: You: **Asseyez-vous!**
           Partner: **Allez au tableau!**

J. Write the command under the activity.

1. _____

2. _____

3. _____

4. _____

5. _____

6. _____

K. Write a list of commands your teacher might give when going over the homework.

1. _____

2. _____

3. _____

4. _____

Prononciation

- Most final consonants in French are not pronounced.

    sport   leçon   restaurant   dessert   délicieux   blond

- Use the consonants in *c a r e f u l* to help you remember to pronounce most final *c, r, f,* and *l* sounds.

lac	bonjour	chef	il
parc	tour	neuf	animal
avec	docteur	sportif	Michel

 Now that you know all of the new words, read the following story and see if you can understand it.

La classe de français.

À l'école il y a **une** classe de français. La classe est intéressante. Le professeur de français est Mme Lefarge. Mme Lefarge est **une** personne intelligente. En classe, les élèves se servent d'**un** stylo, d'**un** crayon, d'**un** bâton de craie et d'**un** livre de français. Il y a un tableau noir. Le grand livre sur le bureau de Mme Lefarge est **un** dictionnaire.

à at   un, une a, an
  de of   français French
Mme (= madame) Mrs.
se servent d' use
Il y a there is
grand big

Il y a beaucoup d'élèves dans la classe. Roger est **un** élève populaire. Pourquoi? Le père de Roger est directeur de l'école. Marie est **une** élève populaire aussi. Pourquoi? Parce que la mère de Marie est championne de karaté. Tous les élèves respectent Roger et Marie. Naturellement ils ont beaucoup d'amis.

beaucoup de a lot of
  dans in
pourquoi why
  le directeur the principal
aussi also
  parce que because
tous all
naturellement naturally
  amis friends
sympathique nice

Les élèves adorent la classe de français. Le français est **une** langue populaire et Mme Lefarge est **un** professeur sympathique.

Activités

L. Complete each sentence about the story.

1. La classe de _____ est intéressante.

2. Le professeur est une personne _____ .

3. _____ est le professeur.

4. En classe les élèves se servent d'_____ , d'_____ ,
   d'_____ et d'_____ .

5. Un dictionnaire est un grand _____ .

6. Le père de Roger est _____ .

7. La mère de Marie est _____ .

8. Les élèves populaires ont beaucoup d' _____ .

9. Les élèves _____ la classe de français.

10. Le français est une langue _____ .

M. How would you describe the people and things in the story? Form sentences by matching the adjectives with the nouns they describe.

EXAMPLE: Le livre/grand   **Le livre est grand.**

1. La classe _____ .   grand

2. Mme Lefarge _____ .   populaire

3. Le dictionnaire _____ .   intelligente

4. Le français _____ .   sympathique

5. Le professeur _____ .   intéressante

5 Look at the story again. There are two little words that appear many times.

What are these two new words? _____ and _____ . These are the words for *a* and *an* in French. Can you figure out when to use **un** and when to use **une?** Look carefully.

I	II
le tableau noir	*un* tableau noir
le livre	*un* livre
le dictionnaire	*un* dictionnaire
*l'*élève	*un* élève

Let's start by comparing the two groups of words. In Group I, are the nouns singular or plural? _____ How do you know? _____

Are the nouns in Group I masculine or feminine? _____

How do you know? _____

What does **le** mean? _____

Now look at Group II. Which word has replaced **le?** _____

What does **un** mean? _____

6 Now look at these examples.

I	II
la classe	*une* classe
la personne	*une* personne
la règle	*une* règle

Are the nouns in Group I singular or plural? _____

How do you know? _____

Are the nouns in Group I masculine or feminine? _____

How do you know? _____

What does **la** mean? _____ Now look at Group II. Which word has replaced **la?** _____ What

does **une** mean? _____

7   Let's try one more group:

I	II
les livres	*des* livres
les classes	*des* classes
les élèves	*des* élèves

Are the nouns in Group I singular or plural? _____

How do you know? _____

Are the nouns in Group I masculine or feminine? _____

Is there any clue to help you figure out the gender of the nouns? _____

What does **les** mean? _____ Now look at Group II. Which word has replaced **les?** _____ What

does **des** mean? _____

Un, une, and **des** are indefinite articles. Indefinite articles refer to things or people not specifically identified.

> **un** is used before masculine singular nouns to express *a* or *an.*
> **une** is used before feminine singular nouns to express *a* or *an.*
> **des** is used before masculine and feminine plural nouns to express *"some."*

> To make most French nouns plural, simply add **s** to the noun.

Activités

N. Listen to your teacher read some words using LE, LA, or LES. Check whether you would replace them with UN, UNE, or DES.

	UN	UNE	DES		UN	UNE	DES
1.	_____	_____	_____	**5.**	_____	_____	_____
2.	_____	_____	_____	**6.**	_____	_____	_____
3.	_____	_____	_____	**7.**	_____	_____	_____
4.	_____	_____	_____	**8.**	_____	_____	_____

O. Here are some people and things you find in a classroom. Match the descriptions with the pictures.

des papiers   des cahiers   un élève
des élèves   une porte   des règles
un professeur   une fenêtre   un bureau

1. _____   2. _____   3. _____

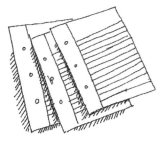

4. _____   5. _____   6. _____

7. _____   8. _____   9. _____

In our story about **la classe de français**, you may have noticed something special about these two sentences:

> **La mère de Marie est championne de karaté.**
> **Le père de Roger est directeur de l'école.**

> We do not use **un** or **une** with a trade, occupation, or profession.

But: **Mme Lefarge est *un professeur sympathique.***

> The indefinite article **un** or **une** is used when a trade, occupation, or profession is accompanied by an adjective.

M. Robert est *professeur*.
M. Robert est *un professeur populaire*.
Mademoiselle Dupont est *secrétaire*.
Mademoiselle Dupont est *une secrétaire excellente*.

Mr. Robert is a teacher.
Mr. Robert is a popular teacher.
Miss Dupont is a secretary.
Miss Dupont is an excellent secretary.

Activités

P. Describe the professions of these people by completing the sentences with **un** or **une** if it is necessary.

1. Mme Détroit est _____ dentiste populaire.

2. Julie est _____ secrétaire.

3. La mère de Pierre est _____ artiste.

4. Le père de Philippe est _____ docteur important.

5. Jean est _____ acteur excellent.

6. Il est _____ président.

Q. You've been practicing your vocabulary. Underline the expression that does not belong in each group.

1. une porte, une fenêtre, un océan, un tableau

2. le crayon, le stylo, le cahier, le café

3. intelligent, excellent, intéressant, stupide

4. l'élève, le fruit, la carotte, le sandwich

5. un train, une bicyclette, un jardin, une auto

6. le menu, l'école, l'université, la classe

CONVERSATION

Vocabulaire

Comment allez-vous?
   How are you?
nous avons we have
ça ne fait rien
   it doesn't matter

aujourd'hui today
demain tomorrow
tu es you are
est-ce is it

difficile difficult
facile easy
bien sûr of course
bonne chance good luck

Parlons français

You are babysitting for your little cousin who wants to play school. Working with a partner, take turns playing the role of the teacher and that of the student. Follow the example and ask about the school supplies you need for various subjects.

EXAMPLE: You: **Pour les maths, il faut quoi?** *(For math what do you need?)*
Partner: **Il faut une règle.** *(You need a ruler.)*

DIALOGUE

Bien, merci!   Comment allez-vous?   Très bien.
Bonne chance!   C'est très facile.   préparé
Ça ne fait rien.   ma classe préférée   difficile
Bien sûr.   un examen   demain

Page culturelle

La vie scolaire *(school life)*

LES ÉCOLES EN FRANCE

LE PRIMAIRE

L'école maternelle (enfants âgés de 2 à 6 ans)
Nursery School and Kindergarten

L'école primaire (enfants âgés de 6 à 10 ans)
Elementary School, Grades 1 to 5

LE SECONDAIRE

Le collège
Middle School, Grades 6 to 9

The students, who are 11 to 14 years old, are evaluated during the last two years of **le collège**. Then they go either to **le lycée professionnel** (or **L.P.**) or to **le lycée**.

Le lycée professionnel (L.P.) Vocational High School	**Le lycée** High School
The students (15 to 17 years old) prepare for an apprenticeship or a job	The students (15 to 17 years old) prepare for a college education and a profession. At the end of the **lycée**, students take a difficult final examination called **le baccalauréat (le bac)** that determines if they are eligible to attend a university. About 75% pass the test.

L'UNIVERSITÉ
****

Note how French grade levels are numbered:

	ÂGE	CLASSE		= U.S.
École primaire	6	cours primaire	CP	1st
	7	cours élémentaire 1	CE1	2nd
	8	cours élémentaire 2	CE2	3rd
	9	cours moyen 1	CM1	4th
	10	cours moyen 2	CM2	5th
Collège	11	sixième	6e	6th
	12	cinquième	5e	7th
	13	quatrième	4e	8th
	14	troisième	3e	9th
Lycée	15	seconde	2e	10th
	16	première	1re	11th
	17	terminale	Ter	12th

In which school and grade would you be in France?

Rappel

Complete the sentences.

1. The French equivalent of nursery school is _____ .

2. A French elementary school is called _____ .

3. The French equivalent of middle school is _____ .

4. In France, students studying a trade in high school go to a _____ .

5. After finishing the lycée, a French student must pass a test called the _____
    _____ to go to the university.

À Vous

1. Find out what is tested on the French **baccalauréat**.

2. Find out how life in a French school is different from what you are accustomed to.

La Chasse au trésor

 http://

Using your best Internet search skills, find the answers to the following questions:

1. What weekday is free or a half day in French schools?
2. Which day may French students have class that American students don't?
3. How long is the typical French school day?
4. What is "le Brevet" and when is it taken?
5. What is the name of the famous French university in Paris?
6. How are French schools named? Give an example.

C'est authentique!

What school supplies do these ads offer?

Authentique
sac à dos japonais
en cuir synthétique à
soufflets et poches
zippées,
très résistant
(118 €)

Sac de sport
Toile enduite P.V.C. et
bandoulière
(35 €)

1. _____   2. _____   3. _____   4. _____

MOTS NÉCESSAIRES

SCHOOL

le bâton de craie piece of chalk
le bureau desk
le cahier notebook
le classeur loose-leaf notebook
le crayon pencil
les devoirs *m. pl.* homework
le dictionnaire dictionary
le drapeau flag
l'élève *m.* or *f.* student
l'étudiant *m.* student
l'étudiante *f.* student
la fenêtre window
la feuille de papier sheet/piece of paper
le livre book
le matériel scolaire school supplies
la note grade
le papier paper
la porte door
la règle ruler
le sac à dos backpack
la salle de classe *f.* classroom
le stylo pen
le tableau (noir) blackboard

SCHOOL SUBJECTS

l'anglais *m.* English
l'art *m.* art
l'éducation physique *f.* gym, physical education
le français French
l'histoire *f.* history
l'informatique *f.* computer science
la langue language
les mathématiques *f. pl.* mathematics
la musique *f.* music
les sciences *f. pl.* science

IMPORTANT WORDS

à at, to
beaucoup de many, much, a lot of
c'est it is
dans in
des some
Mme (madame) Mrs.
parce que because
Qu'est-ce que c'est? What is it?
sympathique nice
un, une a, an, one

VERBS

adorer to adore, love
allez (aller to go**)** go
asseyez-vous (s'asseoir to sit**)** sit down
complétez (compléter to complete**)** complete
corrigez (corriger to correct**)** correct
détester to hate
écoutez (écouter to listen**)** listen
écrivez (écrire to write**)** write
faites attention (faire to do**)** pay attention
fermez (fermer to close**)** close
lever to raise
levez-vous (se lever to stand up**)** stand up
lisez (lire to read**)** read
ouvrez (ouvrir to open**)** open
prenez (prendre to take**)** take
répétez (répéter to repeat**)** repeat
répondez (répondre to answer**)** answer
se servir de to use

Un, deux, trois . . .

Counting in French

1 Repeat the numbers aloud after your teacher:

0	zéro				
1	un, une	11	onze	21	vingt et un
2	deux	12	douze	22	vingt-deux
3	trois	13	treize	23	vingt-trois
4	quatre	14	quatorze	24	vingt-quatre
5	cinq	15	quinze	25	vingt-cinq
6	six	16	seize	26	vingt-six
7	sept	17	dix-sept	27	vingt-sept
8	huit	18	dix-huit	28	vingt-huit
9	neuf	19	dix-neuf	29	vingt-neuf
10	dix	20	vingt	30	trente

Activités

A. Your teacher will read some numbers to you. Write the numerals for the number you hear.

EXAMPLE: You hear: **vingt.**   You write: **20**

1. _____   4. _____   7. _____

2. _____   5. _____   8. _____

3. _____   6. _____   9. _____

B. Work with a partner. Take turns giving a number in English and responding with the number in French.

EXAMPLE: You: Four.
            Partner: **Quatre.** Eleven.

C. Match the French number with the numeral.

1   14   20   11   8   21   5   12   3   16   2   10   15   7   19

1.	trois	_____	6.	quatorze	_____	11.	sept	_____
2.	dix	_____	7.	vingt	_____	12.	vingt et un	_____
3.	huit	_____	8.	seize	_____	13.	un	_____
4.	cinq	_____	9.	quinze	_____	14.	deux	_____
5.	douze	_____	10.	dix-neuf	_____	15.	onze	_____

D. Laure wants to play the lottery and has made a list of her lucky numbers. Write them in French.

7   _____   16   _____

11   _____   23   _____

12   _____   21   _____

29   _____   14   _____

26   _____   13   _____

15   _____   18   _____

2 Now that you know the French numbers from 0 to 30, let's try some arithmetic in French. First you must learn the following expressions.

et	*plus*	(+)
moins	*minus*	(−)
fois	*times*	(×)
divisé par	*divided by*	(÷)
font	*are, equals*	(=)

EXAMPLES:
$3 + 2 = 5$ **trois et deux font cinq**
$5 - 4 = 1$ **cinq moins quatre font un**
$4 \times 4 = 16$ **quatre fois quatre font seize**
$12 \div 2 = 6$ **douze divisé par deux font six**

Activités

E. Read the following numbers in French. Then write out each problem in numerals.

1. Cinq et cinq font dix. _____

2. Vingt moins cinq font quinze. _____

3. Neuf fois deux font dix-huit. _____

4. Quatre divisé par deux font deux. _____

5. Six et trois font neuf. _____

6. Dix-sept moins seize font un. _____

7. Onze fois un font onze. _____

8. Vingt divisé par cinq font quatre. _____

9. Dix-huit divisé par deux font neuf. _____

10. Dix et six font seize. _____

F. Write the following examples in French, then read them aloud.

1. $21 + 3 = 24$ _____

2. $19 - 2 = 17$ _____

3. $4 \times 7 = 28$ _____

4. $8 \div 4 = 2$ _____

5. $12 + 3 = 15$ _____

6. $30 - 5 = 25$ _____

7. $6 \times 5 = 30$ _____

8. $16 \div 2 = 8$ _____

9. $10 + 13 = 23$ _____

10. $28 - 7 = 21$ _____

G. Complete the math problems in French.

1. Treize et sept font _____

2. Trente moins onze font _____

3. Quatre fois six font _____

4. Quinze divisé par cinq font _____

5. Dix et cinq font _____

6. Vingt-neuf moins dix-sept font _____

7. Vingt moins douze font _____

8. Sept fois trois font _____

9. Seize moins douze font _____

10. Vingt et dix font _____

Study and practice the numbers to 100.

40 quarante
50 cinquante
60 soixante

70 soixante-dix	80 quatre-vingts	90 quatre-vingt-dix
71 soixante et onze	81 quatre-vingt-un	91 quatre-vingt-onze
72 soixante-douze	82 quatre-vingt-deux	92 quatre-vingt-douze
73 soixante-treize	83 quatre-vingt-trois	93 quatre-vingt-treize
74 soixante-quatorze	84 quatre-vingt-quatre	94 quatre-vingt-quatorze
75 soixante-quinze	85 quatre-vingt-cinq	95 quatre-vingt-quinze
76 soixante-seize	86 quatre-vingt-six	96 quatre-vingt-seize
77 soixante-dix-sept	87 quatre-vingt-sept	97 quatre-vingt-dix-sept
78 soixante-dix-huit	88 quatre-vingt-huit	98 quatre-vingt-dix-huit
79 soixante-dix-neuf	89 quatre-vingt-neuf	99 quatre-vingt-dix-neuf
		100 cent

Activités

H. **La téléphoniste.** The telephone operator would like you to repeat some numbers in French. You reply: **Madame, donnez-moi le numéro . . .**

EXAMPLE: 01 44 56 32 78   zéro un; quarante-quatre; cinquante-six; trente-deux; soixante-dix-huit

1. 01 48 79 46 21
2. 02 67 37 34 56
3. 04 35 55 67 43
4. 03 24 16 12 66

I. The winning lottery numbers are being read. Write them down and check them against your ticket.

J. Circle the number being read to you.

1. 67 16 66 76	3. 100 16 20 50	5. 37 27 47 57
2. 80 24 44 90	4. 82 72 92 62	6. 13 30 16 60

K. Match the French numbers with the numerals. Write the matching numeral.

63   59   28   34   93   100   47   13   72   83

1. quatre-vingt-treize   _____   6. quarante-sept   _____
2. soixante-douze   _____   7. vingt-huit   _____
3. cinquante-neuf   _____   8. soixante-trois   _____
4. trente-quatre   _____   9. quatre-vingt-trois   _____
5. cent   _____   10. treize   _____

L. Say the following numbers aloud and write the matching numeral.

1. quatre-vingts   _____   7. quatre-vingt-cinq   _____
2. trente-deux   _____   8. quinze   _____
3. douze   _____   9. onze   _____
4. soixante-huit   _____   10. seize   _____
5. cinquante-six   _____   11. treize   _____
6. quatorze   _____   12. dix-sept   _____

M. You have seen that the numbers from 70 to 99 are tricky. Can you recognize these numbers and write the numerals?

1. quatre-vingt-neuf   _____   6. quatre-vingt-dix   _____
2. soixante et un   _____   7. quatre-vingt-seize   _____
3. quatre-vingt-huit   _____   8. soixante-dix   _____
4. quatre-vingt-quinze   _____   9. soixante et onze   _____
5. soixante-six   _____   10. soixante-quatorze   _____

Here is a story about an auction. Auctions can be fun, but be careful. Read the story and then answer the questions about it.

VENDEUR: Voici un tableau exceptionnel. C'est l'œuvre d'un artiste très célèbre, Paul Soupe-de-Poisson. Le tableau s'appelle «Un chien mange du gâteau dans son lit».

TOUT LE MONDE: Aaaaah!

ANDRÉ: Ce tableau est horrible.

SYLVIE: Il est monstrueux.

VENDEUR: Bon. Qui désire ce tableau extraordinaire? Qui me donne cinquante euros?

ACHETEUR nº1 :   Cinquante euros.

ACHETEUR nº2 :   Soixante euros.

un tableau a picture, a painting
  l'œuvre f. the work
célèbre famous
mange eats
  du gâteau m. some cake
  dans in
  son lit his bed
ce this
Qui who
  Qui me donne Who gives me
l'acheteur m. buyer
  nº1=numéro 1 number 1

ANDRÉ: Ils sont fous.   **fous** crazy

SYLVIE: Ce tableau ne vaut pas cinquante centimes.   **ne vaut pas** is not worth
le **centime** cent

ANDRÉ: Ce tableau est affreux.   **affreux** terrible, awful

ACHETEUR nᵒ1:   Soixante-dix euros.

ACHETEUR nᵒ2:   Quatre-vingts euros.

ACHETEUR nᵒ1:   Quatre-vingt-dix euros.

VENDEUR: Quatre-vingt-dix euros une fois, quatre-vingt-dix   **une fois** once
euros deux fois . . . (À ce moment-là Régine entre.) Est-ce   **deux fois** twice
que j'entends cent euros?   **j'entends** I hear

RÉGINE: Tiens! Sylvie, ça va?   **Tiens!** Well! Hey!

Sylvie lève la main pour saluer Régine.   **lève la main** raises her hand
saluer to greet

VENDEUR: Cent euros — pour la demoiselle en rouge. Ce   **la demoiselle** the young
tableau est à elle.   lady   **rouge** red
est à elle is hers

Activités

N. Complete these sentences, based on the conversation you have just read.

1. L'artiste est _____ .

2. Le tableau s'appelle _____ .

3. André pense que le tableau est _____ .

4. Sylvie pense que le tableau est _____ .

5. _____ personnes désirent acheter (*to buy*) le tableau.

6. L'Acheteur nᵒ1 désire payer _____ euros.

7. L'Acheteur nᵒ2 désire payer _____ euros.

8. Sylvie paye _____ euros.

O. More arithmetic in French. Can you solve these problems?

1. Add:

vingt	quarante	quatre-vingt-dix
+ trente	+ soixante	+ dix
_____	_____	_____
_____	_____	_____

2. Subtract:

quinze	douze	quatorze
− cinq	− onze	− un
_____	_____	_____
_____	_____	_____

3. Multiply:

cinq	onze	trente
× quatre	× huit	× trois

_____   _____   _____

_____   _____   _____

4. Divide:

quatre-vingts	seize	vingt-cinq
÷ quatre	÷ deux	÷ cinq

_____   _____   _____

_____   _____   _____

4 There is a special expression that will help you ask for a specific number, **combien de.**

— **Vous regardez** _combien de_ **programmes à la télévision?**
— **Je regarde deux programmes.**

— **Il prépare** _combien de_ **sandwiches?**
— **Il prépare quatre sandwiches.**

— **Tu as** _combien d'_**argent?**
— **J'ai beaucoup d'argent.**

Combien de means _____ when it is followed by a plural noun and _____ when it is followed by a singular noun.

Learn the special expression **il y a.** It means _there is / there are._

Il y a combien d'élèves dans la classe?	_How many students are there in the class?_
Il y a trente élèves dans la classe.	_There are thirty students in the class._
Il y a combien de professeurs?	_How many teachers are there?_
Il y a un professeur.	_There is one teacher._

Activité

P. Little Anne is very curious. Answer her questions.

1. Il y a combien d'élèves dans la classe de français?

   _____

2. Il y a combien d'élèves dans la classe de maths?

   _____

3. Il y a combien de professeurs à l'école?

   _____

4. Il y a combien d'animaux dans le zoo?

   _____

CONVERSATION

Vocabulaire

quel what a
je pense que (qu') I think that
mon frère my brother

Que fais-tu? What are you doing?
une erreur a mistake
le serveur the waiter

l'addition *f.* the check
pourquoi why
fort strong

Parlons français

Work with a partner. Take turns giving each other additions and other math problems in French. Follow the example.

EXAMPLES: You: **Combien font quatre fois trois?**
        Partner: **Quatre fois trois font douze.**

        Partner: **Combien font trois et dix?**
        You: **Trois et dix font treize.**

DIALOGUE

Complete the dialog.

> Quel _____ délicieux!

> Cinq et dix font _____.
> Quinze et _____ font vingt-quatre.

> Que _____ -tu?

> Je _____ l'addition.
> Vingt-quatre et six font _____.

> Quel est _____?

> Mon cousin est _____ et il n'est pas _____ en maths.

Prononciation

- The vowel sound at the end of a word may be dropped in French when the next word starts with a vowel. The dropped vowel is replaced by an apostrophe. This is called ÉLISION.

  Jé adore lé enfant.   J'adore l'enfant.
  Jé admire lá artiste.   J'admire l'artiste.
  Jé étudie lá histoire.   J'étudie l'histoire.

- In many cases the final consonant of one word may be pronounced if the next word begins with a vowel (**a, e, i, o, u, y**) or silent **h**. This is called LIAISON (*linking*).

  un étudiant   Allez au tableau.
  vingt hommes   Faites attention.
  des élèves   Il a six enfants.

Page culturelle

L'argent *(Money)*

Until 2002 the **franc** was the basic monetary unit of France. There were 100 **centimes** in the **franc**. There were five French notes: 20, 50, 100, 200, and 500 francs. There were coins for 1/2 franc, 1 franc, 2, 5, and 10 francs.

In January 1999, the **euro** became the common currency of twelve of the countries in the European Union. At first, banks, businesses, and stock exchanges used the euro. People received phone bills both in francs and euros, and many stores also listed prices in both currencies to accustom people to the euro.

In January 2002, the franc disappeared and was replaced by the euro. One euro is divided into 100 cents, also called "centimes" in popular language. The bank notes (5, 10, 20, 50, 100, 200, and 500 euros) are the same in each country, but the coins have one special side for each country. There are 8 euro coins: 1 cent, 2 cents, 5 cents, 10 cents, 20 cents, 50 cents, 1 euro and 2 euros. It is thought that a common currency will enable Europe to compete more efficiently in the global market place.

Because foreign exchange rates change almost daily, you need to check the foreign exchange table in a newspaper to see how many euros you can buy for a dollar.

When you are in France, you must exchange your dollars for euros. For a good exchange rate, you would go to a bank or a **bureau de change**. Hotels may give a less favorable rate.

FOREIGN EXCHANGE

Currency	Foreign Currency in Dollars Thu.	Wed.	Dollars in Foreign Currency Thu.	Wed.	Currency	Foreign Currency in Dollars Thu.	Wed.	Dollars in Foreign Currency Thu.	Wed.
z-Argentina (Peso)	.4926	.4926	2.0300	2.0300	Kuwait (Dinar)	3.2605	3.2531	.3067	.3074
Australia (Dollar)	.5256	.5227	1.9026	1.9131	Lebanon (Pound)	.000660	.000660	1514.25	1514.25
Bahrain (Dinar)	2.6532	2.6532	.3769	.3769	Malaysia (Ringgit)	.2632	.2632	3.7995	3.7995
Brazil (Real)	.4227	.4253	2.3655	2.3515	z-Mexico (Peso)	.110156	.110116	9.0780	9.0813
Britain (Pound)	1.4281	1.4221	.7002	.7032	N. Zealand (Dollar)	.4308	.4286	2.3213	2.3332
Canada (Dollar)	.6314	.6326	1.5837	1.5807	Norway (Krone)	.1136	.1131	8.8040	8.8448
y-Chile (Peso)	.001499	.001498	667.15	667.45	Pakistan (Rupee)	.0166	.0166	60.08	60.08
China (Yuan)	.1208	.1208	8.2766	8.2765	y-Peru (New Sol)	.2889	.2892	3.462	3.458
Colombia (Peso)	.000436	.000436	2293.75	2294.25	z-Philpins (Peso)	.0197	.0196	50.81	51.01
c-CzechRep (Koruna)	.0278	.0276	35.92	36.23	Poland (Zloty)	.2410	.2410	4.15	4.15
Denmark (Krone)	.1178	.1172	8.4900	8.5300	a-Russia (Ruble)	.0322	.0322	31.0270	31.0560
Dominican (Peso)	.0606	.0606	16.50	16.50	SDR (SDR)	1.25331	1.24684	.7979	.8020
d-Egypt (Pound)	.2159	.2159	4.6325	4.6325	Saudi Arab (Riyal)	.2667	.2667	3.7501	3.7501
Europe (Euro)	.88350	.87640	1.1319	1.1410	Singapore (Dollar)	.5502	.5482	1.8175	1.8242
Hong Kong (Dollar)	.1282	.1282	7.7992	7.7992	SlovakRep (Koruna)	.0208	.0208	47.98	48.12
Hungary (Forint)	.0036	.0036	278.49	279.47	So. Africa (Rand)	.0864	.0907	11.5700	11.0270
y-India (Rupee)	.0205	.0205	48.730	48.680	So. Korea (Won)	.000761	.000760	1314.40	1316.30
Indnsia (Rupiah)	.000101	.000101	9945.00	9915.00	Sweden (Krona)	.0974	.0969	10.2624	10.3198
Israel (Shekel)	.2115	.2119	4.7280	4.7189	Switzerlnd (Franc)	.6000	.5944	1.6668	1.6823
Japan (Yen)	.007871	.007641	127.05	130.88	Taiwan (Dollar)	.0286	.0286	34.94	35.01
Jordan (Dinar)	1.4104	1.4104	.70900	.70900	Thailand (Baht)	.02298	.02293	43.51	43.61
Kenya (Shilling)	.0129	.0129	77.65	77.65	Turkey (Lira)	.000001	.000001	1372500	1385000
					U.A.E. (Dirham)	.2723	.2723	3.6728	3.6726
					f-Uruguay (New Peso)	.0660	.0660	15.1500	15.1500
					z-Venzuel (Bolivar)	.0010	.0010	965.5000	973.0000

a-Russian Central Bank rate.
c-commercial rate, d-free market rate, f-financial rate, y-official rate, z-floating rate.

F was the abbreviation for **francs** and it was commonly used after prices: 10F.

Eur is the abbreviation for **euro**. 0,7 Eur; 18,7 Eur. Its symbol is €.

Note that French uses a comma where we use a period and vice versa:

(French usage) 1.746,70€ (U.S. usage) $1,746.71

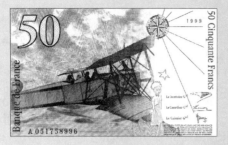 

Rappel

1. In France you can get a good exchange rate for your money at _____ _____ .

2. Less favorable rates of exchange are given out at _____ .

3. The common currency for the European Union is called _____

4. The abbreviation for euro is _____ and its symbol is _____ .

5. The exchange rate shown in the table above is _____ euros to the dollar.

À Vous

1. Design a 1-euro coin with the picture of a famous French person on one side of it.

2. Take an ad from an American newspaper and change 5 prices of items mentioned in it to the equivalent in euros according to the current exchange rate .

La Chasse au trésor
http:// _____

Using your best Internet search skills, find the answers to the following questions:

1. Which king introduced the French franc and in which year?
2. Which 1992 treaty provided for the establishment of the euro?
3. Which countries are now using the euro?
4. Who created the design for the euro banknotes?
5. Who designed the common sides for the euro coins?
6. How much is the euro worth today in dollars?

C'est authentique!

Match the telephone number with the city on the map where you can find the Galeries Lafayette store.

Les Galeries Lafayette in France

Bordeaux:
  11 à 19, rue Ste-Catherine - 33036 - Tél. 05 56 90 92 71
Cannes:
  6, rue du Mal. Foch - 06400 - Tél. 04 93 39 27 55
Dijon:
  41 à 49, rue de la Liberté - 21000 - Tél. 03 80 44 82 12
Grenoble:
  12, place Grenette - 38000 - Tél. 04 76 47 28 54
Lyon les Cordeliers:
  6, place des Cordeliers - 69000 - Tél. 04 72 40 48 00
Marseille:
  40 à 48, rue St-Ferréol - 13001 - Tél. 04 91 54 92 20
Nantes:
  18 et 21, rue du Calvaire - 44000 - Tél. 02 51 25 08 80
Nice:
  6, av. Jean Médecín - 06000 - Tél. 04 92 17 36 36
Paris:
  40, bld Haussmann - 75009 - Tél. 01 42 82 34 56
Reims:
  33 à 45, rue de Vesle - 51000 - Tél. 03 26 40 35 12
Toulon:
  11, bld de Strasbourg - 83000 - Tél. 04 94 22 39 71

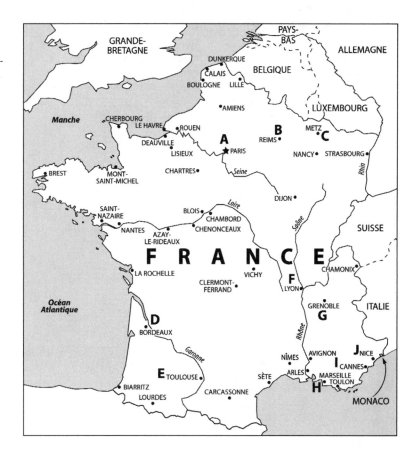

1. zéro quatre, soixante-seize, quarante-sept, vingt-huit, cinquante-quatre _____

2. zéro un, quarante-deux, quatre-vingt-deux, trente-quatre, cinquante-six _____

3. zéro quatre, quatre-vingt-onze, cinquante-quatre, quatre-vingt-douze, vingt _____

4. zéro quatre, quatre-vingt-treize, trente-neuf, vingt-sept, cinquante-cinq _____

5. zéro cinq, cinquante-six, quatre-vingt-dix, quatre-vingt-douze, soixante et onze _____

M O T S   N É C E S S A I R E S

NUMBERS		
zéro zero	**cinq** five	**onze** eleven
un, une one	**six** six	**douze** twelve
deux two	**sept** seven	**treize** thirteen
trois three	**huit** eight	**quatorze** fourteen
quatre four	**neuf** nine	**quinze** fifteen
	dix ten	**seize** sixteen

dix-sept seventeen	**soixante-dix** seventy	ARITHMETIC
dix-huit eighteen	**soixante et onze**	**divisé par** divided by
dix-neuf nineteen	seventy-one	**et** and, plus
vingt twenty	**soixante-douze**	**fois** times
vingt et un twenty-one	seventy-two	**font** equals
vingt-deux twenty-two	**quatre-vingts** eighty	**moins** minus
trente thirty	**quatre-vingt-un** eighty-one	**combien (de)** how many,
quarante forty	**quatre-vingt-dix** ninety	how much
cinquante fifty	**cent** one hundred	**il y a** there is/there are
soixante sixty		**pourquoi** why

Quelle heure est-il?

Telling Time in French

 Quelle heure est-il?

Il est midi *(noon)*.
Il est minuit *(midnight)*.

Il est une heure.

Il est deux heures.

Il est trois heures.

Il est quatre heures.

Il est cinq heures.

Now see if you can do the rest.

_____

_____

_____

_____   _____   _____

 How do you say "What time is it?" in French? _____

How do you express "it is"? _____

How do you express the time? _____

Why is the spelling of **heures** different for **"Il est une heure"**? _____

_____

How do you say "it is noon"? _____

How do you say "it is midnight"? _____

For "noon" and "midnight," which word do you leave out? _____

 Now study these.

Il est deux heures cinq.

Il est deux heures moins cinq.

Il est trois heures cinq.

Il est trois heures moins cinq.

Continue writing these times.

_____   _____   _____

_____   _____   _____

How do you express time after the hour? _____

How do you express time before the hour? _____

To express time AFTER the hour, add the number of minutes.

To express time BEFORE the hour, use **moins** and subtract the number of minutes

How would you say?

 _____

 _____

 _____

 _____

 Now study these.

Il est une heure et quart.

Il est une heure moins le quart.

Il est deux heures et quart.

Il est deux heures moins le quart.

What is the special word for "quarter"? _____

Which little word do you add for "a quarter after"? _____

Which little words do you add for "a quarter before the hour"? _____

How would you express:

_____

_____

 Now study these.

Il est une heure et demie.

Il est deux heures et demie.

Il est trois heures et demie.

Il est midi et demi.
Il est minuit et demi.

What is the special word for "half past"? _____

What is the special spelling for "half past" when it is used with **midi** or **minuit?** _____

Which little word do you add to show that "half past" is after the hour? _____

How would you say:

_____

_____

Activités

A. When you awaken to your clock radio, an announcer is giving the time. Pick the clock showing the correct time.

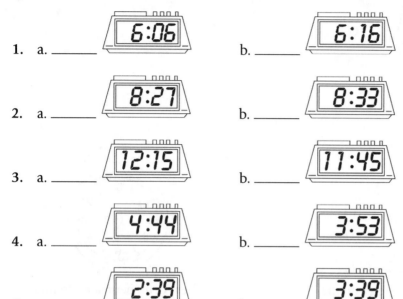

1. a. _____ 6:06   b. _____ 6:16

2. a. _____ 8:27   b. _____ 8:33

3. a. _____ 12:15   b. _____ 11:45

4. a. _____ 4:44   b. _____ 3:53

5. a. _____ 2:39   b. _____ 3:39

B. You will hear the times that various flights will be arriving. Write the number of the flight and the time of arrival.

LE VOL *(the flight)*   ARRIVE À

1. _____   _____

2. _____   _____

3. _____   _____

4. _____   _____

C. Write out these times in numbers.

EXAMPLE: **Il est une heure.**   1h00

1. Il est neuf heures moins le quart.   _____

2. Il est six heures et demie.   _____

3. Il est quatre heures dix.   _____

4. Il est trois heures moins cinq.   _____

5. Il est midi et quart.   _____

6. Il est deux heures vingt.   _____

7. Il est dix heures moins dix.   _____

8. Il est onze heures moins vingt.   _____

D. Write out these times in French.

1. 10:20 _____ .
2. 7:55 _____ .
3. 11:30 _____ .
4. 6:45 _____ .
5. 4:35 _____ .
6. 8:10 _____ .

E. Here are some broken clocks. Each one has the minute hand missing. Can you replace it according to the correct time?

1. Il est trois heures et quart.

2. Il est onze heures cinq.

3. Il est six heures moins vingt-cinq.

4. Il est minuit.

5. Il est quatre heures et demie.

6. Il est cinq heures moins dix.

F. Here are some clocks. Express in French the time each shows.

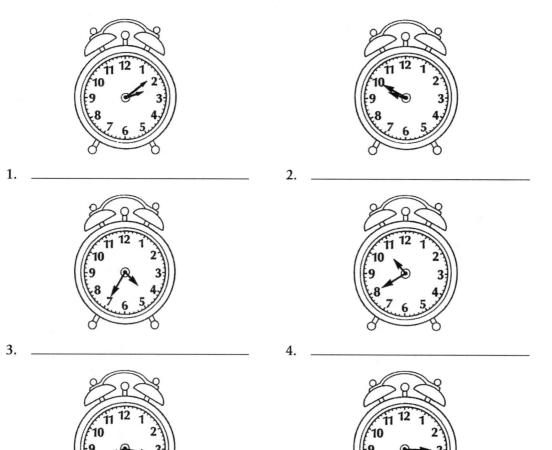

1. _____   2. _____

3. _____   4. _____

5. _____   6. _____

 Now you know what to say when someone asks **Quelle heure est-il?** But how do you reply if someone asks **À quelle heure?** *(At what time?).* Look at these questions and answers.

À quelle heure dînez-vous? *(do you dine)* — **Je dîne à six heures.**
À quelle heure préparez-vous les leçons? *(do you prepare)* — **Je prépare les leçons à huit heures.**
À quelle heure regardez-vous la télé? *(do you watch)* — **Je regarde la télé à neuf heures.**

If you want to express "at" a certain time, which French word do you use before the time? _____

 If you want to be more specific about the time of day, here is what you do.

Je mange *(I eat)* **les flocons de maïs** *(corn flakes)* **à huit heures** *du matin.*
Je mange un sandwich à une heure *de l'après-midi.*
Je mange le dîner à six heures *du soir.*

How do you express "in the morning" or "A.M." in French? _____

How do you express "in the afternoon" or "P.M."? _____

How do you express "in the evening"? _____

Activités

G. Here are ten daily activities. Choose the most likely answer to the question **À quelle heure?** for each picture and write it in numbers.

À une heure et demie du matin.
À sept heures du matin.
À trois heures de l'après-midi.

1. _____ 7:00 a.m. _____

À neuf heures et demie du soir.
À quatre heures du matin.
À sept heures et demie du matin.

2. _____

À huit heures dix du matin.
À onze heures du soir.
À une heure et quart de l'après-midi.

3. _____

À sept heures du soir.
À deux heures du matin.
À midi.

4. _____

À trois heures de l'après-midi.
À onze heures et demie du soir.
À deux heures moins vingt du matin.

5. _____

À huit heures du soir.
À deux heures de l'après-midi.
À dix heures du matin.

6. _____

À deux heures et demie du matin.
À cinq heures cinq du matin.
À huit heures moins cinq du soir.

À six heures du matin.
À dix heures moins dix du soir.
À une heure de l'après-midi.

7. _____

8. _____

À quatre heures moins dix de l'après
    midi.
À sept heures du matin.
À dix heures et quart du soir.

À minuit.
À dix heures cinq du matin.
À sept heures et demie du soir

9. _____

10. _____

H. You do certain things at the same time every day. Write at what time you usually do the following.

EXAMPLE: aller à pied *(walk)* à l'école — **à sept heures et demie du matin.**

1. arriver à l'école

   _____

2. entrer dans la classe de français

   _____

3. parler *(speak)* avec mon ami au téléphone

   _____

4. écouter *(listen to)* la radio

   _____

5. préparer les devoirs

   _____

6. regarder mon programme favori à la télévision

   _____

7. étudier *(study)* la leçon de français

    _____

8. jouer *(play)* au football ou au base-ball

    _____

Prononciation

*   To pronounce **a** or **à**, open wide and say *ahhh,* as in *ah ha.*

à	ça	va	madame	Marie-Anne	Nathalie
là	la	ma	papa	Madagascar	Canada

Ça va, Nathalie?
Papa va là-bas, au Canada.
Madame Canard va à Madagascar avec Marie-Anne.

Now read this dialog and answer the questions that follow.

ANDRÉ: Maman, quelle heure est-il?

MAMAN: Écoute la radio! Il est neuf heures et demie.

ANDRÉ: Neuf heures et demie? Impossible. Il est huit heures dix à ma montre.

MAMAN: Ta montre ne marche pas. Achète une autre montre.

ANDRÉ: Oui, oui. Mais je suis en retard. Il y a un examen dans la classe de français aujourd'hui.

MAMAN: Il y a un examen aujourd'hui? Mais c'est dimanche. Il n'y a pas de classes aujourd'hui.

ANDRÉ: C'est dimanche? Vraiment? Dieu merci!

Écoute listen to

à ma montre on my watch

ta your   **ne marche pas** doesn't work
    achète buy
je suis I am
    en retard late
    un examen a test
aujourd'hui today
    dimanche Sunday
il n'y a pas de there are no
Vraiment really
    Dieu merci! thank goodness!

Activité

I. Answer the following questions in French.

1. Qui parle avec *(who speaks with)* maman?

    _____

2. Selon *(according to)* la radio, quelle heure est-il?

    _____

3. Selon la montre d'André, quelle heure est-il?

    _____

4. Dans quelle classe est-ce qu'il y a un examen?

    _____

5. Pourquoi *(why)* est-ce qu'il n'y a pas de classes aujourd'hui?

    _____

CONVERSATION

Vocabulaire

Tu es You are
nerveux nervous
pourquoi why

un rendez-vous a date
Calme-toi! Calm down
Elle s'appelle Her name is

précises exactly
Mon Dieu! My goodness
C'est ma sœur It's my sister

Parlons français

Have a conversation with a partner in which you discuss at what time you have various classes. Go back and forth three times alternating the person who starts the conversation. Follow the example.

EXAMPLE   You: **À neuf heures.**

          Partner: **À neuf heures j'ai maths. Et toi?** *(And you?)*

           You: **À neuf heures j'ai anglais. À dix heures?**

Page culturelle

L'heure *(Time)*

France, like European countries in general, uses the 24-hour system for official time: schedules for planes, trains, radio and television programs, movies, sports events, and the like.

CONVENTIONAL TIME	OFFICIAL TIME
Noon	12 h 00
1:15 p.m	13 h 15
5:30 p.m	17 h 30
9:45 p.m	21 h 45
Midnight	24 h 00
10 past midnight	0 h 10

Official time may also be written as follows.

12.00	13.15

To calculate official time, add 12 to the conventional time for the hours between noon and midnight.

3:45 a.m.	03 h 45
3:45 p.m.	15 h 45

To calculate the conventional time, subtract 12 from the official time for the hours between noon and midnight.

14 h 30	2:30 p.m.

Rappel

1. European countries use the _____ system for official time schedules.

2. These time schedules are used for _____ .

3. Half past midnight would be written _____ in official time.

4. 14h45 is _____ in conventional time.

5. To convert official time to conventional time, simply _____

_____

À Vous

1. Write an arrival and departure board for an imaginary French airline that has flights to various famous French cities.

2. List the official time in French for your favorite television programs for a week.

La Chasse au trésor

| http: |

Using your best Internet search skills, find the answers to the following questions:

1. In which time zone is France located?
2. If it's 1PM in Paris today, what time is it in:
   a. Algiers, Algeria?   e. Libreville, Gabon?
   b. Cairo, Egypt?   f. Casablanca, Morocco?
   c. Hanoi, Vietnam?   g. Fort-de-France, Martinique?
   d. Montreal, Canada?   h. Los Angeles, California?

C'est authentique!

Write in conventional time in French at what times you can see movies on the following days.

jeudi *(Thursday)*   **samedi** *(Saturday)*

_____   _____

_____   _____

_____   _____

M O T S   N É C E S S A I R E S

TIME
l'après-midi *m./f.*
   afternoon
demi(e) half
l'heure *f.* hour, o'clock
le matin morning
le midi noon

minuit *m.* midnight
le quart quarter
le soir evening

EXPRESSIONS
à at
quel(le) what, which

à quelle heure? at what
   time?
quelle heure est-il? what
   time is it?
aller à pied à to walk to

Révision 1
(LEÇONS 1–4)

Leçon 1

a. There are four ways to say *the* in French.

> **le** is used before masculine singular nouns beginning with a consonant: *le* **cahier**
>
> **la** is used before feminine singular nouns beginning with a consonant: *la* **fille**
>
> **l'** is used before masculine and feminine singular nouns beginning with a vowel sound: *l'***enfant** *l'***hôtel**
>
> **les** is used before ALL plural nouns: *les* **cahiers**

le, la, l', and **les** are definite articles. Definite articles are used to refer to something specific.

b. To make most French nouns plural, add **s** to the singular form of the noun.

les cahiers	les enfants
les filles	les hôtels

To make a noun that ends in **-eau** plural, add **x** to the singular form of the noun.

le bureau	les bureaux

To make a noun that ends in **-al** plural, change **-al** to **-aux**.

l'anim*al*	les anim*aux*
le journ*al*	les journ*aux*

Leçon 2

There are two ways to say *a* or *an* in French.

> **un** is used before masculine singular nouns: *un* **livre**
>
> **une** is used before feminine singular nouns: *une* **fille**

> **des** is used before all plural nouns: *des* **cahiers**   *des* **enfants**
>
>   *des* **filles**   *des* **animaux**

Note that **des** may mean "some."

Un, une, and **des** are indefinite articles. Indefinite articles are used to refer to things not specifically mentioned.

Leçon 3

0 zéro	20 vingt	76 soixante-seize
1 un	21 vingt et un	77 soixante-dix-sept
2 deux	22 vingt-deux	78 soixante-dix-huit
3 trois	23 vingt-trois	79 soixante-dix-neuf
4 quatre	24 vingt-quatre	80 quatre-vingts
5 cinq	25 vingt-cinq	81 quatre-vingt-un
6 six	26 vingt-six	82 quatre-vingt-deux
7 sept	27 vingt-sept	90 quatre-vingt-dix
8 huit	28 vingt-huit	91 quatre-vingt-onze
9 neuf	29 vingt-neuf	92 quatre-vingt-douze
10 dix	30 trente	93 quatre-vingt-treize
11 onze	40 quarante	94 quatre-vingt-quatorze
12 douze	50 cinquante	95 quatre-vingt-quinze
13 treize	60 soixante	96 quatre-vingt-seize
14 quatorze	70 soixante-dix	97 quatre-vingt-dix-sept
15 quinze	71 soixante et onze	98 quatre-vingt-dix-huit
16 seize	72 soixante-douze	99 quatre-vingt-dix-neuf
17 dix-sept	73 soixante-treize	100 cent
18 dix-huit	74 soixante-quatorze	101 cent un
19 dix-neuf	75 soixante-quinze	

+ et   − moins   × fois   ÷ divisé par

Leçon 4

a. Time is expressed as follows.

Quelle heure est-il?	*What time is it?*
Il est une heure.	*It's one o'clock.*
Il est deux heures cinq.	*It's 2:05.*
Il est trois heures dix.	*It's 3:10.*
Il est quatre heures et quart.	*It's a quarter past four. (4:15)*
Il est cinq heures vingt.	*It's 5:20.*
Il est six heures vingt-cinq.	*It's 6:25.*
Il est sept heures et demie.	*It's half past seven. (7:30)*
Il est huit heures moins vingt-cinq.	*It's 7:35.*
Il est neuf heures moins vingt.	*It's 8:40.*
Il est dix heures moins le quart.	*It's 9:45.*
Il est onze heures moins dix.	*It's 10:50.*
Il est midi moins cinq.	*It's 11:55.*
Il est minuit.	*It's midnight*

b. To express "*at*" a specific time, use **à**:

À quelle heure mangez-vous? — Je mange *à* six heures.

Activités

A. Find 16 French nouns hidden in this puzzle. Circle them in the puzzle and list them below. The words may be read from left to right, right to left, up or down, or diagonally.

```
D  T  A  B  L  E  A  U  S  S
N  R  A  N  É  F  A  C  P  T
L  I  A  R  R  E  F  A  E  Y
S  A  A  P  T  S  E  R  L  L
O  R  T  R  E  N  H  O  G  O
U  T  O  R  T  A  C  T  È  E
P  P  L  V  A  D  U  T  R  L
E  E  T  O  N  I  L  E  S  B
D  H  C  I  W  D  N  A  S  A
N  O  I  S  I  V  É  L  É  T
```

1. _____   2. _____
3. _____   4. _____
5. _____   6. _____
7. _____   8. _____
9. _____   10. _____
11. _____   12. _____
13. _____   14. _____
15. _____   16. _____

B. Identify the pictures. Then write the letters in the boxes on page 69. The solution completes the sentence.

Les élèves adorent _____

1. __ ☐ __ ☐ __ __ __ ☐ __ ☐
    1   2   3   4

2. ☐☐☐ __ __ __
   5 6 7

3. __ ☐ __ ☐☐
    8   9 10

4. ☐ __ __ __ ☐ __ ☐ __ ☐☐ __ __
   11   12   13   14 15

5. __ __ ☐ __ __ __ ☐
       16   17

Solution: ☐☐ ☐☐☐☐☐ ☐☐
          8 3   5 15 9 4 10 11 6

☐☐☐☐☐☐☐☐
2 1 16 13 7 14 12 17

C. How many of these words do you remember? Fill in the French words, then read down the boxed column of letters to find the name of everyone's favorite subject.

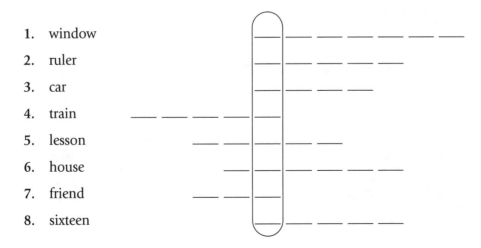

1. window
2. ruler
3. car
4. train
5. lesson
6. house
7. friend
8. sixteen

D. Bureau des objets trouvés *(Lost and Found)*

You are working in a lost-and-found office. The following objects have been brought in. List them below in French.

1. _____	2. _____
3. _____	4. _____
5. _____	6. _____
7. _____	8. _____
9. _____	10. _____
11. _____	12. _____
13. _____	14. _____

E. All the following people are saying some numbers. What are they?

1. _____

2. _____

3. _____   4. _____

5. _____   6. _____

F. Would you like to tell your future? Follow these simple rules to see what the cards have in store for you. Choose a number from two to eight. Starting in the upper left corner and moving from left to right, write down all the letters that appear under that number.

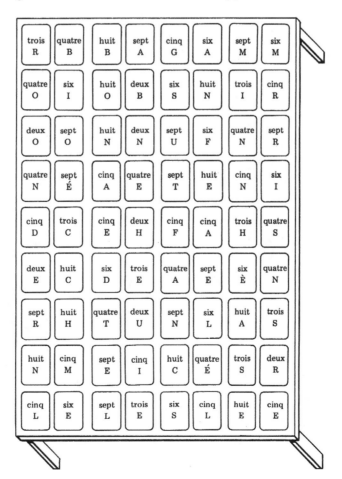

G. **Combien?** To find out, solve the math problems. Then write the letters indicated in the solution boxes below.

1. Trente-deux et vingt-huit font

___ ___ ⬜ ⬜ ___ ⬜ ___ ⬜ .
      1 2   3   4

2. Sept fois sept font

⬜ ___ ⬜ ⬜ ___ ___ ___ ⬜ – ⬜ ___ ___ ⬜ .
5   6 7   8   9   10

3. Quarante moins douze font

⬜ ___ ___ ⬜ ___ – ___ ⬜ ___ ⬜ .
11   12   13   14

4. Trente-six divisé par deux font

⬜ ⬜ ___ – ___ ⬜ ___ ⬜ .
15 16   17   18

Solution: ⬜ ⬜ ⬜ ⬜ ⬜ ⬜ – ⬜ ⬜ ⬜ ⬜ ⬜
           5 13 6 18 7 4   11 16 3 12 14

⬜ ⬜ ⬜ – ⬜ ⬜ ⬜ ⬜
15 1 2   9 8 17 10

H. Write the times in French.

1. _____   2. _____

3. _____   4. _____

I. Quelle heure est-il?

1. _____

2. _____

3. _____

4. _____

5. _____

6. _____

The Cognate Connection

French (as well as Spanish, Italian, Portuguese, and Romanian) is called a Romance language because it is derived from Latin, the language spoken by the Romans.

Since more than half of all English words are also derived from Latin, there is an important relationship between French and English vocabulary, with large numbers of words being related. These words are called cognates.

More importantly, the portion of our English language coming from Latin includes most of our "hard" words — words that are complex or scientific.

Here are some examples of how these languages relate to one another.

LATIN	FRENCH	SPANISH	ITALIAN	ENGLISH COGNATE
mater *(mother)*	**mère**	**madre**	**madre**	**maternal** (motherly)
pater *(father)*	**père**	**padre**	**padre**	**paternal** (fatherly)
veritas *(truth)*	**vérité**	**verdad**	**verità**	**verify** (establish truth)
malus *(bad)*	**mal**	**malo**	**malo**	**malice** (ill will)
juvenis *(young)*	**jeune**	**joven**	**giovane**	**juvenile** (youthful)
unus *(one)*	**un**	**uno**	**uno**	**unilateral** (one-sided)
canto *(to sing)*	**chanter**	**cantar**	**cantare**	**chant** (to sing)
dormire *(to sleep)*	**dormir**	**dormir**	**dormire**	**dormant** (inactive)

In this and succeeding lessons, we will explore more of the fascinating relationship between the English and French languages.

Write the meanings of the following French and English words.

FRENCH   ENGLISH COGNATE

1. maison _____ mansion _____

2. stylo _____ stylus _____

3. répondre _____ response _____

4. cent _____ century _____

5. douze _____ dozen _____

2

deuxième partie

5

Les activités

*Using **-ER** Verbs; Asking Questions and Saying No*

Vocabulaire

chanter

danser

écouter

gagner

goûter

jouer

marcher

parler

77

préparer

regarder

Activités

A. Your friend mumbles and often can't be understood by the end of a sentence. Complete the sentences you hear.

1. **a.** Paris   **b.** à l'école   **c.** des amis

2. **a.** le professeur   **b.** au cinéma   **c.** les livres

3. **a.** Pierre   **b.** le français   **c.** huit heures

4. **a.** dans le sac   **b.** à midi   **c.** cinq garçons

5. **a.** dans le parc   **b.** à neuf heures   **c.** une grande maison

B. Your friend Nathalie tells you about things she loves to do. After she explains each preference, write the number of the sentence you hear next to the activity in which she would engage.

a. étudier   _____   **d.** écouter des CD   _____

b. danser   _____   **e.** jouer au football   _____

c. téléphoner à des amis   _____   **f.** regarder la télé   _____

C. Work with a partner. Take turns matching the verb with the noun that could be used with it. Then write your answers.

la radio   la télévision   à l'école
avec des amis   le rock   Frère Jacques
français   la mousse   une salade
le match

1. goûter _____   6. gagner _____

2. regarder _____   7. marcher _____

3. écouter _____   8. chanter _____

4. danser _____   9. parler _____

5. préparer _____   10. jouer _____

Many people will be involved in the conversation later in this lesson. Who are they?

je *(I)*

nous *(we)*

tu *(you)*

vous *(you)*

il *(he)*

ils *(they* [boys; boys and girls])

elle *(she)*

elles *(they* [girls])

These words are called subject pronouns. Subject pronouns refer to the persons or things doing the action.

> **tu** is used when you are speaking to a close relative, a friend, or a child — someone with whom you are familiar.
>
> **vous** is used when you are speaking to a stranger or a grown-up — a person with whom you should be formal — or when addressing more than one person.

Activités

D. Listen as your teacher refers to different people. Check the box to show which pronoun you would use to speak to the people mentioned.

	TU	VOUS
1.	_____	_____
2.	_____	_____
3.	_____	_____
4.	_____	_____
5.	_____	_____

E. Would you use **tu** or **vous** if you were speaking to these people?

1. le vendeur _____
2. la mère _____
3. Marie et Sylvie _____
4. le président _____
5. Roger _____
6. un élève _____
7. les professeurs _____
8. un bébé _____

3 Which pronoun would you use if you wanted to speak about **Charles** without using his name? _____ , which means _____ .

Which pronoun would you use if you wanted to speak about **Marie** without using her name? _____ , which means _____ .

Which pronoun would replace **Charles et Paul?** _____ **Marie et Anne?** _____ **Marie et Paul?** _____ , which mean _____ .

Il and **elle** may also mean *it.* Which one would you use to refer to **le livre?** _____ **la règle?** _____

Ils and **elles** mean *they.* Which one would you use to refer to **les livres?** _____ **les maisons?** _____

> The pronoun ON (*one, you, we*) is frequently used when speaking about people in general.
> **On étudie si on est intelligent.**
> *You study if you're smart.*

Activités

F. Everyone is talking about his or her friend. Check the pronouns that could be used to replace the name or names.

	IL	ILS	ELLE	ELLES
1.	_____	_____	_____	_____
2.	_____	_____	_____	_____
3.	_____	_____	_____	_____
4.	_____	_____	_____	_____
5.	_____	_____	_____	_____

G. Imagine that you were speaking about your family. Write the pronoun you would use to substitute for each name or noun.

1. Pierre est intelligent. _____ est intelligent.

2. Oncle Henri et Tante Michelle sont professeurs. _____ sont professeurs.

3. Les animaux sont adorables. _____ sont adorables.

4. Jeanne et Joséphine sont étudiantes. _____ sont étudiantes.

5. La famille est grande. _____ est grande.

6. Anne est artiste. _____ est artiste.

Prononciation

- To pronounce **i**, **î**, or **y** show your teeth and say *eee*.

il	midi	visiter	mystère	Didier	Italie	fille
île	ici	dîner	timide	Brigitte	Sylvie	livre

À midi, il explique le mystère à Sylvie.
Brigitte dîne ici à dix heures et demie.
Didier est timide mais il visite l'île avec Philippe.

 Now read this story about an interesting French lesson.

La mousse au chocolat

ANNE: **Tu goûtes** la mousse au chocolat de Mme Navet?

JEAN: Oui, **je goûte** la mousse. Elle est délicieuse. **Claude goûte** la mousse aussi?

ANNE: Oui, **il goûte** la mousse. Et Marie. **Elle goûte** la mousse aussi. Et les autres filles, **elles goûtent** la mousse aussi. Paul et Roger, **vous goûtez** la mousse délicieuse?

autres other

PAUL ET ROGER: Oui, **nous goûtons** la mousse. (Ils commencent à agir d'une façon étrange.)

commencer à to begin
agir to act
  la façon the way
  étrange strange
sont are **trop** too
  incroyable unbelievable

ANNE: Mais Madame, regardez! **Ils goûtent** beaucoup de mousse! Ils sont très comiques et trop actifs. C'est incroyable! Pourquoi? Ils continuent à manger beaucoup de mousse!

MADAME NAVET: Oh là là! Ne vous inquiétez pas. Il y a beaucoup de chocolat dans la mousse. Ils mangent tant de mousse qu'ils ont un excès d'énergie. Eh, Paul, Roger, lavez le tableau, rangez les chaises, fermez les fenêtres, ramassez les livres . . .

Ne vous inquiétez pas
  Don't worry
tant de so much
un excès an excess
  lavez wash
rangez straighten
  les chaises the chairs
  fermez close
  ramassez gather (up)

Activité

H. Oui ou non? Change the wrong words to correct the sentence.

1. Les élèves goûtent la mousse **à la vanille.**

   _____

2. La mousse est **horrible.**

   _____

3. Paul et Roger sont très **sincères** et trop **timides.**

   _____

4. Il y a beaucoup de **carottes** dans la mousse.

   _____

5. Paul et Roger ont un excès de **problèmes.**

   _____

 Goûter is a verb, an **-ER** verb. All of the verbs in this lesson belong to the **-ER** family because all their infinitives (their basic forms) end in **-ER** and because they all follow the same rules of conjugation.

CONJUGATION, what's that? CONJUGATION refers to changing the ending of the verb so that the verb agrees with the subject. We do the same in English without even thinking about it. For example, we say *I taste* but *he tastes*. Look carefully at the forms of the verb **goûter** in bold type in the conversation and see if you can answer these questions.

To conjugate an **-ER** verb in the present tense (making subject and verb agree), which letters are dropped from the infinitive? _____ Which endings are added to the stem for the following subject pronouns?

je goût	_____	nous goût	_____
tu goût	_____	vous goût	_____
il/elle goût	_____	ils/elles goût	_____

5 Let's see how the present tense works. Take the verb **parler** (*to speak*). If you want to say *I speak*, take **je,** remove the -er from **parler** and add the ending **-e:**

parl~~er~~
je parle   *I speak, I am speaking*

Do the same for all the other subjects:

tu parl*es*	*you speak, you are speaking* (familiar singular)
il/elle parl*e*	*he/she speaks, he/she is speaking*
nous parl*ons*	*we speak, we are speaking*
vous parl*ez*	*you speak, you are speaking* (formal singular and plural)
ils/elles parl*ent*	*they are speaking*

There are two possible meanings for each verb form: **je parle** may mean *I speak* or *I am speaking;* **tu parles** may mean *you speak* or *you are speaking;* and so on.

NOTE: **J'écoute la musique.**

What happened to the **e** in **je?** _____

What did we put in place of the **e** in **je?** _____

Why did we do so? _____

Je becomes **j'** before a vowel sound.

Activités

I. Work with a partner. Take turns asking about your activities. Then write your answer.

EXAMPLE: You: **Vous regardez la télévision?**
Partner: **Nous regardons la télévision.**

1. écouter la musique _____ .
2. danser à une fête _____ .
3. jouer avec des amis _____ .
4. parler avec les grands-parents _____ .

J. A reporter for the school newspaper is asking what you do in your French class. Write what you do.

      EXAMPLE: regarder le tableau.   **Je regarde le tableau.**

    1.   écouter le professeur _____ .

    2.   préparer la leçon _____ .

    3.   parler français _____ .

    4.   chanter «Frère Jacques» _____ .

K. Talk to a friend about what she does on weekends.

      EXAMPLE: regarder la télévision   **Tu regardes la télévision.**

    1.   écouter la radio _____ .

    2.   parler au téléphone _____ .

    3.   marcher dans le parc _____ .

    4.   préparer un dessert _____ .

L. Madame Bernard wants to see if her students understand verb conjugation. Can you help Daniel fill in his chart for the present tense? Supply the correct verb forms.

	chanter	danser	préparer	regarder
je	_____	_____	_____	_____
tu	_____	_____	_____	_____
il	_____	_____	_____	_____
elle	_____	_____	_____	_____
nous	_____	_____	_____	_____
vous	_____	_____	_____	_____
ils	_____	_____	_____	_____
elles	_____	_____	_____	_____

M. Tell what the members of the Chevalier family are doing.

      EXAMPLE: Georges / écouter la radio
                Georges écoute la radio.

    1.   Marie et Joseph / parler français

       _____

    2.   Le père / jouer avec les enfants

       _____

    3.   L'oncle et la tante / marcher dans le parc

       _____

4. La mère / préparer la mousse au chocolat

_____

5. Les grands-parents / regarder la télévision

_____

6. La fille / goûter le chocolat

_____

 Here are some more activities.

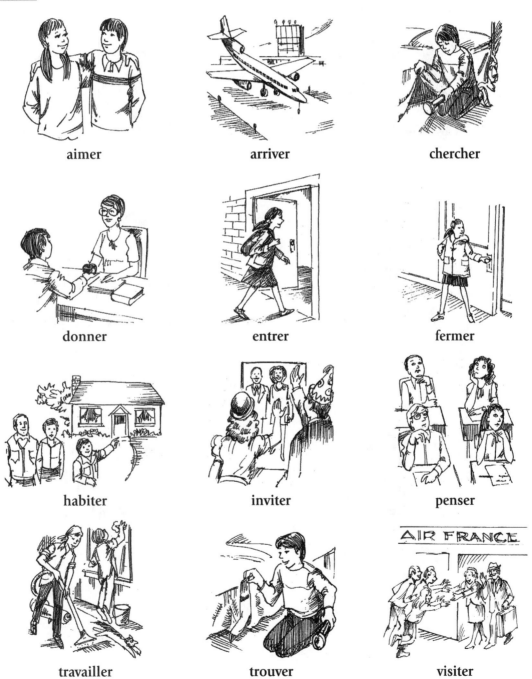

aimer

arriver

chercher

donner

entrer

fermer

habiter

inviter

penser

travailler

trouver

visiter

Activités

N. Match the descriptions with the pictures.

L'étudiant cherche un livre.
Vous entrez dans le cinéma.
Tu arrives à l'école.
Elles trouvent le CD.
Il ferme la fenêtre.

Nous visitons Paris.
J'habite un appartement.
Béatrice travaille à la maison.
Les élèves aiment le professeur.
Vous invitez les grands-parents.

1. _____

2. _____

3. _____

4. _____

5. _____

6. _____

7. _____   8. _____

9. _____   10. _____

O. Here are eight "action words." Tell who "is doing the action" by writing every pronoun that can be used with the verb as it is written.

EXAMPLE: **je, il, elle parle**

1. _____ prépare
2. _____ arrive
3. _____ habitent
4. _____ joues

5. _____ gagnent
6. _____ travaillons
7. _____ aimez
8. _____ entre

P. Write what each person is doing today.

EXAMPLE: parler: je **parle**

1. (travailler)   je _____ .
2. (jouer)   tu _____ au football.
3. (marcher)   il _____ dans le parc.
4. (gagner)   Marie _____ le match.
5. (inviter)   vous _____ des amis chez vous.
6. (chanter)   nous _____
7. (arriver)   Marie et Sylvie _____ à New York.
8. (visiter)   Paul _____ la France.

Now look at these negative sentences.

	I	II
	Je marche.	Je *ne* marche *pas.*
	Philippe danse.	Philippe *ne* danse *pas.*
	Ils entrent.	Ils *n'*entrent *pas.*

How are the sentences in Group II different from the sentences in Group I? _____

_____

Which two little words are used in French to make a sentence negative? _____

Where do we put **ne** in relation to the verb? _____ Where do we put

pas? _____ Look at the last sentence. What happened to the **e** in **ne?**

_____ What did we put in its place? _____ Why did we

do so? _____

What do the sentences in Group II above mean in English? Each sentence has two meanings.
What are they?

1. _____

2. _____

3. _____

No matter what we say in English (*don't, doesn't, aren't, isn't,* and the like), in French the rule is
always the same.

> To make a sentence negative, use **ne (n')** before the verb and **pas** after it.

Je *ne* marche *pas* avec des amis.	{ *I don't walk with friends.* *I'm not walking with friends.*
Tu *ne* parles *pas* français.	{ *You don't speak French.* *You're not speaking French.*
Il *n'*écoute *pas* la musique.	{ *He doesn't listen to the music.* *He's not listening to the music.*

Activités

Q. Listen to what your friend has to say about Robert. Then check whether you agree or disagree
with your friend's opinion.

	OUI	NON			OUI	NON
1.	_____	_____		4.	_____	_____
2.	_____	_____		5.	_____	_____
3.	_____	_____				

R. You like to contradict your older brother. Make the following statements negative and write the English meanings of each negative sentence on the line below.

1. Paul danse bien.

   _____

   _____

2. Nous travaillons dans le jardin.

   _____

   _____

3. Vous écoutez la radio.

   _____

   _____

4. Les filles préparent le dîner.

   _____

   _____

5. Un ami arrive à la maison.

   _____

   _____

6. Elle invite les garçons.

   _____

   _____

7. Tu visites la France.

   _____

   _____

8. Les étudiants chantent beaucoup.

   _____

   _____

S. **Félicitations!** Congratulations! The senior class has just chosen you as the student most likely to succeed. Tell your friends what you do (or don't do) to make you so successful.

EXAMPLES: **J'écoute les professeurs à l'école.**
             Je ne regarde pas beaucoup la télévision.

1. _____
2. _____
3. _____
4. _____
5. _____

Formidable! You now know how to make a French sentence negative. Now let's see how to ask a question in French.

You'll have a choice of several ways to ask a question that requires a yes or no answer. The first way is the easiest of all. It's called intonation. Repeat the two groups of sentences after your teacher.

Je chante bien.	Je chante bien?
Tu marches avec des amis.	Tu marches avec des amis?
Elle goûte la mousse.	Elle goûte la mousse?
Vous parlez français.	Vous parlez français?
Ils habitent Paris.	Ils habitent Paris?

> The simplest way to ask a *yes-no* question in French, and the way that is most often used in conversation, is to raise your voice at the end of the sentence and add _____ in writing.

 Look at another group of sentences to find the second way to express questions in French that require a *yes-no* answer. Repeat after your teacher.

I	II
Je danse bien.	EST-CE QUE je danse bien?
Tu entres dans la maison.	EST-CE QUE tu entres dans la maison?
Il chante en classe.	EST-CE QU'il chante en classe?
Nous parlons français.	EST-CE QUE nous parlons français?
Vous travaillez beaucoup.	EST-CE QUE vous travaillez beaucoup?
Elles marchent avec des amis.	EST-CE QU'elles marchent avec des amis?

What did we add to all the statements in Group I to form the questions in Group II?

_____

What happens to the **e** in **que** before **il, ils, elle, elles**? _____

Why is the **e** of **que** dropped? _____

What do the sentences in Group II above mean in English?

1. _____

2. _____

3. _____

4. _____

5. _____

6. _____

> To ask a question, you may put **est-ce que** at the beginning of the sentence.

Activités

T. You have an earache and can't hear very well today. You have to question everything you hear. Change the following statements to questions using EST-CE QUE.

1. Jean arrive à l'école avec amis.

   _____

2. Tu travailles après (*after*) l'école.

   _____

3. Ta mère prépare le dîner.

   _____

4. Nous chantons bien.

   _____

5. Elles habitent un appartement.

   _____

6. Les élèves préparent les exercices.

   _____

7. Vous dansez en classe.

   _____

8. Les étudiants visitent la France.

   _____

U. Answer the questions in French.

1. Est-ce que vous regardez la télévision tous les jours?

   _____

2. Vous chantez bien?

   _____

3. Vous parlez beaucoup au téléphone?

   _____

4. Est-ce que vous écoutez la radio?

   _____

5. Est-ce que vous aimez danser?

_____

6. Vous préparez le dîner?

_____

 # CONVERSATION

Vocabulaire

les feuilletons soap operas   **je suis** I am
un chic type a nice guy   **flatté** flattered

DIALOGUE

Choose one response.

Parlons français

Work with a partner. Take turns asking each other and then answering as many personal questions as you can. Vary your questions as much as possible. Ask yes-no questions but also ask for information.

EXAMPLE: You: **Tu aimes la classe de français?**
Partner: **Oui, j'aime beaucoup la classe de français.**
You: **Tu arrives à l'école à quelle heure?**
Partner: **J'arrive à huit heures et quart.**

C'est authentique!

Match the ad with the activity.

a.

b.

c.

d.

BALLETS DE MONTE-CARLO

*Sous la Présidence de S.A.S. la
Princesse Caroline de Monaco*

Salle Garnier

•

COMPAGNIE DE BALLETS
DE MONTE-CARLO

*

*Location tous les jours de 10h à 12h 30
au Casino de Monte-Carlo*

1. _____

MONTE-CARLO SPORTING CLUB

SALLE DES ETOILES

•

THE PLATTERS

•

ORCHESTRES DE DANSE

Le Vendredi: Gala à 21 heures
Tenue de soirée

Du Samedi au Lundi
Dîner dansant à 21 heures
Tenue de ville

Réservations : 93.50.80.80

2. _____

THÉÂTRE DU
FORT ANTOINE

•

LE SONGE D'UNE NUIT D'ÉTÉ
par le
Drama Group

•

•

ENSEMBLE INSTRUMENTAL
DE VENISE

*Location le soir même au Théâtre
à partir de 20 h 30*

•

3. _____

CAFÉ DE PARIS

•

DÉJEUNERS SPÉCIAUX
GRAND PRIX

•

"LE GRAND PRIX" Déjeuner : 40€
–Boissons incluses–

•

RÉSERVATIONS OBLIGATOIRES

•

Téléphone : 93.50.57.75

4. _____

Page culturelle

Les gourmandises *(Delicacies)*

If dessert is your favorite part of a meal, you will find a great variety of desserts in French restaurants and cafés. Here are a few favorites. What would you choose?

Chocolat (café) liégeois [Chocolate (coffee) ice cream with whipped cream]

Crème caramel [Egg custard with caramel sauce]

Crêpes Suzette [Dessert crêpes made with orange flavoring and served flambées (flaming) with Grand Marnier (orange-flavored liqueur)]

Marquise [Sliced, thick, rich chocolate dessert with whipped cream]

Mousse au chocolat [Light, fluffy chocolate pudding with whipped cream]

Omelette norvégienne [Baked Alaska, a cake, ice cream, and meringue dessert]

Poire Belle Hélène [Poached pear with vanilla ice cream, chocolate sauce, and whipped cream]

Profiteroles [Cream puffs with hot chocolate sauce]

As a special treat for family and friends, try your hand at making **la mousse au chocolat.** Just follow this simple recipe:

MOUSSE AU CHOCOLAT

1 8-oz. bar of semisweet chocolate
1 square of unsweetened chocolate
2 tbs. butter
1 tb. very strong black coffee
2 eggs, separated
1 pint heavy sweet cream

In a double boiler, melt the chocolate, the unsweetened chocolate, and the butter, stirring into a smooth paste. Add the coffee and egg yolks. Stir. Remove from heat and let cool slightly.

Beat the egg whites until stiff and the cream until whipped but not stiff.

Add the egg whites to the chocolate mixture, blending it in slowly. Add the whipped cream. Mix slowly so that the cream remains high.

Spoon into individual dessert cups and chill for at least four hours. Serve with whipped cream.

Rappel

1. If you don't like chocolate, you can order _____ .
2. If you love chocolate, you'd probably love _____ .

3. For an ice cream dessert pick _____ .

4. Crêpes Suzette have an _____ flavor.

5. Crème Caramel is a type of _____ .

À Vous

1. Create a French dessert menu with realistic prices in euros.

2. Find another recipe for a French dessert.

3. Prepare a dessert for your class.

La Chasse au trésor

http://

Using your best Internet search skills, find a description for the following French desserts:

a. Une bûche de Noël
b. Une crème brûlée
c. Une tarte Tatin
d. Un pot de crème
e. Des œufs à la neige
f. Des marrons glacés

MOTS NÉCESSAIRES

VERBS

aimer to like, love	habiter to live (in)	**PRONOUNS**
arriver to arrive	inviter to invite	je I
chanter to sing	jouer to play	tu you
chercher to look for	marcher to walk	il he, it
danser to dance	parler to speak	elle she, it
donner to give	penser to think	on one, you, we
écouter to listen	préparer to prepare	nous we
entrer to enter	regarder to look at	vous you
fermer to close	travailler to work	ils they
gagner to win, earn	trouver to find	elles *f.* they
goûter to taste	visiter to visit	

6

La famille

Expressing Possession

 Vocabulaire

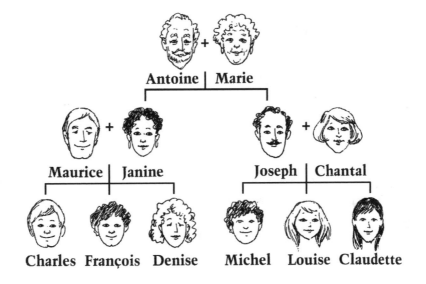

Antoine | Marie

Maurice | Janine   Joseph | Chantal

Charles   François   Denise   Michel   Louise   Claudette

 Here we have a big, happy family. It's obvious from the family tree who all the members are. Let's take a closer look.

Antoine et Marie sont **les grands-parents**. Les **petits-enfants** sont Charles, François, Denise, Michel, Louise et Claudette. Antoine est **le grand-père** et Marie est **la grand-mère**. Maurice et Janine sont **les parents de Charles, de François et de Denise**. Charles et François sont **frères**. Ils sont **les fils** de Maurice et de Janine. Louise et Claudette sont **sœurs**. Elles sont **les filles** de Joseph et de Chantal. Joseph et Chantal sont **mari** et **femme**.

Janine est **la sœur** de Joseph, **la mère** de Charles, de François et de Denise et **la tante** de Michel, de Louise et de Claudette. Joseph est **le frère** de Janine, **le père** de Michel, de Louise et de Claudette et **l'oncle** de Charles, de François et de Denise.

les petits-enfants *m. pl.* grandchildren

de of

le mari husband
la femme wife

97

Charles est **le cousin** de Michel, de Louise et de Claudette.
Denise est **la cousine**. Ils sont **cousins**.

Il y a aussi un chien, Féroce, et un chat, Tigre, dans la famille.
Féroce et Tigre sont amis.

La famille Dupont est de Paris, en France.

il y a there is
aussi also
le chien the dog
le chat the cat

Activités

A. Using the family tree of the Duponts, complete each sentence with the correct words.

1.   Janine est _____ de Charles, de François et de Denise.

2.   Les enfants de Maurice et de Janine sont _____ ,
     _____ et _____ .

3.   Charles est _____ de Maurice.

4.   Charles et Michel sont _____ .

5.   Antoine est _____ de Joseph.

6.   Féroce et Tigre sont _____ .

7.   Maurice et Janine sont _____ .

8.   Joseph est _____ de Charles.

9.   Denise est _____ de Claudette.

10. Antoine est _____ et Marie est _____
     de Charles, François, Denise, Michel, Louise et Claudette.

B. Work with a partner. Take turns identifying the people in the story.

EXAMPLE: You: **Chantal?**
                Partner: **C'est la femme de Joseph et la mère de Michel, de Louise
                           et de Claudette. Charles?**

C. Identify the members of the Dupont family, matching the words with the pictures.

la mère   les parents   les sœurs
le père   les grands-parents   les frères
le grand-père   le chat   la tante
la grand-mère   le chien   les cousins

1. _____   2. _____

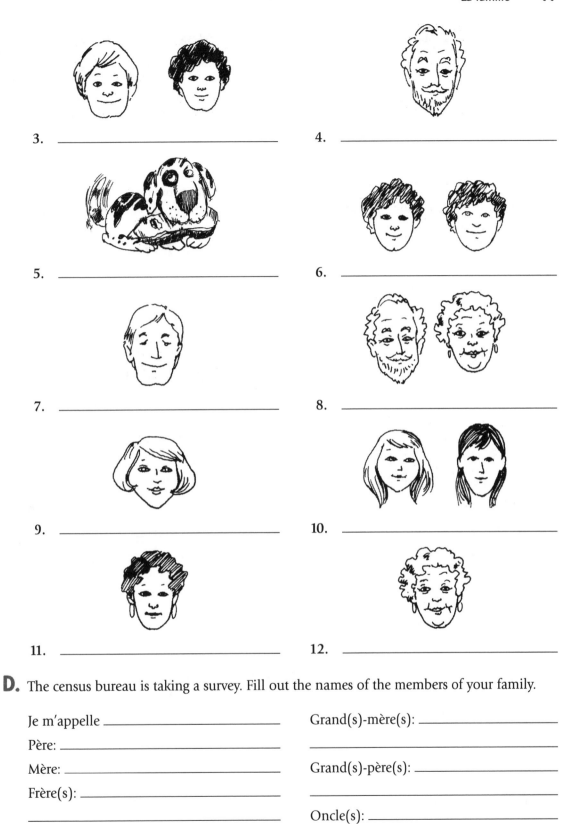

3. _____   4. _____

5. _____   6. _____

7. _____   8. _____

9. _____   10. _____

11. _____   12. _____

D. The census bureau is taking a survey. Fill out the names of the members of your family.

Je m'appelle _____   Grand(s)-mère(s): _____

Père: _____   _____

Mère: _____   Grand(s)-père(s): _____

Frère(s): _____   _____

_____   Oncle(s): _____

Sœur(s): _____   _____

_____

Tante(s): _____   Cousine(s): _____

_____   _____

Cousin(s): _____   _____

_____   Chien(s) _____

_____   Chat(s): _____

 In this chapter you are going to learn how to say that something belongs to someone. You will learn about possession and possessive adjectives. Look at the pictures and pay special attention to each group of sentences.

I	II
C'est *le* chien.	C'est *mon* chien.
C'est *le* père.	C'est *mon* père.
C'est *le* frère.	C'est *mon* frère.

C'est *mon* chien.

Look at the nouns in Group I. Are they masculine or feminine? _____

Singular or plural? _____

How do you know? _____

Do they begin with consonants or vowels? _____

Now look at Group II. In Group II we are listening to a girl describing a dog that belongs to her.

She says : **C'est mon chien.** Which word has replaced **le** from Group I? _____

What does **mon** mean? _____

Before what kinds of nouns is it used? _____

3

I	II
C'est *la* mère.	C'est *ma* mère.
C'est *la* sœur.	C'est *ma* sœur.
C'est *la* cousine.	C'est *ma* cousine.

Look at the nouns in the first group of sentences. Are they masculine or feminine? _____ .

Singular or plural? _____

How do you know? _____

Do they begin with consonants or vowels? _____

Now look at the Group II. Which word has replaced **la** from Group I? _____

What does **ma** mean? _____

Before what kinds of nouns is it used? _____

I	II
C'est *l'*ami.	C'est *mon* ami.
C'est *l'*amie.	C'est *mon* amie.

Look at the nouns in Group I. Are they masculine or feminine? _____

Singular or plural? _____

Do they begin with a consonant or vowel? _____

Now look at Group II. Which possessive adjective is used before all singular nouns that start with a

vowel in order to avoid the repetition of two vowel sounds next to each other? _____ .

I	II
Ce sont *les* chiens.	Ce sont *mes* chiens.
Ce sont *les* livres.	Ce sont *mes* livres.
Ce sont *les* photos.	Ce sont *mes* photos.
Ce sont *les* amis.	Ce sont *mes* amis.

Ce sont *mes* chiens.

Look at the nouns in Group I. Are they masculine or feminine? _____

Singular or plural? _____

How do you know? _____

Do they begin with consonants or vowels? _____

Now look at Group II. In Group II we are listening to a girl describing two dogs that belong to her.

She says : **Ce sont mes chiens.** Which word has replaced **les** from Group I? _____

What does **mes** mean? _____

Before what kinds of nouns is it used? _____

How many ways are there to say MY? _____

You use **mon**	_____
	_____
	_____
ma	_____
	_____
mes	_____

Activités

E. Paul Legrand is talking about his family. Write the letter of the person he is describing next to the appropriate number.

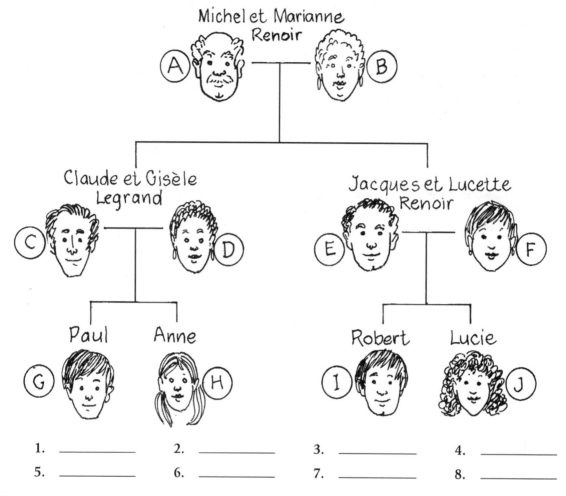

1. _____ 2. _____ 3. _____ 4. _____

5. _____ 6. _____ 7. _____ 8. _____

F. You have been asked to show the class pictures of your family and friends. Identify them using **mon, ma,** or **mes**.

EXAMPLE: tante   **C'est ma tante.**
cousins   **Ce sont mes cousins.**

1. mère _____

2. grand-père _____

3. oncle _____

4. amis _____

5. frères _____

6. amie _____

7. tantes _____

8. parents _____

Can you apply these rules to other possessive adjectives?

I	**II**
C'est *le* chien.	C'est *ton* chien.
C'est *le* père.	C'est *ton* père.
C'est *la* mère.	C'est *ta* mère.
C'est *l'*amie.	C'est *ton* amie.
Ce sont *les* cousins.	Ce sont *tes* cousins.

C'est *ton* chien.

In group II, a boy says to the girl who is holding her dog : **C'est ton chien.**

What subject pronoun do **ton, ta,** and **tes** bring to mind? _____

What do **ton, ta,** and **tes** mean? _____

You use **ton** _____

_____

ta _____

tes _____

When you use **ton, ta,** and **tes,** are you being familiar or formal? _____

Activité

G. Some things have been left behind in your classroom. Work with a partner asking and answering questions about the items that remain. Then write the questions and answers in French. Follow the example.

EXAMPLE:    C'est ton livre?
C'est mon livre.

    Ce sont tes cahiers?
Ce sont mes cahiers.

1.   _____

_____

2. _____

3. _____

4. _____

5. _____

Keeping in mind what you have already learned, look at the next group of possessive adjectives.

I	II
C'est *le père de Paul.*	C'est *son père.*
C'est *le père de Marie.*	C'est *son père.*
C'est *la mère de Paul.*	C'est *sa mère.*
C'est *la mère de Marie.*	C'est *sa mère.*
C'est *l'amie de Paul.*	C'est *son amie.*
C'est *l'amie de Marie.*	C'est *son amie.*
Ce sont *les cousins de Paul.*	Ce sont *ses cousins.*
Ce sont *les cousins de Marie.*	Ce sont *ses cousins.*

C'est *son père.*

In group II, we are listening to a girl who says that the man holding a little boy in his arms is the boy's father. **C'est *son* père.**)

You use **son**	_____
	_____
sa	_____
ses	_____

Son, sa, and **ses** have two meanings. What are they? _____

Do the possessive adjectives **son, sa, ses** agree with the possessor or with the person or thing "possessed"? _____

Possessive adjectives agree with _____ ,
not with _____ .

Activités

H. You're curious about your new neighbor, Jean-Pierre. What do your friends tell you about his family?

EXAMPLE:

C'est son chien.

Ce sont ses grands-parents.

1. _____ .

2. _____ .

3. _____ .

4. _____ .

5. _____ .

6. _____ .

I. Your mother has asked you to pick up your things from the living room. You tell her that they are your sister's.

EXAMPLES: sac   C'est son sac.
            crayons   **Ce sont ses crayons.**

1. livres _____ .
2. cahier _____ .
3. règle _____ .
4. papiers _____ .
5. stylo _____ .
6. radio _____ .

J. You are speaking to Robert about yourself and Alice. Assign the objects listed below to their proper owners by following the examples.

	YOURSELF	ROBERT	ALICE
	un fruit	deux crayons	un oncle
	des carottes	une règle	une amie
	un sandwich	un stylo	un frère
	une soupe	trois cahiers	deux sœurs

C'est mon fruit.   Ce sont tes crayons.   C'est son oncle.

_____   _____   _____

_____   _____   _____

_____   _____   _____

8 Let's learn some more about the possessive:

C'est *le* père.   C'est *notre* père.
C'est *la* mère.   C'est *notre* mère.
C'est *l'*amie.   C'est *notre* amie.
Ce sont *les* cousins.   Ce sont *nos* cousins.

C'est *notre* père.

Which subject pronoun do **notre** and **nos** bring to mind? _____

What do **notre** and **nos** mean? _____

When do you use **notre**? _____

nos? _____

9

C'est *le* père.   C'est *votre* père.
C'est *la* mère.   C'est *votre* mère.
C'est *l'*amie.   C'est *votre* amie.
Ce sont *les* cousins.   Ce sont *vos* cousins.

Which subject pronoun do **votre** and **vos** bring to mind? _____

What do **votre** and **vos** mean? _____

When do you use **votre**? _____

vos? _____

Are you being familiar or formal? _____

Activités

K. Members of your family are browsing through a photo album. Listen to the questions they ask and select the best answer to each question

1. a. Non, ce sont nos parents.
   b. Non, ce sont tes parents.
   c. Oui, ce sont nos parents.

2. a. Oui, c'est son oncle.
   b. Oui, c'est mon oncle.
   c. Oui, c'est notre oncle.

3. a. Oui, ce sont nos cousines.
   b. Oui, ce sont nos cousins.
   c. Oui, c'est notre cousin.

4. a. Oui, c'est mon frère.
   b. Oui, c'est notre frère.
   c. Oui, c'est ton frère.

L. You are talking with your twin friends about things that belong to them. Write the questions you ask and their answers. Follow the example.

EXAMPLES:

C'est votre radio?
C'est notre radio.

Ce sont vos chats?
Ce sont nos chats.

1. _____

2. _____

3. _____

4. _____

C'est *le* père.   C'est *leur* père.
C'est *la* mère.   C'est *leur* mère.
C'est *l'*amie.   C'est *leur* amie.
Ce sont *les* cousins.   Ce sont *leurs* cousins.

C'est leur père.

What do **leur** and **leurs** mean? _____

When do you use **leur?** _____

                    leurs? _____

Activité

M. Now give the information in Activité L to another friend who is part of your group.

    EXAMPLES: **C'est leur radio.**   **Ce sont leurs chats.**

    1. _____

    2. _____

    3. _____

    4. _____

Prononciation

The letter **o** has two different sounds in French.

- **o** may be pronounced *oh* like the *o* in *no*. The sound *o* may be written as **o** (when it is the last pronounced sound of the word, or before *s* + vowel) or **ô**, **au**, or **eau**.

radio	chose	allô	aussi	eau	trop
mot	rose	hôpital	autre	beaucoup	bientôt

- **o**, when followed by a pronounced consonant other than **s**, is pronounced like the *o* in the English word *love*.

olive   homme   octobre   donner   note   téléphone   Georges

Practice the two different sounds of **o** in these words.

nos	notre	pose	poste
vos	votre	trop	tropical
Rose	Roger	idiot	idiote

Auguste donne beaucoup de manteaux jaunes et roses à Olivier.
Colette donne trop tôt notre beau cadeau à Roger.
En octobre, un homme téléphone à Nicole à l'hôtel Saumon.

CONVERSATION

Vocabulaire

tu es you are   **calme-toi!** Calm down!   **ton** your
nerveuse nervous   **précises** exactly   **c'est** he is, it is
rendez-vous date   **Mon Dieu!** My goodness

Parlons français

Have a conversation with a partner about your family. Take turns asking for the names of certain members.

EXAMPLE: You: **Comment s'appelle ton frère?**
          Partner: **Il s'appelle Jean.**
              You: **Comment s'appelle ta mère?**
          Partner: **Elle s'appelle Marie.**

Page culturelle

Salut! Je m'appelle . . . *(Hi! My name is . . .)*

Here is a list of popular French first names. Your teacher will help you pronounce them.

GARÇONS	FILLES	GARÇONS	FILLES
André	Andrée	Joël	Joëlle
Bernard	Bernadette	Laurent	Laurence
Christian	Christiane	Louis	Louise
Claude	Claude, Claudine	Martin	Martine
Daniel	Danielle (Dinièle)	Michel	Michelle (Michèle)
Denis	Denise	Nicolas	Nicole
Dominique	Dominique	Noël	Noëlle
François	Françoise	Paul	Pauline
Gabriel	Gabrielle	Simon	Simone
Jacques	Jacqueline	Stéphane	Stéphanie
Jean	Jeanne	Yves	Yvette

Some first names are formed by joining two names with a hyphen, usually beginning with Jean for a boy or Marie for a girl.

GARÇONS		FILLES	
Jean-Claude	Jean-Michel	Marie-Claire	Marie-France
Jean-Luc	Jean-Paul	Marie-Chantal	Marie-Hélène
Jean-Marc	Jean-Pierre	Marie-Christine	Marie-Laure

Rappel

1. Two French names that are exactly the same for boys and girls are: _____ and _____ .

2. Many girls' names are formed by adding _____ , _____ , _____ , or _____ to boys' names.

3. Hyphenated boys' names usually use _____ as the first name.

4. Hyphenated girls' names usually use _____ as the first name.

5. Some French names that are the same as English names are _____

_____ .

À Vous

1. Write the first and last name of as many famous French people as you can. Label whether they were historic figures, artists, musicians, authors, or scientists.

2. Keep a log of French-speaking people mentioned in the news. Explain why they are important.

La Chasse au trésor

 http://

Using your best Internet search skills, find the answers to the following questions:

1. What are the most recent top ten popular names for French baby boys and girls? Identify your sources.

2. Find ten French boys' and girls' names that you think are very unusual. (Do not use names from your list of top ten baby names.)

C'est authentique!

les jeunes au micro

la famille

On demande aux jeunes Français: tu as une grande famille?

Éric Bertrand
quatorze ans

Oui ! J'ai une grande famille. J'ai trois sœurs et un frère. Mes sœurs s'appellent Valérie, Brigitte et Christine. Mon frère s'appelle Nicolas. Valérie a sept ans. Brigitte a onze ans, Christine a dix-neuf ans et Nicolas a dix ans. Moi, j'ai quatorze ans. Nicolas est sérieux. Christine est intelligente. Brigitte est timide et Valérie est amusante.

What information does this article give you about Éric's family? _____

1. It is small.

2. Éric is the oldest child.

3. Éric has more brothers than sisters.

4. There are five children in his family.

MOTS NÉCESSAIRES

FAMILY
le chat cat
le chien dog
le cousin cousin
la cousine cousin
la femme wife; woman
la fille daughter
le fils son
le frère brother
la grand-mère grandmother

le grand-parent
   grandparent
le grand-père grandfather
le mari husband
la mère mother
l'oncle *m.* uncle
le parent parent
le père father
la sœur sister
la tante aunt

POSSESSIVES
mon, ma, mes my
ton, ta, tes your
son, sa, ses his, her
notre, nos our
votre, vos your
leur, leurs their

EXPRESSION
il s'appelle his name is

"To Be or Not to Be"

*Expressing Professions and Trades; Using the Verb **être***

 Vocabulaire

le professeur

le professeur

le docteur/le médecin

le docteur/le médecin

le dentiste

la dentiste

l'artiste

l'artiste

le secrétaire

la secrétaire

l'acteur

l'actrice

l'infirmier   l'infirmière   l'avocat

l'avocate   le facteur   la factrice

l'agent de police   l'agent de police   le pompier

Activités

A. Your friends describe what their relatives do for a living. Match the person with the appropriate picture.

a.   b.   c.

d.   e.

1. _____   2. _____   3. _____   4. _____   5. _____

B. **Qui est-ce?** *(Who is it?)* The people in your family have different professions. Match their occupation with the correct picture.

un agent de police   un secrétaire   un professeur   une avocate
une infirmière   un artiste   un pompier   un facteur

1. _____

2. _____

3. _____

4. _____

5. _____

6. _____

7. _____

8. _____

C. Now identify these professions:

1. _____   2. _____

3. _____   4. _____

5. _____   6. _____

 Read the following story and see if you can answer the questions about it. All of the verb forms in bold type are some form of the verb **être** (*to be*):

JEAN: Madame Renard **est** votre professeur de français. Est-ce qu'elle **est** sympathique?

sympathique nice

ROBERT: Oui, elle **est** très sympathique. Marie et Janine, les deux filles blondes, **sont** sympathiques aussi, n'est-ce pas?

n'est-ce pas isn't that so

JEAN: Oui, elles **sont** sympathiques. Roland **est** drôle.

drôle funny

ROLAND: Oui, je **suis** drôle, mais tu **es** drôle aussi, Jean.

JEAN ET ROBERT: Nous **sommes** drôles, nous deux. Mais Madame Renard, vous n'**êtes** pas drôle.

nous deux the two of us

MME RENARD: Non, je ne **suis** pas drôle. Mais je **suis** sympathique, dynamique, aimable, sociable et formidable.

aimable friendly
formidable terrific

Activité

D. Répondez aux questions.

1. Qui (*who*) est sympathique?

   _____

2. Comment sont Marie et Janine?

   _____

3. Qui est drôle?

   _____

4. Qui n'est pas drôle?

   _____

5. Comment est Mme Renard?

   _____

2 In the story you have just read there is a new verb—**être** (*to be*). **Être** is a special verb because it is one of a kind. No other French verb is conjugated like **être**. For this reason, **être** is called irregular. Can you pick out the correct forms of **être** from the story to match the subjects below?

je _____   nous _____

tu _____   vous _____

il _____   ils _____

elle _____   elles _____

Memorize all forms of **être**.

Activités

E. There's a lot of gossip at school. Check who is being spoken about.

	ROGER	LUCIE	PAUL ET JACQUES	ALICE ET YVETTE
1.	___	___	___	___
2.	___	___	___	___
3.	___	___	___	___
4.	___	___	___	___
5.	___	___	___	___
6.	___	___	___	___

F. You have a pen pal in France who wants to know details about your family. Complete these sentences with the correct form of the verb **être**.

1. Mon grand-père _____ avocat.

2. Mon père _____ professeur et ma mère _____ docteur.

3. Mes parents _____ sympathiques.

4. Mon frère et moi, nous _____ populaires.

5. Nous _____ étudiants.

6. Mes deux sœurs _____ infirmières; elles _____ très intelligentes.

7. Tu _____ mon ami. Tu _____ français; je _____ américain.

G. Choose five people you know and write their professions in complete sentences. (Remember that the indefinite article is omitted in French before an unmodified profession or trade following a form of **être**.)

EXAMPLE: **Tom Cruise est acteur.**

1. _____

2. _____

3. _____

4. _____

5. _____

H. Here are some sentences in which a form of **être** is used. Match the sentences with the pictures they describe.

Terreur est un petit chien.   **Mes grands-parents sont acteurs.**
Je suis président de la classe.   **Nous sommes amies.**
Tu es agent de police.   **Vous êtes une artiste populaire.**

1. _____   2. _____

3. _____

4. _____

5. _____

6. _____

I. Today is a day set aside for visiting a relative on the job. Express who the relatives are and what their professions are.

EXAMPLE:  elle/oncle/
Elle est avec son oncle qui *(who)* est professeur.

1.  nous/mère _____
_____

2. elles/frère _____
_____

3. je/père _____
_____

4.  vous/grand-mère _____
_____

5. tu/sœur _____

_____

6. il/grand-père _____

_____

J. Answer the following questions about yourself in complete sentences.

1. Est-ce que vous êtes sociable ou *(or)* timide?

_____

2. Est-ce que vous êtes grand(e) ou petit(e)?

_____

3. Est-ce que vous êtes français(e)?

_____

_____

4. Est-ce que vous êtes riche?

_____

_____

5. Est-ce que vous êtes célèbre?

_____

_____

Prononciation

There is no equivalent English sound for **u** or **û**. First say the French word **si**. Then round your lips as if to whistle and say **si** again with rounded lips. Now remove the **s** and you get a sound close to a French **u**.

une	du	sûr	salut	menu	bus
tu	sur	mûr	minute	dispute	Lulu

Salut Lulu! Tu discutes le menu avec Luc? Super!
Une minute! Il y a du jus sur le pull de Lucette.

CONVERSATION

Vocabulaire

tu veux you want
sortir to go out

Ça dépend. That depends.

C'est dommage. That's too bad.

Parlons français

Work with a partner. Using the conversation you just read, speak on the phone with a new friend and describe yourselves and ask each other questions.

EXAMPLE: You: **Tu veux sortir avec moi?**
            Partner: **Ça dépend. Tu es dynamique?**

DIALOGUE

Complete the dialog with suitable expressions of your own choice.

Page culturelle

L'agriculture et l'industrie en France

What do French people do to earn a living?

French farmers make France a leading agricultural producer in Europe. Transportation, telecommunications, chemical products, food products, and fashion are important industries in France.

Study the maps and identify the products and industries of the various regions in France. (See map page 332 in chapter 19 to identify the regions)

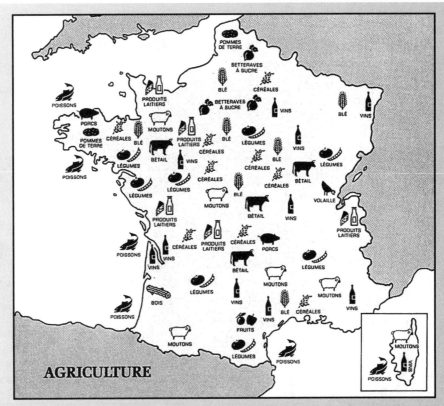

bétail cattle; **betterave à sucre** sugar beet; **blé** wheat; **légumes** vegetables; **pommes de terre** potatoes; **produits laitiers** dairy products; **volaille** poultry

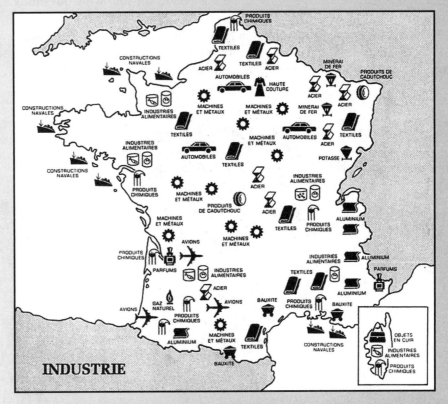

acier steel; **caoutchouc** rubber; **cuir** leather; **minerai de fer** iron ore; **parfums** perfumes; **métaux** metals; **produits chimiques** chemical products; **industries alimentaires** food products

Rappel

1. France is a leading agricultural force in Europe because there are many
   _____ in the country.

2. Two important industries are _____ and _____ .

3. _____ is an important coastal industry.

4. A beverage produced in France is _____ .

5. The French produce bread by using the _____ that is grown
   throughout the country.

À Vous

1. Cheese is an important dairy product in France. Take a trip to the supermarket and
   find out the names of different French cheeses. Then find out as much as you can
   about each cheese.

2. Create a poster advertising French fashions.

La Chasse au trésor

http://

Using your best Internet search skills, find the answers to the following questions:

1. What does France export to the United States? Give examples, where possible.
2. What does France import from the United States? Give examples, where possible.
3. Why is France the most important agricultural nation of Western Europe?

C'est authentique!

Match the ads with the employees being sought.

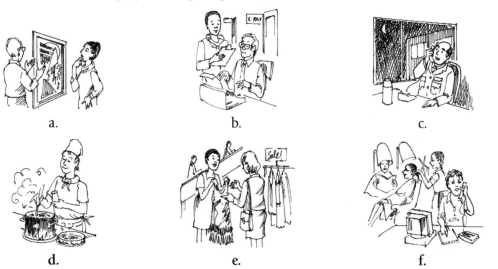

a.   b.   c.

d.   e.   f.

CMC de la Porte de Choisy
Paris 13ᵉ recherche

**SECRÉTAIRES
MÉDICALES**

Postes fixes

Écrire à Mme LANCIAN
6, place de la Liberté
75013 Paris

1. _____

**RESPONSABLE
SALON COIFFURE**

Caissière-Réceptionniste

40 ans environ
Env. C. V. SCI JOURDAIN

2. _____

Magasin Prêt-à-Porter

Centre Commercial 4 TEMPS

**VENDEUSE
QUALIFIÉE**

Env. photo + C. V.
au Journal Petites Annonces
Réf. 1292

3. _____

**CONSULTANTES
ARTISTIQUES**
Possib. temps partiel
Formation assurée
Voiture indispensable
Pouvant concilier vie
familiale et vie
professionnelle.
LIBRE IMMÉDIATEMENT
Se présenter mardi 16h.

4. _____

EUREST

pour résidences services de
luxe recherche pour Paris et
région parisienne

CHEFS H/F

5. _____

URGENT
Clinique Chirurgicale
Paris 13ᵉ recherche

**GARDIEN DE NUIT
STANDARDISTE**
Bonne présentation
tél. 01 45 65 15 15 pour r.v.

6. _____

M O T S   N É C E S S A I R E S

PROFESSIONS
l'**acteur** *m.* actor
l'**actrice** *f.* actress
l'**agent de police** *m.* police
  officer
l'**artiste** *m./f.* artist
l'**avocat** *m.* lawyer
l'**avocate** *f.* lawyer
le/la **dentiste** dentist
le **docteur** doctor

le **facteur** letter carrier
la **factrice** letter carrier
l'**infirmier** *m.* nurse
l'**infirmière** *f.* nurse
le **médecin** doctor
le **pompier** firefighter
le/la **professeur** teacher,
  professor
le/la **secrétaire** secretary

ÊTRE : TO BE
être to be
je suis I am
tu es you are
il est he is
elle est she is
nous sommes we are
vous êtes you are
ils/elles sont they are

Les vêtements; les couleurs

Describing Things in French

Can you guess the meanings of these new words?

les vêtements *m.*

le pantalon

le survêtement

le jean

les baskets *f.*

la cravate

les tennis *f.*

le chapeau

la ceinture

les chaussures *f.*

la veste

le manteau

la chemise

126

Activité

A. Jean-Louis just went shopping. Identify the new clothes in his closet by putting the number under the correct picture. Listen to your teacher.

a. _____   b. _____   c. _____   d. _____

e. _____   f. _____   g. _____   h. _____

 Now try to figure out the meanings of these words.

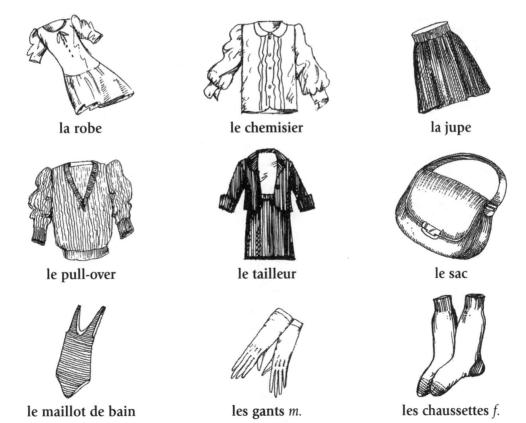

la robe   le chemisier   la jupe

le pull-over   le tailleur   le sac

le maillot de bain   les gants *m.*   les chaussettes *f.*

Activités

B. Marianne also bought some new clothes. Identify her purchases.

1. _____   2. _____   3. _____

4. _____   5. _____   6. _____

7. _____   8. _____   9. _____

C. Daniel has just gotten a job in a clothing store. The boss asks him to pin labels on the models so that the prices can be put on later. Can you help him?

la chemise	la jupe	le manteau
les chaussures	le chemisier	le chapeau
la veste	le sac	le pull-over
le pantalon	les gants	la ceinture
la cravate	le tailleur	

When you want to give your opinion about clothing, use these expressions.

C'est **trop court.** It's too short.

C'est **trop long.** It's too long.

C'est **trop étroit.** It's too narrow.

C'est **moche.** It's awful.

C'est **démodé.** It's out of date.

C'est **criard.** It's loud.

C'est **laid.** It's ugly.

C'est **affreux.** It's horrible.

C'est **magnifique.** It's magnificent.

C'est **super.** It's great!

C'est **formidable.** It's terrific.

C'est **chouette.** It's great!

C'est **à la mode.** It's in style.

C'est **chic.** It's fashionable.

C'est **élégant.** It's elegant.

C'est **parfait.** It's perfect.

Activité

D. Work with a partner. Take turns giving your opinion of the clothing shown in Activité C.

EXAMPLE: You: **Le manteau?**
Partner: **C'est démodé. La robe?**

Prononciation

- **e** at the end of a one-syllable word, or in the middle of a word followed by only one consonant is pronouned like the **e** in *the*.

  je   le   de   ne   regarder   demander   menu   devoirs

  Je regarde le menu devant le neveu de Denis.

- **é**, final **-er**, **-ez**, and most **-es** in one-syllable words, as well as a few **-ai** and **-et** combinations, have the sound *ay* as in *may*.

élégant	arriver	nez	ces	ai	et
téléphone	parler	chez	des	aider	est
bébé	danser	allez	les	serai	béret

  En été les bébés de Roger et de Renée portent des bérets.

- è, ê, and e (+two consonants or +a final pronounced consonant) and **et, ei,** or **ai** when followed by a consonant have a slightly more open *eh* sound like the **e** in *get*.

mère	être	vêtement	ouest	avec
très	même	intelligent	sept	quel
achète	tête	intéressant	belle	chef
bonnet	fête	seize	mais	Seine
ballet	complet	treize	aide	air

Suzette est à l'est de Paris près de la Seine.

 Can you understand these two stories?

Jean est un garçon français. Il est grand et blond. Il est très fort. Il est aussi élégant et charmant. Il porte des vêtements français chics. Il est très intelligent, intéressant et populaire. C'est un garçon parfait.

fort strong
porte wears
chics fashionable

Jeanne est une jeune fille africaine. Elle est petite et brune. Elle est élégante et charmante, surtout quand elle porte des vêtements très à la mode: un pantalon et un pull-over court. Elle est intéressante et très intelligente. Elle adore les garçons mais elle est timide. Elle est populaire. C'est une jeune fille parfaite.

jeune young
  africaine african
  brune brunette
surtout especially
  quand when
mais but

Activités

E. Change all the words in bold type to make the sentences true.

1. Jean est un garçon **africain**.   _____

2. Jean est **petit**.   _____

3. Il est **brun**.   _____

4. Il porte des vêtements **intéressants**.   _____

5. C'est un garçon **cruel**.   _____

6. Jeanne est une jeune fille **américaine**.   _____

7. Elle est **blonde** et **grande**.   _____

8. Elle porte **une jupe** et **une chemise**.   _____

9. Elle est **stupide**.   _____

10. Elle adore **le professeur**.   _____

F. Make a list of all the adjectives that describe Jean.

1. _____   5. _____   8. _____
2. _____   6. _____   9. _____
3. _____   7. _____   10. _____
4. _____

G. Make a list of all the adjectives that describe Jeanne.

1. _____   5. _____   8. _____
2. _____   6. _____   9. _____
3. _____   7. _____   10. _____
4. _____

4 Have you been observant? Look at the adjectives on the left that could describe Jean. Compare them with the adjectives on the right that could describe Jeanne.

élégant	élégante
charmant	charmante
intelligent	intelligente
intéressant	intéressante
blond	blonde
brun	brune
fort	forte
grand	grande
petit	petite
parfait	parfaite

Adjectives in French agree in gender with the person or thing they describe. Which letter do we add to the MASCULINE form of the adjective to get the FEMININE form? _____ .

Repeat the adjectives in both groups after your teacher. Do the masculine and feminine adjectives sound the same or different? _____ What is the difference you hear?

_____

Activités

H. You are asked to give your opinion about some people and things. Complete the sentence with the correct form of the adjective.

1. Jean est _____ (fort, forte).

2. Marie est _____ (petit, petite).

3. La classe est _____ (excellent, excellente).

4. Le livre est _____ (intéressant, intéressante).

5. L'étudiante est _____ (élégant, élégante).

6. Le message est _____ (important, importante).

7. La mère est _____ (charmant, charmante).

8. La famille est _____ (grand, grande).

I. You are making some observations about people and things. Complete the sentence with the correct French form of the adjective.

1. (grand)   Le livre est _____ .

2. (surpris)   La femme est _____ .

3. (important) La musique est _____ .

4. (blond)   Le garçon est _____ .

5. (français) La sœur est _____ .

6. (excellent) La classe est _____ .

7. (petit)   La mère est _____ .

8. (intéressant) Le menu est _____ .

9. (parfait)   La robe est _____ .

10. (américain) Marie est _____ .

5 Now look at these adjectives that describe both Jean and Jeanne.

Jean:	Jeanne:	Jean:	Jeanne:
timide	**timide**	**superbe**	**superbe**
populaire	**populaire**	**splendide**	**splendide**
riche	**riche**	**magnifique**	**magnifique**
ordinaire	**ordinaire**	**stupide**	**stupide**
pauvre *(poor)*	**pauvre**	**mince** *(thin)*	**mince**

What do you notice about the adjectives in both columns? _____

_____ . Adjectives in French agree in gender with the person

or thing they describe. For these adjectives, however, we did not add **e** to get the feminine form.

Why do you think we did not have to add **e**? _____ . A good

rule to remember is: When the masculine form of an adjective ends in a silent **e**, the feminine

form _____ .

Activité

J. You are making some more observations today. Complete each sentence with the correct form of the adjective.

1. Le livre est rouge; la table est _____ aussi.

2. Le professeur est riche; l'étudiante est _____ aussi.

3. Le pantalon est superbe; la robe est _____ aussi.

4. Pierre est timide; Marie est _____ aussi.

5. Le restaurant est splendide; la boutique est _____ aussi.

6. Le président est populaire; la secrétaire est _____ aussi.

 There is still more to learn about adjectives. Can you complete the second column?

	I	**II**
	élégant	élégants
	charmant	charmants
	riche	riches
	pauvre	pauvres

intelligent	_____
intéressant	_____
blond	_____
brun	_____
fort	_____
grand	_____
petit	_____
timide	_____
populaire	_____

Look at Group I. How many people are we describing? _____

Look at Group II. How many people are we describing? _____

Which letter did we add to the adjective to express that we are describing more than one? _____

Adjectives in French agree in GENDER and NUMBER with the person or thing they describe.

Think carefully. What is the plural form of the adjective if the singular form already ends in **s**?

EXAMPLE: **Le garçon est** *surpris.* **Les garçons sont** _____ .

If you wrote **surpris,** you are correct.

Can you finish Group II?

	I	II
	élégante	élégantes
	charmante	charmantes
	intelligente	intelligentes
	intéressante	intéressantes
blonde	_____	
brune	_____	
forte	_____	
grande	_____	
petite	_____	
timide	_____	
populaire	_____	
riche	_____	
pauvre	_____	

Look at Group I. What is the gender of the noun we are describing? _____ .
What letter did we have to add to get the feminine form? _____ How many people are we
describing in Group I? _____ Look at Group II. How many people are we describing? _____ Which letter did we add to the adjective to express that we are
describing more than one? We added the letter _____ .

Activités

K. Circle the adjective you would use to describe the articles of clothing you hear.

1.	grand	grande	grands	grandes
2.	petit	petite	petits	petites
3.	joli	jolie	jolis	jolies
4.	élégant	élégante	élégants	élégantes
5.	étroit	étroite	étroits	étroites
6.	parfait	parfaite	parfaits	parfaites

L. Describe the members of your family. Add an ending to the adjective if necessary.

    1. (moderne)   Mes parents sont _____ .

    2. (joli)   Ma cousine est _____ .

    3. (riche)   Mon oncle est _____ .

    4. (intelligent)   Mes sœurs sont _____ .

    5. (grand)   Mes cousines sont _____ .

    6. (fort)   Mes frères sont _____ .

    7. (américain)   Mes grands-parents _____ .

    8. (timide)   Mes cousins sont _____ .

    9. (élégant)   Ma mère est _____ .

  10. (petit)   Ma tante est _____ .

M. Your parents bought you some new clothes. Tell them what you think by completing the sentences with the correct form of the French adjective.

    1. (criard)   Les chapeaux sont _____ .

    2. (super)   Le pantalon est _____ .

    3. (élégant)   La robe est _____ .

    4. (chouette)   Le sac est _____ .

    5. (petit)   Les chaussettes sont _____ .

    6. (parfait)   La cravate est _____ .

    7. (court)   Les jupes sont _____ .

    8. (laid)   Le pull-over est _____ .

N. You are the editor of the school yearbook. Fill in the students' names and describe each of them by using three adjectives.

Il est

Ils sont

_____   _____

_____   _____

_____   _____

Elle est

Elles sont

_____   _____

_____   _____

_____   _____

  Look at the phrases below.

un garçon fort	un programme intéressant
une école moderne	des restaurants excellents
une fille sympathique	des livres rouges

Where is the adjective? Does the adjective come before or after the noun? _____ .

In French, most adjectives come AFTER the noun they modify. There are some exceptions. Four common adjectives come before the nouns they modify:

petit   **grand**   **jeune**   **joli**

EXAMPLES: **le grand garçon**   **le jeune homme**
            la petite fille   **la jolie robe**

NOTE: As you have learned in Lesson 2, the plural indefinite article is **des** (*some*).

des écoles modernes   *des* livres rouges

The plural indefinite article is often **de** if the adjective comes BEFORE the noun.

de grands garçons   *de* jolies robes

Activités

O. Describe the clothes you love. Take out the verb **être** to make a new phrase with the adjective.

EXAMPLE: La robe est chic.   **J'adore la robe chic.**

1. La veste est moderne. _____

2. La chemise est élégante. _____

3. Les manteaux sont longs. _____

4. Les chaussures sont confortables. _____

5. La ceinture est petite. _____

6. Les vêtements sont jolis. _____

 Can you figure out the color of each object?

La tomate est rouge.

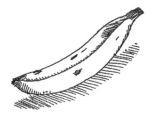

La banane est jaune.

Le chat est noir.

Le lait est blanc.

La fleur est rose.

L'orange est orange.

L'éléphant est gris.

L'arbre est vert.

Le ciel est bleu.

Le chocolat est brun.

La prune *(plum)* **est mauve.**

Colors are adjectives and follow the rules for adjectives. Compare:

le pantalon bleu	la robe bleu*e*
le chapeau blanc	la cravate blan*che*
les pantalons bleu*s*	les robes bleu*es*
les chapeaux blanc*s*	les cravates blan*ches*

Note the feminine form of the color **blanc(s): blanche(s).**

Activités

P. Listen as your teacher reads the names of certain things. Write the corresponding number next to the appropriate color.

jaune _____   orange _____   gris _____

rouge _____   bleu _____   brun _____

Q. Identify the articles of clothing purchased by the Lamartine family. Follow the example.

1. _____la jupe bleue_____
(blue)

2. _____
(yellow)

3. _____
(black)

4. _____
(pink)

5. _____
(white)

6. _____
(green)

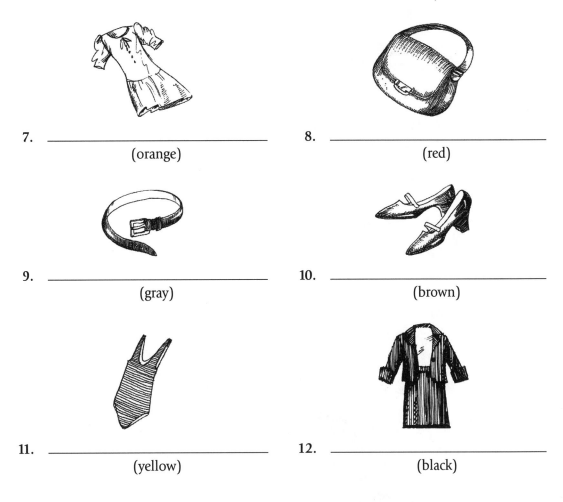

7. _____
(orange)

8. _____
(red)

9. _____
(gray)

10. _____
(brown)

11. _____
(yellow)

12. _____
(black)

R. You are making a list of new clothes you want to buy. Write the names and colors of the items in French.

EXAMPLE: **une robe rouge**

1. _____

2. _____

3. _____

4. _____

5. _____

6. _____

Work with a partner. Take turns describing what you are wearing.

> EXAMPLE   You: **Ma jupe est courte et bleue.**
> Partner: **Mon pantalon est brun et chic.**

CONVERSATION

Vocabulaire

De quelle couleur What color
le ciel the sky

Quelles What
Tiens ! Hey !

DIALOGUE

You are the first speaker in this dialog, the one asking all the questions.

 ### Page culturelle

Les tailles *(Sizes)*

If you should buy a French article of clothing, don't be too frightened or too overjoyed by the sizes.

1 = small 2 = medium 3 = large

When you buy clothing, keep the following sizes in mind:

GIRLS—DRESSES, PANTS, BLOUSES, COATS, etc.

USA	3	5	7	9	11	13
FRANCE	34	36	38	40	42	44

GIRLS—SHOES

USA	4–4½	5–5½	6–6½	7–7½	8–8½	9–9½
FRANCE	35	36	37	38	39	40

BOYS—SUITS, PANTS, COATS, etc.

USA	26	28	30	32	34	36	38	40
FRANCE	36	38	40	42	44	46	48	50

BOYS—SHOES

USA	7	7½	8	8½	9	10	11
FRANCE	39	40	41	42	43	44	45

BOYS—SHIRTS

USA	14	14½	15	15½	16	16½	17
FRANCE	36	37	38	39	40	41	42

Which sizes do you wear?

French sizes are based on the metric system.

$$1 \text{ meter} = 39.37 \text{ inches} \qquad 1 \text{ inch} = 2.5 \text{ centimeters (cm)}$$
$$= 3.28 \text{ feet} \qquad 1 \text{ foot} = 0.3 \text{ meter}$$
$$= 1.09 \text{ yards} \qquad 1 \text{ yard} = 0.9 \text{ meter}$$

How tall are you in meters? Check the chart.

(approximately)

FEET/ INCHES	METERS/ CENTIMETERS	FEET/ INCHES	METERS/ CENTIMETERS
5	1 m 50	5.7	1 m 67½
5.1	1 m 52½	5.8	1 m 70
5.2	1 m 55	5.9	1 m 72½
5.3	1 m 57½	5.10	1 m 75
5.4	1 m 60	5.11	1 m 77½
5.5	1 m 62½	6	1 m 80
5.6	1 m 65		

How much do you weigh metrically?

(approximately)   1 kilo(gram) = 2.2 pounds
1 pound = 0.45 kilograms

POUNDS	KILOGRAMS	POUNDS	KILOGRAMS
90	40.5	150	67.5
100	45	160	72
110	49.5	170	76.5
120	54	180	81
130	58.5	190	85.5
140	63	200	90

Rappel

1. If you wear a size "small" expect to see the number _____ in French clothing to indicate this size.

2. French sizes are based on the _____ system.

3. There are _____ inches in a meter.

4. One foot is equal to _____ meter.

5. One pound is equal to _____ kilogram.

À Vous

1. Do a survey of all the members of your immediate family. Record everyone's height, weight, clothing, and shoe size in American and French sizes.

2. Draw a clothing chart for a store that sells French and American style clothing.

La Chasse au trésor

http://

Using your best Internet search skills, find the answers to the following questions.

1. What are the names of five French fashion designers? Explain why they are famous.
2. What are the names of five French fashion models?

C'est authentique!

You are reading the personal ads in a French newspaper. Match the man writing with the girl he is looking for.

a.   b.   c.   d.

> **FRANÇAIS, 25 ans**, plein de charme, romantique et cultivé, aimerait rencontrer Jeune Française dynamique et moderne.

1. _____

> **Ingénieur, Alexis, 30 ans**, charmant et élégant. C'est un homme sincère, généreux qui désire rencontrer une J.F. simple et naturelle.

2. _____

> **27 ANS**, excellente situation, dentiste. Il est dynamique et sympa. Il est sentimental. Il voudrait faire connaissance d'une J.F. tendre, petite et blonde, qui adore les animaux.

3. _____

> **JEUNE AMÉRICAIN, 26 ans**, sincère, intelligent, bonne situation financière, 1m79, cherche française sincère et intelligente.

4. _____

M O T S   N É C E S S A I R E S

VÊTEMENTS
les baskets *f. pl.* basketball sneakers
la ceinture belt
le chapeau hat
la chaussette sock
la chaussure shoe
la chemise shirt
le chemisier shirt, blouse
la cravate tie
le gant glove
le jean jeans
la jupe skirt
le maillot de bain bathing suit
le manteau coat
le pantalon pants
le pull-over pullover sweater
la robe dress

le sac pocketbook
le survêtement jogging suit
le tailleur woman's suit
les tennis *f. pl.* tennis shoes
la veste jacket
les vêtements *m. pl.* clothing

ADJECTIVES
blanc (*f.* **blanche**) white
bleu blue
brun brown
chic fashionable
chouette great
court short
criard loud
démodé out of style
étroit narrow
formidable terrific

fort strong
gris gray
jaune yellow
laid ugly
long (*f.* **longue**) long
mauve purple
mince thin
moche awful
noir black
orange orange
rose pink
rouge red
super great
vert green

MOTS IMPORTANTS
à la mode fashionable
porter to wear

Révision II
(LEÇONS 5–8)

Leçon 5

a. The subject pronouns are:

je	*I*	nous	*we*
tu	*you*	vous	*you*
il	*he*	ils	*they*
elle	*she*	elles	*they*

b. In order to have a correct verb with each subject, the infinitive of the verb is changed so that the verb form agrees with the subject pronoun or noun. Drop the ending **-er** and add the endings for the different subjects. This step is called CONJUGATION.

EXAMPLE: **parler** – Drop the infinitive ending **-er**.

If the subject is		add	to the remaining stem:		
	je	e		je	parl*e*
	tu	es		tu	parl*es*
	il/elle	e		il/elle	parl*e*
	nous	ons		nous	parl*ons*
	vous	ez		vous	parl*ez*
	ils/elles	ent		ils/elles	parl*ent*

We have just conjugated **parler** in the present tense.

c. To make a sentence negative in French, that is, to say that a subject does NOT do something, use **ne** and **pas.** Put **ne** before the verb and **pas** after the verb.

Je *ne* **parle** *pas* **italien.**

d. To ask a question, you may:

1. Simply raise your voice at the end of the sentence.

   Tu aimes danser?

2. Put **est-ce que** at the beginning of the sentence.

   Est-ce que je parle?

   Put **est-ce qu'** before a vowel (**il** or **elle**).

   *Est-ce qu'*il parle?

145

Leçon 6

A possessive adjective expresses that something belongs to someone.

Use **mon**   *my*
   ton   *your*
   son   *his, her, its*   before masculine singular nouns beginning with a consonant.
   notre   *our*   before all singular nouns beginning with a vowel.
   votre   *your*
   leur   *their*

Use **ma**   *my*
   ta   *your*
   sa   *his, her, its*   before feminine singular nouns beginning with a consonant.
   notre   *our*
   votre   *your*
   leur   *their*

Use **mes**   *my*
   tes   *your*
   ses   *his, her, its*   before ALL plural nouns.
   nos   *our*
   vos   *your*
   leurs   *their*

Leçon 7

a. The verb **être** is an irregular verb that means *to be*. Memorize all its forms.

je suis	nous sommes
tu es	vous êtes
il/elle est	ils/elles sont

b. The same rules as the rules for **-er** verbs apply for making a sentence negative or for asking a question.

Elle *n'*est *pas* contente.
*Est-ce qu'*elle est contente?

Leçon 8

a. Adjectives agree in GENDER and NUMBER with the nouns they describe. If the noun is masculine, the adjective is masculine. If the noun is feminine, the adjective is feminine. If the noun is plural, the adjective is plural. An adjective modifying two or more nouns of different gender is masculine plural.

Le garçon et la fille sont charmants.

b. For most adjectives, add **e** to the masculine form to get the feminine form.

> **Le livre est grand.**
> **L'école est grande.**

c. When the masculine form of the adjective already ends in **e**, no **e** is added to form the feminine adjective.

> **Le garçon est populaire.**
> **La jeune fille est populaire.**

d. Add **s** to get the plural form of the adjectives.

> **Les acteurs sont américains.**
> **Les actrices sont françaises.**

e. An adjective that ends in **s** in the singular does not change in the plural.

> **Les chefs sont français.**
> **Les sandwiches sont exquis.**

f. Adjectives normally follow the nouns they describe. Exceptions are **grand, petit, jeune, joli.**

> **un** *grand* **hôpital** *moderne*
> **une** *petite* **école** *populaire*

Activités

A. Here are eight pictures of people doing things. Describe each picture, using the correct form of one of the following verbs.

chanter	écouter	goûter	regarder
chercher	fermer	habiter	travailler
demander	gagner	préparer	visiter

1. Ils _____
   la télévision.

2. Il _____
   le match.

3. Maman _____ le dîner.

4. Jean _____ beaucoup.

5. Nous _____ Frère Jacques.

6. Les élèves _____ le professeur.

7. Vous _____ le livre.

8. Elles _____ des CD.

B. Qui est-ce?

1. La mère de ma mère est _____ .

2. Le père de mon père est _____ .

3. La sœur de mon père est _____ .

4. Le frère de ma mère est ————————————— .

5. La fille de mon oncle est ————————————— .

6. Le fils de ma tante est ————————————— .

C. Mots croisés

HORIZONTALEMENT	VERTICALEMENT
1. secretary	1. bags
4. nurse	2. hats
8. tie	3. police officer
11. artist	4. he
12. you	5. mail carrier
14. four	6. coat
15. doctor	7. dress
16. skirt	9. actress
17. dentist	10. lawyer
19. she	11. to love
21. ten	13. shirt
22. to enter	14. fifteen
23. socks	18. they
	20. the

D. Write the French word for each clothing item you see. Then circle the French word in the puzzle. The words may be read from left to right, right to left, up or down or diagonally.

1. _____

2. _____

3. _____

4. _____

5. _____

6. _____

7. _____

8. _____

9. _____

10. _____

11. _____

12. _____

E	S	T	N	A	G	U	S	M	P
T	I	E	G	N	A	A	I	A	J
A	E	S	S	E	C	A	N	I	N
V	V	S	P	I	U	L	N	L	O
A	R	A	U	N	M	E	E	L	L
R	H	U	O	E	R	E	T	O	A
C	E	E	U	T	L	T	H	T	T
C	P	B	T	S	E	B	O	C	N
A	U	O	L	E	P	S	A	R	A
S	J	R	E	V	O	L	L	U	P

E. Use an adjective to describe these people or things.

1. Le livre de français est _____ .
2. Le professeur est _____ .
3. Le directeur de l'école est _____ .
4. Les garçons sont _____ .
5. Les jeunes filles sont _____ .

F. Unscramble the colors. Then unscramble the circled letters to find out Annick's favorite colors.

N G R A E O   ⓞ ⓞ _ ⓞ ⓞ _

S G R I   _ _ ⓞ _

E N U J A   _ _ ⓞ _ _

A V U M E   _ _ _ _ ⓞ

E R S O   ⓞ ⓞ _ _

Les couleurs préférées d'Annick sont le _____ et le _____ .

The Cognate Connection

Write the meanings of the following French and English words.

FRENCH

ENGLISH COGNATE

1. avocat _____   advocate _____

2. donner _____   donate _____

3. habiter _____   to inhabit _____

4. infirmier _____   infirmary _____

5. jaune _____   jaundice _____

3

troisième partie

Les parties du corps

*Using the Verb **avoir**; Using Expressions with **avoir***

 L_E M O N S T R E

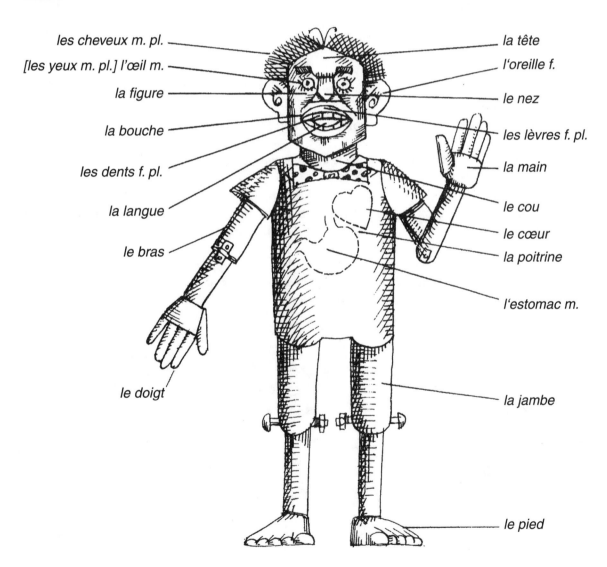

les cheveux m. pl.

[les yeux m. pl.] l'œil m.

la figure

la bouche

les dents f. pl.

la langue

le bras

le doigt

la tête

l'oreille f.

le nez

les lèvres f. pl.

la main

le cou

le cœur

la poitrine

l'estomac m.

la jambe

le pied

Activités

A. You will hear Jean-Luc speak about what he can do with different parts of the body. He says: **Je peux** . . . *(I can)*. Match the body part with the activity it performs.

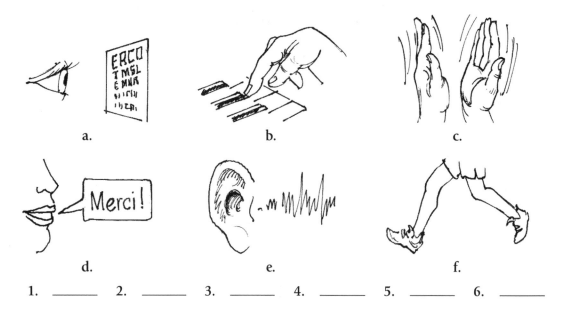

a.   b.   c.

d.   e.   f.

1. _____ 2. _____ 3. _____ 4. _____ 5. _____ 6. _____

B. Work with a partner. Take turns pointing to and identifying a body part.

EXAMPLE: You: **Qu'est-ce que c'est?** *(points to head.)*
              Partner: **C'est la tête.**

C. This monster may look weird, but the parts of his body are the same as yours and mine. Study the French names and match the words with the correct pictures.

la figure	l'oreille	la langue
les cheveux	la bouche	les dents
les yeux	les lèvres	la tête

1. _____ 2. _____ 3. _____

4. _____ 5. _____ 6. _____

D. Label these parts of the body.

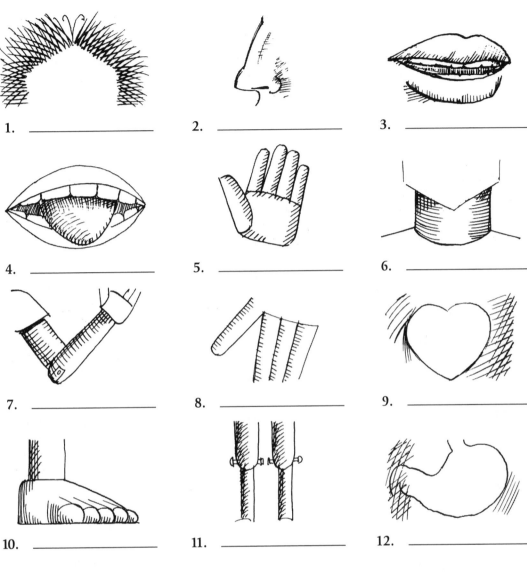

1. _____   2. _____   3. _____

4. _____   5. _____   6. _____

7. _____   8. _____   9. _____

10. _____   11. _____   12. _____

E. Every part of the body can do something. Match the part of the body with the action it can perform. Sometimes more than one part of the body will be appropriate. Write the matching part(s) next to the correct verb.

1.	parler	_____	les pieds
2.	danser	_____	les dents
3.	chanter	_____	les mains
4.	étudier	_____	la bouche
5.	regarder	_____	les lèvres
6.	goûter	_____	les oreilles
7.	marcher	_____	la langue
8.	écouter	_____	les jambes

les bras
les yeux
les doigts

Prononciation

- **ou**, **où**, and **oû** are pronounced like *ou* in *you*.

nous	fou	toujours	écouter	kangourou	coucou
où	douze	cousin	beaucoup	Toulouse	coûter

Le kangourou trouve toujours le coucou de Toulouse.
Où est la cousine qui écoute ses douze cousins?

- Practice the difference between **u** and **ou**

une	ou	cure	cour	tu	tout
bu	bout	dur	doux	rue	roue

Now that you are an expert on the parts of the body, you are ready to read the amazing story of the mad scientist Dr. François Frankenpierre and the horrible monster he created. All the forms of the irregular French verb **avoir** (*to have*) are in this story. See if you can find them all.

Le docteur Frankenpierre

LIEU: Laboratoire d'un savant fou, le docteur François Franken-pierre.

PERSONNAGES: Le docteur Frankenpierre; Marcel, son secrétaire; le Monstre, une combinaison de différentes parties du corps.

LE DOCTEUR FRANKENPIERRE: **J'ai** une idée magnifique. Je veux créer une créature terrible.

MARCEL: Oui, maître.

DR. F.:   D'abord un corps. **Nous avons** un corps, Marcel?

MARCEL: **Vous avez** un corps ici, monsieur, un vieux corps laid.

DR. F.:   Bon. Bon. Et maintenant, deux bras, Marcel.

MARCEL: Voilà deux bras. **Ils ont** beaucoup de poils.

DR. F.:   Bon. Et les mains?

MARCEL: Deux mains. Une main d'homme et l'autre de gorille.

DR. F.:   **Les mains ont** combien de doigts?

MARCEL: Dix doigts, monsieur.

DR. F.:   Parfait

MARCEL: Il y a sept doigts à une main et trois à l'autre.

DR. F.:   Bon. Les pieds. **Nous avons** des pieds?

MARCEL: Certainement, monsieur. Un grand pied et un très petit pied.

Glossary (right margin):

lieu place
un savant a scientist
fou crazy
une combinaison a combination
parties parts

créer to create

maître master

d'abord first
un corps a body
vieux old

poils (body) hair

l'autre the other

certainement certainly

DR. F.:   Très bien. Mais **il n'a pas** de tête.

MARCEL: La voici, monsieur. Une petite tête avec une figure stupide.

DR. F.:   Formidable. L'électricité va donner vie au monstre.

BZZZZZZZZZZZZZ

MARCEL: Regardez le monstre. . . . Il va parler!

DR. F.:   **Tu as** une bouche. Parle! Parle!

LE MONSTRE: Je parle, tu parles, il parle . . .

DR. F.:   Quel monstre formidable! C'est un professeur de fran-çais. C'est (*Fill in someone's name, someone who won't get too angry with you.*) —————————

il n'a pas de tête he does not have a head
La voici here it is

va is going to   **la vie** life

Activités

F. **Oui ou non?** If the sentence is incorrect, change it to make it correct.

1. Le Docteur Frankenpierre est un savant fou.

    _____

2. Le monstre a le corps d'un jeune homme.

    _____

3. Le monstre n'a pas de bras.

    _____

4. Chaque main a cinq doigts.

    _____

5. Le monstre danse bien.

    _____

6. Le monstre a une figure intelligente.

    _____

7. L'électricité donne vie au monstre.

    _____

8. Le monstre parle italien.

    _____

G. Fill in the names of the labeled parts of the body.

Did you find the forms of the irregular verb **avoir** in the story? Remember: **Avoir** is a special verb because it is one of a kind. No other verb in French is conjugated like **avoir. Avoir** means *to have.* Fill in the proper verb forms for each subject. MEMORIZE them.

j' _____

tu _____

il/elle _____

nous _____

vous _____

ils/elles _____

Activités

H. You are talking on the phone with a blind date. You want some information from that person. Work with a partner. Then write your questions and your partner's answers. Ask the questions following the example.

> EXAMPLE: les cheveux longs
> You: **Tu as les cheveux longs?**
> Partner: **Oui, j'ai les cheveux longs.**

1. un petit nez

   _____

   _____

2. de petites oreilles

   _____

   _____

3. les cheveux noirs

   _____

   _____

4. des yeux bleus

   _____

   _____

I. You are writing a letter to a pen pal. Tell him/her some things about yourself and your family.

> EXAMPLE: **Mon père/les cheveux noirs**
> **Mon père a les cheveux noirs.**

1. Ma sœur / un grand nez

   _____

2. je / les yeux verts

   _____

3. Mes parents / les yeux gris

   _____

4. Nous / de petites mains

   _____

5. Mon frère et moi / de grands pieds

   _____

J. Talk about some things you and your friends don't have.

> EXAMPLE: **Charles / beaucoup d'amis.**
> **Charles n'a pas beaucoup d'amis.**

1. je / deux chats noirs

    _____

2. Georges et Marie / de petits enfants.

    _____

3. vous / beaucoup de travail.

    _____

4. tu / les yeux verts.

    _____

5. nous / le grand dictionnaire

    _____

6. Rose / de longs cheveux

    _____

 More about **avoir**. There are some very common expressions in French that use the verb **avoir**. The comparable English expressions use the verb _to be_.

avoir chaud	_to be warm_
avoir froid	_to be cold_
avoir faim	_to be hungry_
avoir soif	_to be thirsty_
avoir raison	_to be right_
avoir tort	_to be wrong_
avoir peur (de)	_to be afraid (of)_
avoir sommeil	_to be sleepy_
avoir _____ ans	_to be _____ old_

> EXAMPLES: **J'ai faim.** _I am hungry_
> **Il a soif.** _He is thirsty._

<u>NOTE:</u> The expressions **avoir chaud** and **avoir froid** are used only if the subject is a person or an animal. For objects, use the verb **être**:

> **L'élève** _a chaud._ _The student is (feels) warm._

But:

> **La soupe** _est chaude._ _The soup is warm._

Activités

K. Your friend Jean-Pierre is describing some of his friends. Put the letter of each picture next to the appropriate number.

a.

b.

c.

d.

e.

f.

1. _____   2. _____   3. _____   4. _____   5. _____   6. _____

L. Work with a partner. Ask if you are having the following problems and then give truthful answers. After your conversation, write the questions and answers.

1.   2.   3.   4.

1. _____ .

2. _____ .

3. _____ .

4. _____ .

M. Here are some sentences in which a form of **avoir** is used. Match these sentences with the pictures they describe.

Le bébé a un an.
J'ai très chaud.
Le chien a soif.
Jean a un long cou.
Les enfants n'ont pas froid.

Nous avons soif.
Tu as faim?
Les filles ont les cheveux longs.
Tu as deux bras forts.
Elle a de grands yeux.

1. _____

2. _____

3. _____

4. _____

5. _____

6. _____

7. _____

8. _____

9. _____

10. _____

Parlons français

Take turns with a partner. One person acts out a physical condition. The other person must guess the situation and ask an appropriate question. Follow the examples.

EXAMPLES: (*act out: hungry*)   You: **Tu as soif?**
    Partner: **Non, tu as tort; j'ai faim.**

    (*act out: long hair*)   You: **Tu as les cheveux longs?**
    Partner: **Oui, tu as raison; j'ai les cheveux longs.**

CONVERSATION

Vocabulaire

penser to think
au contraire on the contrary

qu'est-ce que vous avez what's the matter with you?
avoir peur to be afraid

DIALOGUE

Answer the following questions with a suitable response.

Quand avez-vous froid?

Quand avez-vous chaud?

Avez-vous toujours raison?

Qu'est-ce que vous avez à dix heures du soir?

Page culturelle

Les gestes *(Gestures)*

In every culture, gestures play an important role in communicating ideas and feelings. Gestures may be accompanied by a word or phrase. In most instances, however, the meaning of a gesture is clear to a native speaker or listener. Gestures, like pictures, are often more expressive than words and contribute to a more lively conversation.

Here are some typical French gestures:

1. **Un, deux, trois . . .**
   (The French start counting with their thumbs.)

2. **Salut!**
   (French people kiss on both cheeks to greet relatives or friends.)

3. **Magnifique!** *(Magnificent!)*

4. **Parfait!** *(Great!)*

5. **Allons boire quelque chose.**
   (Let's go drink something.)

6. **Que c'est ennuyeux!**
   (It's so boring.)

7. **J'en ai par-dessus la tête.**
   (I've had it up to here!)

8. **Mon œil!**
   (You must be kidding!)

9. **Je ne sais pas.**
   (I don't know.)

10. **Pas un sou! Rien!**
    (Not a penny! Nothing!)

Rappel

1. Gestures are important in communicating _____ and _____ .

2. Gestures may be accompanied by a _____ or a _____ .

3. The meaning of most gestures is _____ .

4. Gestures contribute to a lively _____ .

5. An example of a typical French gesture for greeting someone is _____ .

À Vous

1. Write a list of gestures you use to express your various moods.

2. Draw a poster showing your favorite French gestures or comparing those used in America with those used in France.

La Chasse au trésor

http://

Using your best Internet search skills, find the answers to the following questions:

1. How is a French handshake different from an American handshake?
2. What do the French say when someone is twiddling his thumbs?
3. What French gesture indicates that someone needs money? What phrase would be used to accompany this gesture?
4. What French gesture indicates that someone is lazy? What phrase would be used to accompany this gesture?
5. What French gesture indicates that someone is fed up? What phrase would be used to accompany this gesture?

C'est authentique!

Imagine that you are not feeling well while visiting France and that you go to a doctor. Complete the form the nurse gives you. Make sure to list the parts of your body that are painful.

FRÉDÉRIC A. PIERROT
Médecin des hôpitaux
68, Rue Napoléon Paris France
Tel: 01 47 35 19 56 Fax: 01 47 22 80 04

FICHE MÉDICALE

Date _____

Nom _____ Prénoms _____

Adresse _____

_____

N° de téléphone _____

Date de naissance _____ âge _____

Profession _____

Situation de famille:
célibataire (*single*) ____ , marié(e) ____ , divorcé(e) ____ , veuf/veuve (*widowed*) ____

Parties du corps douloureuses (*painful*)

_____

_____

_____

_____

_____

_____

_____

_____

_____

M O T S   N É C E S S A I R E S

BODY PARTS
la bouche mouth
le bras arm
les cheveux *m. pl.* hair
le cœur heart
le corps body
le cou neck
la dent tooth

le doigt finger
l'estomac *m.* stomach
la figure face
la jambe leg
la langue tongue
la lèvre lip
la main hand
le monstre monster

le nez nose
l'œil *m.* eye
l'oreille *f.* ear
la partie part
le pied foot
la poitrine chest
la tête head
les yeux *m. pl.* eyes

AVOIR

avoir to have
j'ai I have
tu as you have
il/elle a he/she has
nous avons we have
vous avez you have
ils/elles ont they have

EXPRESSIONS

avoir chaud to be warm
avoir froid to be cold
avoir faim to be hungry
avoir peur (de) to be
 afraid (of)
avoir raison to be right
avoir soif to be thirsty

avoir sommeil to be sleepy
avoir tort to be wrong
avoir _____ **ans** to
 be _____ years old

10
Les jours et les mois

Expressing the Days and the Months

1 **Les jours de la semaine sont:**

lundi	mercredi	vendredi	dimanche
mardi	jeudi	samedi	

Activités

A. Listen to Anne tell her schedule for the week. Circle the day after the one you hear to complete her sentences.

1. **a.** lundi   **b.** vendredi   **c.** mercredi
2. **a.** samedi   **b.** lundi   **c.** mardi
3. **a.** mardi   **b.** dimanche   **c.** samedi
4. **a.** jeudi   **b.** vendredi   **c.** mardi
5. **a.** lundi   **b.** dimanche   **c.** vendredi

B. Work with a partner. One person gives the name of a day and the other person gives the name of the day that comes before.

EXAMPLE   You: **Lundi?**
               Partner: **Dimanche. Samedi?**

C. Fill in the name of the day of the week.

1. l __ n __ i
2. m __ __ d __
3. d __ m __ __ __ __ e
4. m __ r __ __ __ d __
5. s __ __ __ __ i
6. ve __ dr __ __ i
7. __ e __ __ i

D. Complete with the correct information.

1. Il y a _____ jours dans une semaine.

2. Les jours de travail sont _____

    _____ .

3. Il n'y a pas de classes le _____ et le _____ .

E. Fill in the days before and after the day given.

1. _____   lundi   _____

2. _____   mercredi   _____

3. _____   vendredi   _____

4. _____   dimanche   _____

Now you can read this conversation about the days of the week.

Quel est votre jour préféré? Pourquoi?

ANDRÉ: Samedi et dimanche. Il n'y a pas de classes.

FRANÇOISE: Lundi. J'aime aller à l'école.

SYLVIE: Lundi, mardi, mercredi, jeudi et vendredi. Je parle avec
Paul, un garçon formidable dans la classe d'histoire.

ROGER: Samedi et dimanche. J'aime regarder les sports à la télé.

MICHEL: Samedi. J'ai rendez-vous tous les samedis avec une
jeune fille différente.

ANNE: Mercredi. J'ai un cours de karaté. J'aime me défendre.

un cours a course
me myself

Activités

F. Match the person with his/her favorite day. Write the matching letter in the space provided.

1. Anne   ____   4. Sylvie   ____   a. samedi
2. André   ____   5. Michel   ____   b. lundi
3. Françoise   ____   6. Roger   ____   c. mercredi
                                            d. samedi et dimanche
                                            e. dimanche
                                            f. lundi, mardi, mercredi, jeudi, vendredi

G. Give the reason in French why each person prefers his/her favorite day.

1. Roger   _____

2. Anne   _____

3. André _____

4. Françoise _____

5. Michel _____

6. Sylvie _____

H. Quel est votre jour favori? _____

Pourquoi? _____

2 Look at the spelling of the days of the week. What do you notice about the first letters of each day when they appear in the middle of the sentence? _____

_____

How does each day end except for **dimanche?** _____

How does **dimanche** begin? _____

One more little point about the days of the week. Compare these examples:

Il n'y a pas de classes *lundi.*	*There's no school Monday* [next Monday].
Il n'y a pas de classes *le samedi.*	*There's no school (on) Saturday(s)* [each Saturday].

> When referring to every Saturday, Sunday, etc.
> use **le** before the name of a day.
> When referring to one specific day (next Monday . . .) use no article.

3 **Les mois de l'année sont:**

janvier	février	mars
avril	mai	juin

juillet   août   septembre

octobre   novembre   décembre

Activités

I. Fill in the months before and after the months given.

1. _____ février _____

2. _____ mai _____

3. _____ août _____

4. _____ novembre _____

J. Below each picture, write the French name of the month(s) commonly associated with the activity shown. (In some situations, more than one month may be correct.).

1. _____ 2. _____ 3. _____

4. _____ 5. _____ 6. _____

7. _____   8. _____   9. _____

10. _____   11. _____   12. _____

 Now you can read this conversation about the months of the year.

Quel est votre mois préféré? Pourquoi?

SOLANGE: J'aime janvier parce que j'aime le ski.

MARIE: J'aime nager dans l'océan en août.

ARTHUR: En octobre j'aime jouer au football américain.

ANDRÉ: Je préfère avril parce que j'aime jouer au base-ball.

CHANTAL: J'aime la rentrée des classes en septembre.

PAUL: J'aime juillet parce que j'adore les grandes vacances.

ÉRIC: Décembre. J'aime Noël.

MICHÈLE: Je préfère mai parce que j'aime les jolies fleurs.

nager to swim

la rentrée des classes back to school day
les vacances the vacation

Activités

K. Match the person with his / her favorite month. Write the matching letter in the space provided.

1. Paul _____   5. Solange _____   a. mai
2. André _____   6. Éric _____   b. janvier
3. Michèle _____   7. Marie _____   c. décembre
4. Arthur _____   8. Chantal _____   d. avril
                                     e. juillet
                                     f. octobre
                                     g. août
                                     h. septembre

L. Give the reason in French why each person prefers his / her month.

1. Éric _____

2. Michèle _____

3. Marie   _____

4. André   _____

5. Chantal   _____

6. Paul   _____

7. Solange   _____

8. Arthur   _____

M. Work with a partner. Take turns asking and answering the question.

Quel est votre mois préféré? _____

Pourquoi? _____

 Look at the spelling of the months. What do you notice about the first letters when these words are in the middle of the sentence? _____

_____

 Quelle est la date aujourd'hui? *(What is today's date?)*

Let's see how the date is expressed in French. Look at the dates circled in the calendar (**le calendrier**):

	JANVIER	FÉVRIER	MARS	AVRIL
LUNDI	7 14 21 28	4 11 18 25	4 ⑪ 18 25	1 8 15 22 29
MARDI	1 8 15 22 29	⑤ 12 19 26	5 12 19 26	2 9 16 23 30
MERCREDI	2 9 16 23 30	6 13 20 27	6 13 20 27	3 10 17 24
JEUDI	3 10 17 24 31	7 14 21 28	7 14 21 28	4 11 18 25
VENDREDI	4 11 18 25	1 8 15 22	1 8 15 22 29	5 12 19 26
SAMEDI	5 12 19 26	2 9 16 23	2 9 16 23 30	6 13 20 27
DIMANCHE	6 13 20 27	3 10 17 24	3 10 17 24 31	7 14 21 28
	MAI	JUIN	JUILLET	AOÛT
LUNDI	6 13 20 27	3 10 17 24	1 8 15 22 29	5 12 19 26
MARDI	7 14 21 28	4 11 18 25	2 9 16 23 30	6 13 20 27
MERCREDI	1 8 ⑮ 22 29	5 12 19 26	3 10 17 24 31	7 14 21 28
JEUDI	2 9 16 23 30	6 13 20 27	4 11 18 25	1 8 15 22 29
VENDREDI	3 10 17 24 31	7 14 21 28	5 12 19 26	2 9 16 23 30
SAMEDI	4 11 18 25	1 8 15 22 29	6 13 20 27	3 10 17 24 ㉛
DIMANCHE	5 12 19 26	2 9 16 23 30	7 14 21 28	4 11 18 25
	SEPTEMBRE	OCTOBRE	NOVEMBRE	DÉCEMBRE
LUNDI	2 9 16 23 30	7 14 21 28	4 11 18 25	2 9 16 23 30
MARDI	3 10 17 24	1 8 15 22 29	5 12 19 26	3 10 17 24 31
MERCREDI	4 11 18 25	2 9 16 23 30	6 13 20 27	4 11 18 25
JEUDI	5 12 19 26	3 10 17 24 31	7 14 21 28	5 12 19 26
VENDREDI	6 13 20 27	4 11 18 25	1 8 15 22 29	6 13 20 27
SAMEDI	7 14 21 28	5 12 19 26	2 9 16 23 30	7 14 21 28
DIMANCHE	1 8 15 22 29	6 13 20 27	3 10 17 24	① 8 15 22 29

C'est le cinq février.
C'est mardi, le cinq février.

C'est le onze mars.
C'est lundi, le onze mars.

C'est le quinze mai.
C'est mercredi, le quinze mai.

C'est le trente et un août.
C'est samedi, le trente et un août.

Can you fill in the blanks? To express the date, use:

C'est + _____ + _____ + _____

If you want to include the day of the week, use:

C'est + _____ + _____ + _____ + _____

There is just one exception:

C'est le premier décembre.
C'est dimanche, le premier décembre.

The first of the month is always expressed as **le premier.**

Notice how we write dates in numbers and how the French write them:

	ENGLISH	FRENCH
July 11, 1947	7/11/47	**11/7/47**
May 3, 1974	5/3/74	**3/5/74**
September 27, 1953	9/27/53	**27/9/53**

In French, the _____ comes first, then the _____ , and finally the
_____ .

Activités

N. Your teacher is telling you when you'll have days off this term. Write the dates you hear.

EXAMPLE: you hear: **samedi, le trente octobre**
you write: Saturday, October 30.

1. _____
2. _____
3. _____
4. _____
5. _____

O. These are your friends' birthdays. Express them in French.

1. April 22 _____

2. August 7 _____

3. February 1 _____

4. July 29 _____

5. January 12 _____

6. Monday, March 30 _____

7. Saturday, December 4 _____

8. Wednesday, June 15 _____

9. Sunday, September 14 _____

10. Thursday, November 16 _____

P. Give the dates in French for these important events

1. your birthday _____

2. Christmas _____

3. New Year's Day _____

4. Thanksgiving _____

5. Independence Day _____

6. your mother's birthday _____

7. your father's birthday _____

8. your favorite day of the year _____

Q. For your French pen pal, you want to express all the dates in Activité P in numbers, French style.

1. _____   5. _____

2. _____   6. _____

3. _____   7. _____

4. _____   8. _____

Now you can read this conversation about dates.

Quelle est votre date préférée? Pourquoi?

ANDRÉ: Le vingt-cinq décembre. J'aime l'arbre de Noël et toutes les décorations.

l'arbre the tree

FRANÇOISE: Le quatre juillet. J'aime regarder le feu d'artifice.

le feu d'artifice the fireworks

SYLVIE: Le quinze avril. C'est mon anniversaire. J'aime les cadeaux.   **le cadeau** the gift

ROGER: Le premier janvier. Je mange un grand dîner dans un
restaurant élégant.

ANNE: Le premier juillet. L'école ferme et les vacances com-   **commencer** to start
mencent.

Activités

R. Match the person with his / her favorite date. Write the matching letter next to the names.

1. Anne   _____   **a.** le vingt-cinq décembre

2. Sylvie   _____   **b.** le quatre juillet

3. André   _____   **c.** le quinze avril

4. Roger   _____   **d.** le premier juillet

5. Françoise _____   **e.** le premier janvier

S. Give the reason in French why each person prefers his / her favorite date.

1. Roger _____

2. Anne _____

3. André _____

4. Françoise _____

5. Sylvie _____

Prononciation

• **h** at the beginning of a word is usually silent. Words starting with **h** begin with a vowel
sound.

l'heure	l'histoire	l'homme	l'herbe	Henri
l'hôtel	l'hiver	l'hôpital	habiter	Hélène

Les hommes habitent en bas.
Henri et Hélène sont à l'hôpital.

• In some words the **h** is not silent, though it is not pronounced. It is called aspirate **h**, with
which there is no liaison and no elision.

le haricot   le hareng   la harpe   le hasard   le haut   la hauteur

CONVERSATION

Vocabulaire

viens célébrer come celebrate   **mignon** cute

Parlons français

Work with a partner. Take turns giving information about your daily activities. Make sure you speak about all seven days of the week. Follow the example.

EXAMPLE   You: **Qu'est-ce que tu fais** *(do)* **le dimanche?**
            Partner: **Le dimanche, je regarde la télévision. Et toi?**

Page culturelle

Les jours fériés *(Days off)*

What is the first thing many students look for on the school calendar? Days off! All French people are given time off for the following eleven legal holidays (**jours fériés**). In addition students often have longer vacations before or after those dates. (See chapter 24).

1- **La Toussaint** *(All Saint's Day)*, November 1st, is a day celebrating all the saints. Many people visit cemeteries and place chrysanthemums on graves of relatives. November 2nd, **le Jour des Morts** *(All Souls' Day)*, is not a legal holiday. Schools are closed for about a week at this time.

2- **L'Armistice** *(Armistice Day)*, November 11, is the day that commemorates the end of World War I in 1918. In the U.S., this holiday is called Veterans Day.

3- **Noël**, December 25, is *Christmas*. Christmas Eve is celebrated with a midnight mass and **un réveillon**, a festive dinner. **La bûche de Noël** (a cake in the form of a Yule log) is the traditional dessert.

4- New Year's Eve is celebrated on December 31st, **la Saint-Sylvestre**, with another late festive **réveillon**. On **le Jour de l'An**, also called **le Nouvel An** *(New Year's Day)*, January 1st, it is a French tradition to visit family and friends to wish each other **une bonne année**.

French school children have a two-week winter recess (**les vacances d'hiver**) in February, which usually includes **Mardi Gras** *(Shrove Tuesday)*, the last day of carnival before Lent (**le Carême**). It is celebrated with parades in some French-speaking cities such as Nice in France and New Orleans in Louisiana. People wear costumes and dance in the streets, but it is not a legal holiday.

5- Around **Pâques** *(Easter)*, students usually enjoy a spring vacation which includes **le Vendredi Saint** *(Good Friday)*. Easter eggs and chocolates are given to children. For their parents, however, only the Monday after Easter, known as **le lundi de Pâques**, is a **jour férié**.

6- On **le 1er mai, la Fête du Travail** *(Labor Day)*, May 1st, workers celebrate in the streets with parades. The lily of the valley (**le muguet**) is considered the good-luck symbol of this day and is offered to relatives and close friends.

7- **Le 8 mai** celebrates the Allied victory in 1945 and the end of World War II in Europe. There are military ceremonies and parades throughout France. On this date also, the French remember Joan of Arc (**Jeanne d'Arc**), a young peasant girl who helped deliver France from the English in 1429.

8- **L'Ascension** is a Catholic holiday which takes place forty days after Easter.

9- **La Pentecôte** *(Pentecost)* occurs seven weeks after Easter. The next day, le **lundi**, is a jour férié.

During the school summer vacation, two more legal holidays are celebrated:

10- **la Fête Nationale** *(Bastille Day)* takes place on July 14, **le 14 juillet.** This holiday marks the storming of the Bastille prison in 1789 and the beginning of the French Revolution. There are military parades, parties, dancing in the streets, and, of course, magnificent fireworks.

11- August 15 is another religious holiday, **l'Assomption.** In many towns there are religious processions or folkloric festivals, such as the blessing of the boats in seaside towns.

Rappel

1. The special Christmas dinner is called _____ .

2. People wear costumes and dance in the streets to celebrate _____ .

3. We celebrate Easter and the French celebrate _____ .

4. _____ is the good luck symbol that is given to family and friends to celebrate Labor Day.

5. The end of World War II is celebrated on _____ .

6. Bastille Day, **la Fête Nationale,** is celebrated on _____ .

À Vous

1. Pick a holiday that is celebrated differently in France. Compare and contrast what the French and Americans do.

2. Prepare a diorama depicting a French holiday.

3. Describe how Mardi Gras is celebrated.

La Chasse au trésor

http://

Using your best Internet search skills, find the answers to the following questions:

1. What does Bastille Day symbolize?
2. When was Bastille Day declared a national holiday?
3. What began with the storming of the Bastille?
4. Who was the king of France at that time?
5. Who was the queen at that time?
6. What famous quote is attributed to that queen?
7. Why did this quote enrage the people?
8. What happened to this queen?

C'est authentique!

When can you visit this museum? _____

MUSÉUM NATIONAL D'HISTOIRE NATURELLE

Visitez la Grande Galerie de l'Évolution

Ouvert de 10 h à 18 h, nocturne le jeudi jusqu'à 22 h. Fermé mardi et 1ᵉʳ mai.

Jardin des Plantes

36, rue Geoffroy Saint-Hilaire, Paris Vᵉ

Téléphone : 01 40 79 30 00

métro Austerlitz, Jussieu, Censier-Daubenton ou RER C
http://www.mnhn.fr/evolution

1. On Wednesday, May 1ˢᵗ at 2 pm?

2. On Tuesday, May 7, at 10 am?

3. On Thursday, November 14, at 9 pm?

4. On Friday, November 15, at 9 pm?

MOTS NÉCESSAIRES

DAYS
le jour day
lundi m. Monday
mardi m. Tuesday
mercredi m. Wednesday
jeudi m. Thursday
vendredi m. Friday
samedi m. Saturday

dimanche m. Sunday
le jour férié day off

MONTHS
le mois month
janvier m. January
février m. February
mars m. March
avril m. April

mai m. May
juin m. June
juillet m. July
août m. August
septembre m. September
octobre m. October
novembre m. November
décembre m. December

11

Quel temps fait-il?

Expressing the Weather and the Seasons;
*Using the Verb **faire***

 Quel temps fait-il?

le printemps

l'été

Au printemps il fait beau.
Il pleut quelquefois *(sometimes).*

En été il fait chaud.
Il fait du soleil.

l'automne

l'hiver

En automne il fait du vent.
Il fait mauvais.

En hiver il fait froid.
Il neige.

Activités

A. Match the descriptions you hear with the seasons being described.

a. l'hiver _____
b. l'été _____

c. le printemps _____
d. l'automne _____

B. Quel temps fait-il aujourd'hui? You are a weather forecaster. Match the following expressions with the correct pictures:

Il fait du vent.	Il neige.
Il fait du soleil.	Il pleut.
Il fait froid.	Il fait beau.
Il fait chaud.	Il fait mauvais.

1. _____ .

2. _____ .

3. _____ .

4. _____ .

5. _____ .

6. _____ .

7. _____ .   8. _____ .

C. What's the weather in France? Listen to the forecast and match the city with its weather.

a. _____

b. _____

c. _____

d. _____

e. _____

D. Do you know which months belong to each season?

le printemps	l'été	l'automne	l'hiver
_____	_____	_____	_____
_____	_____	_____	_____
_____	_____	_____	_____

 Did you notice how the weather is expressed in French? You use the verb **faire** (*to make, to do*). **Faire** is an irregular verb, and all of its forms must be memorized. In the story that follows, all the forms of **faire** appear. Can you find them all?

Quand **il fait** chaud, je suis très contente. Mes amis et moi, **nous faisons** une promenade au parc. Au parc, **les garcons font** une partie de football et **les filles font** une partie de volley. Après le match **nous faisons** un pique-nique et nous mangeons beaucoup.

une promenade a walk

mangeons eat

Le lendemain matin le professeur demande: «Pourquoi est-ce que **tu fais** tes devoirs en classe?» Et moi, je réponds: «Quand **il fait** chaud, **je** ne **fais** pas mes devoirs à la maison. Qu'est-ce que **vous faites** quand **il fait** chaud?» Alors le professeur répond: «Hélas, quand **il fait** chaud, je punis les élèves.»

le lendemain matin the next morning
réponds answer
à la maison at home

hélas alas
   je punis I punish

Activité

E. Complete the sentences.

1. Quand il fait chaud, l'élève est _____ .

2. Elle _____ avec ses amis.

3. Au parc les garçons _____ .

4. Au parc les filles _____ .

5. Après le match les garçons et les filles _____ .

6. Le lendemain le professeur demande à l'élève: _____ .

7. L'élève répond: _____ .

8. Quand il fait chaud, le professeur _____ .

2 Did you find all the forms of the verb **faire** *(to make, to do)* in the story? Fill in the proper forms of **faire** for each subject.

je _____   nous _____

tu _____   vous _____

il / elle _____   ils / elles _____

Look carefully at these sentences.

Il *fait* chaud.   Il *fait* du vent.
Il *fait* froid.   Il *fait* du soleil.

The verb **faire** is used in most weather expressions. Exceptions:

Il pleut.   *It rains. It is raining.*
Il neige.   *It snows. It is snowing.*

Activités

F. Make a list of what you do every day.

EXAMPLE: **(les devoirs) Je fais les devoirs.**

1. (une promenade)   _____

2. (une partie de tennis)   _____

3. (le dîner)   _____

4. (des exercices)   _____

5. (attention)   _____

G. Describe the weather in these pictures.

1. _____

2. _____

3. _____

4. _____

5. _____

6. _____

H. Work with a partner. Ask your friend what he or she does after school. Then record your questions and your partner's answers.

EXAMPLE: (un pique-nique)
    YOU: **Est-ce que tu fais un pique-nique?**
    PARTNER: **Oui, je fais un pique-nique.**

1. (beaucoup de sport) _____
   _____

2. (de bons sandwichs) _____
   _____

3. (le dîner) _____
   _____

4. (les devoirs) _____
   _____

I. The weather forecast was wrong again. Disagree with the predictions.

EXAMPLE: **(chaud) Il ne fait pas chaud.**

1. (froid) _____ .
2. (beau _____ .
3. (mauvais) _____ .

J. Tell what these people are doing. Complete the sentences with the correct form of **faire**.

1. Vous _____ attention.
2. Je _____ la valise.
3. Il _____ un long voyage.
4. Nous _____ nos devoirs.
5. Elles _____ un pique-nique.
6. Tu _____ une omelette.
7. Elle _____ la liste.
8. Ils _____ les sandwiches.

K. There's a substitute teacher in your class today and the students are misbehaving. Using the verb **faire** tell what the students are not doing.

EXAMPLE: **Richard ne fait pas les mots croisés.**

attention	**les devoirs**
les exercices	**la liste de vocabulaire**
la grammaire	**le travail scolaire**

1. Vous _____ .
2. Je _____ .
3. Tu _____ .
4. Marie _____ .
5. Nous _____ .
6. Les garçons _____

L. Il y a quatre saisons. En quelle saison sommes-nous?

1. Cette saison est très belle. Il fait beau. Il y a beaucoup
de fleurs dans le parc. Tout est vert. Les oiseaux chantent
dans les arbres. Les gens ne portent pas beaucoup de
vêtements. Pâques est une fête importante de cette
saison. Il y a aussi la fête des Mères et la fête des Pères.

   Cette saison est _____ .

belle beautiful
la fleur flower
  les oiseaux birds
la fête holiday

2. C'est la saison préférée de beaucoup d'enfants parce qu'il y a les grandes vacances et il n'y a pas de classes. Il fait très chaud et il fait du soleil. Les enfants vont à la plage. Les jours sont longs et les nuits sont courtes. Les fêtes importantes sont: le jour de l'Indépendance et la fête du Travail.

vont go
   la plage beach
les nuits nights
   courtes short

Cette saison est _____ .

3. En cette saison, les enfants sont un peu tristes parce que les écoles ouvrent et c'est la rentrée des classes. Mais c'est une saison agréable. Il ne fait ni très froid ni très chaud. Il fait beau. Il y a beaucoup de fêtes: le jour de l'arrivée de Christophe Colomb en Amérique, Halloween et le jour d'Action de grâce.

ouvrent open
   la rentrée return
ni . . . ni neither . . . nor

Action de grâce
   Thanksgiving

Cette saison est _____ .

4. En cette saison, il neige et il fait très froid. Les gens portent beaucoup de vêtements pour se protéger. Les nuits sont longues et il y a beaucoup de gens qui trouvent que c'est une saison triste. Pourtant il y a beaucoup de fêtes populaires. Il y a Noël, le jour de l'An, les anniversaires de Martin Luther King Jr., d'Abraham Lincoln et de George Washington et la Saint-Valentin.

se protéger to protect
   oneself

triste sad
   pourtant still

Cette saison est _____ .

M. Complete the sentences based on the stories.

1. Il y a _____ saisons.

2. Les saisons sont _____

_____ .

3. La saison des fleurs s'appelle _____ .

4. Les enfants ne vont pas à l'école en _____ .

5. En été il fait _____ et il fait du _____ .

6. Les jours sont longs et les nuits sont courtes en _____ .

7. En _____ il neige beaucoup.

8. Le premier janvier s'appelle _____ .

N. Which holidays are suggested by these pictures? Write your answer under each picture, choosing from the following list.

le jour de l'An	l'anniversaire de Lincoln
l'anniversaire de Washington	la fête des Pères
le jour d'Action de grâce	la Saint-Valentin
le jour de l'Indépendance	Noël
l'arrivée en Amérique	Pâques
de Christophe Colomb	Halloween
la fête des Mères	

1. _____

2. _____

3. _____

4. _____

5. _____

6. _____

7. _____

8. _____

9. _____

10. _____

11. _____

12. _____

O. Pick your favorite season and write a short paragraph in French about it using the following cues: the season you like; the weather during that season; the holidays during that season; two things you like to do during the season.

_____

_____

_____

_____

_____

CONVERSATION

Vocabulaire

la chaleur the heat
affreuse awful
Tiens! hey!

Je vais I go
Tu vas you go

pendant during
je viens I come

on va? shall we go?
je ne sais pas I don't know

DIALOGUE

You are the second person in the dialog. Respond in complete French sentences.

Prononciation

- **ill** often represents the sound of *y* as in *yes*.

famille   **fille**   **billet**   **feuille**   **travailler**   **gentille**   **brillant**   **gorille**

<u>NOTE:</u> Exceptions: **ill** has the sound of *eel* in these and related words:

     ville   **village**   **mille**   **million**   **tranquille**   **tranquillement**

- **il** often has the sound of *y* as in *yes* when it is preceded by a vowel.

         travail   **soleil**   **œil**   **détail**

     Il y a mille familles tranquilles dans le village.
     La fille gentille travaille avec les gorilles en plein soleil.

Parlons français

Have a conversation with a partner in which you take turns asking about and discussing the weather and your activities in various seasons.

EXAMPLE: You: **Quel temps fait-il en été?**
    Partner: **En été il fait très beau.**

    You: **Qu'est-ce que tu fais en été?**
    Partner: **En été, je fais un voyage.**

C'est authentique!

Look at the weather symbols and see if you can guess what they mean. Then using the expressions given below, give today's forecast for the cities listed.

Il fait beau. _____   Il pleut. _____   Il fait du vent. _____

Il neige. _____   Il fait mauvais. _____

1. Ajaccio

    _____ .

2. Cherbourg

    _____ .

3. Dijon

    _____ .

4. Strasbourg

    _____ .

5. Grenoble

    _____ .

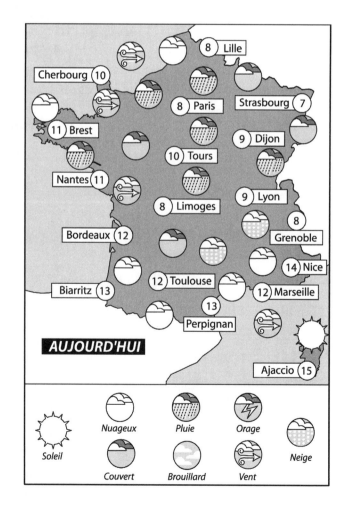

Page culturelle

Les vacances d'été et d'hiver

During the month of August, many French businesses close for vacation and everyone seems to leave the city to go to the beach or the mountains. Swimming and camping are very popular summer activities.

Winter ski vacations are also popular in France. During Christmas and February breaks, many French youths take to the slopes. Some schools even provide special **classes de neige.** In the morning, students attend their regular courses, and in the afternoon they learn to ski.

Look at the map below and see in which French cities you could spend a summer or winter vacation.

If you want to know if the temperature is right for swimming or skiing, keep in mind that the French use the Celsius rather than the Fahrenheit scale:

To convert Fahrenheit to Celsius or vice versa, use the following formulas:

$$\text{CELSIUS} = C \qquad\qquad \text{FAHRENHEIT} = F$$
$$C = \tfrac{5}{9}(F - 32) \qquad F = \tfrac{9}{5}C + 32$$

To change Fahrenheit to Celsius, subtract 32 from the Fahrenheit reading, multiply by 5, and divide by 9. To change Celsius to Fahrenheit, multiply the Celsius reading by 9, divide by 5, and add 32.

Rappel

1. Many French businesses close during the month of _____ .
2. Big cities are deserted as the French head to _____ or the _____ .
3. In the winter, _____ vacations are popular.
4. A popular city for summer vacations is _____ .
5. A popular city for winter vacations is _____ .

À Vous

1. Create an accurate weather map for a typical day in France. Make sure to include the major cities.
2. Write a travel brochure for a ski or beach vacation in France.

La Chasse au trésor

`http://`

Using your best Internet search skills, find the answers to the following questions:
What is today's weather in:

a. Toronto, Canada?
b. Port-au-Prince, Haiti?
c. Rabat, Morocco?
d. Phnom Penh, Cambodia?
e. Lomé, Togo?
f. Monaco?

MOTS NÉCESSAIRES

SEASONS
la **saison** season
l'**automne** *m.* autumn
l'**hiver** *m.* winter
le **printemps** spring
l'**été** *m.* summer

WEATHER EXPRESSIONS
quel temps fait-il? what is
   the weather like?
il fait beau the weather is
   nice
il fait chaud it is hot
il fait du soleil it is sunny
il fait du vent it is windy

il fait froid it is cold
il fait mauvais the weather
   is bad
il neige it's snowing
il pleut it's raining

ACTIVITÉS
faire les devoirs to do one's
   homework
faire un pique-nique to go
   on a picnic
faire une partie de to play a
   game of
faire une promenade to go
   for a walk

VERB: FAIRE
faire to make, do
je fais I make, do
tu fais you make, do
il/elle fait he/she makes,
   does
nous faisons we make, do
vous faites you make, do
ils/elles font they make, do

ADVERB
quelquefois sometimes

promance nous fu zms
as

12
Les sports

*Using **IR** Verbs; Using Inversion and Question Words*

1 **Vocabulaire**

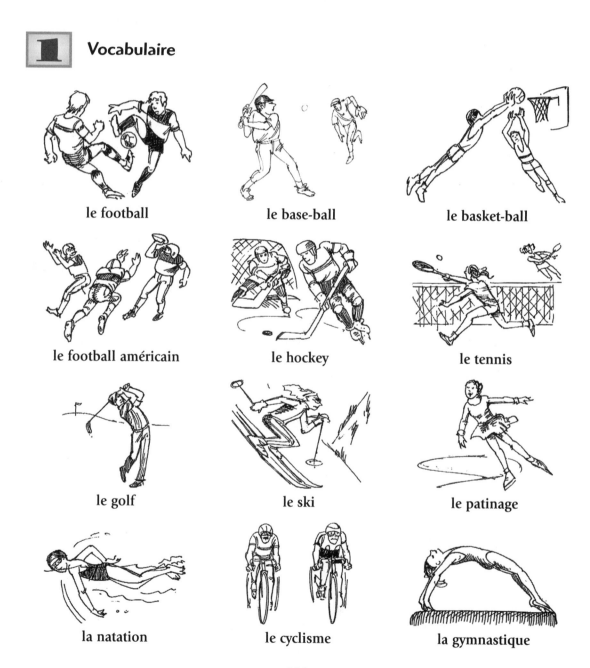

le football

le base-ball

le basket-ball

le football américain

le hockey

le tennis

le golf

le ski

le patinage

la natation

le cyclisme

la gymnastique

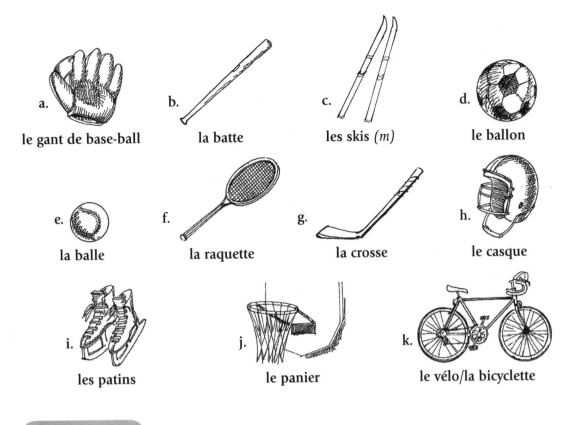

a. le gant de base-ball
b. la batte
c. les skis *(m)*
d. le ballon
e. la balle
f. la raquette
g. la crosse
h. le casque
i. les patins
j. le panier
k. le vélo/la bicyclette

Activités

A. What equipment do you and your friends need to practice each sport? Listen to your teacher read the name of a sport. Then put the letter of the equipment above next to the appropriate number.

1. ___d___   3. _____   5. _____   7. _____

2. _____   4. _____   6. _____   8. _____

B. Work with a partner. Take turns giving a sport and the equipment needed.

EXAMPLE: You: J'aime le base-ball.
            Partner: Il te faut (*you need*) un gant. J'aime le basket
            You   **Il te faut . . .**

C. Monsieur Durand needs sports equipment for his gym classes. Can you help him choose some items?

1. Pour le base-ball: _____ .

2. Pour le basket-ball: _____ .

3. Pour le cyclisme: _____ .

4. Pour le football américain: _____ .

5. Pour le football: _____ .

6. Pour le tennis: _____ .

7. Pour le patinage: _____ .

D. What are your likes and dislikes? Rate the sports listed below.

<table>
<tr><td>le base-ball</td><td>la gymnastique</td></tr>
<tr><td>le basket-ball</td><td>le hockey</td></tr>
<tr><td>le cyclisme</td><td>la natation</td></tr>
<tr><td>le football</td><td>le patinage</td></tr>
<tr><td>le football américain</td><td>le ski</td></tr>
<tr><td>le golf</td><td>le tennis</td></tr>
</table>

1. J'adore _____ .

2. J'aime beaucoup _____ .

3. J'aime _____ .

4. Je n'aime pas _____ .

5. Je déteste _____ .

E. What sports are these people engaged in?

1. _____

2. _____

3. _____

4. _____

5. _____

6. _____

7. _____

8. _____

The verb **faire** may be used with the sports you take part in.

> **Je fais du football.**
> **Elles font de la natation.**

What is the gender of football? _____ After **faire**, use _____ when referring to the name of a masculine singular sport.

What is the gender of natation? _____ After **faire**, use _____ when referring to the name of a feminine singular sport.

The verb **jouer + à** and the definite article (**à la, au, aux**) may also be used with the names of sports in which you play a match.

Je joue au football, au basket.

Activités

F. All your friends are into sports. Using **faire** and **du** or **de la**, express the sport that each person takes part in.

1. Nous _____

2. Les garçons _____

3. Tu _____

4. Odette _____

5. Je _____

6. Vous _____

G. Using the verb **jouer + à / au,** write a list of three sports that you enjoy.

1. _____
2. _____
3. _____

Prononciation

• **qu** generally represents the sound *k* as in *kick*.

qui	quoi	quatre	quand	cinq
que	quel	pourquoi	quelques	quinze

Quatre filles font un pique-nique à Québec.
Qu'est-ce qui arrive? Qui quitte la maison? Quand?

 This new group of verbs belongs to the **-IR** conjugation. Can you guess their meanings?

applaudir   choisir   finir

punir   remplir   saisir

Here are six more action words. You probably noticed that these verbs don't end in **-er** but in _____ . You will recall how we made changes in **-ER** verbs by dropping the **-er** and adding certain endings. Well, we must do the same with **-IR** verbs, dropping the **-ir** and adding endings. The endings, however, are slightly different. Let's see what happens.

Read this story, look for the -IR verbs, and see if you can spot the endings.

Comment choisir un sport

Le directeur prépare les équipes de l'école. Il demande aux élèves: — Quel sport est-ce que **vous choisissez** et pourquoi? André dit qu'**il choisit** le cyclisme parce que son père refuse de lui donner sa voiture. **Liliane et Chantal choisissent** la gymnastique parce qu'elles sont très athlétiques.

Denis et Nathalie répondent: — **Nous choisissons** la natation parce que grand-père est maître-nageur.

— Et toi, Christophe, demande le directeur, — quel sport est-ce que **tu choisis?**

— Moi, **je choisis** le football parce que je pratique ce sport chaque après-midi avec ma sœur cadette, Marie.

Quelques jours après le directeur annonce les équipes:

André — cyclisme
Liliane et Chantal — gymnastique
Denis et Nathalie — natation
Christophe — base-ball

— Le base-ball! crie Christophe. — Mais pourquoi?

Le directeur répond: — Parce que j'ai vu ta sœur Marie jouer au football. Elle est formidable! Elle va jouer avec l'équipe!

les équipes the teams	
de of	
Quel which	
dit says	
parce que because	
lui to him	
sa voiture his car	
répondent answer	
maître-nageur lifeguard	
toi you	
pratique play, do **ce** this	
chaque every	
cadette younger	
quelques a few	
après after	
mais but **pourquoi** why?	
j'ai vu I saw	
va jouer is going to play	

Activités

H. Match the students with the sport they choose. Then add why the students like the sport.

le football   la gymnastique
la natation   le vélo

1. Denis et Nathalie choisissent _____ .

   _____

2. Christophe _____ .

   _____

3. Chantal et Liliane _____ .

   _____

4. André _____ .

   _____

I. Complete the sentences with the appropriate information.

1. Le directeur prépare _____ .

2. Il demande aux élèves: — Quel sport _____ ?

3. L'équipe de Christophe est _____ .

4. Le directeur répond que Marie est _____ .

4 Look again at our story. Can you fill in the correct endings of the verb choisir?

je chois _____	I choose, I am choosing
tu chois _____	you choose, you are choosing
il/elle chois _____	he/she chooses, he/she is choosing
nous chois _____	we choose, we are choosing
vous chois _____	you choose, you are choosing
ils/elles chois _____	they choose, they are choosing

NOTE:

j'applaudis. What happened to the **e** in **je?** _____

What did we put in place of **e?** _____

Why do we do this? _____

Activités

J. Let's practice with the other -**IR** verbs.

	applaudir	finir	punir	remplir	saisir
je (j')	_____	_____	_____	_____	_____
tu	_____	_____	_____	_____	_____
il/elle	_____	_____	_____	_____	_____
nous	_____	_____	_____	_____	_____
vous	_____	_____	_____	_____	_____
ils/elles	_____	_____	_____	_____	_____

K. Tell what these people do by completing each sentence with the correct form of the verb in parentheses.

1. (applaudir) J' _____ les acteurs.
2. (choisir) Vous _____ la classe de français.
3. (remplir) Elles _____ les pages des cahiers..
4. (saisir) Marie _____ le petit enfant.
5. (choisir) Sylvie et Régine _____ un exercice.
6. (remplir) Je _____ mon sac.
7. (applaudir) Nous _____ l'artiste.
8. (saisir) Je _____ l'occasion.
9. (punir) Vous _____ l'élève bavard. (*talkative*)
10. (choisir) Tu _____ le verbe correct.

L. Match the sentences with the pictures they describe.

L'élève remplit le sac.
Nous applaudissons en classe.
Le chef saisit la poule.

La mère punit les enfants.
Elle choisit la réponse correcte.
Tu finis le dîner?

1. _____ .   2. _____ .

3. _____ .   4. _____ .

5. _____ .   6. _____ .

M. Your friends asked you what the members of your family do not do at home. Tell them.

> EXAMPLE: Jean / choisir le film à la télévision
> Jean **ne choisit pas** le film à la télévision.

1. Mes parents / punir mon chien

   _____

2. Paulette / applaudir les acteurs

   _____

3. Mes petites sœurs / saisir les balles

   _____

4. Nicolas / finir l'exercice

   _____

5. Papa / remplir les verres (*glasses*)

   _____

N. Work with a partner. Your partner asks what you do in school. You answer, then reverse roles.

> EXAMPLE: Partner: **Est-ce que tu réfléchis (*think*)?**
> You: **Oui, je réfléchis. Est-ce que tu . . .**

1. finir les devoirs
2. applaudir le professeur
3. choisir les réponses correctes
4. remplir le cahier avec des exercices

 There is another way to form a question in French. Observe these sentences.

Tu parles.	**Parles-tu?**
Nous chantons.	**Chantons-nous?**
Vous dansez bien.	**Dansez-vous bien?**
Ils écoutent la musique.	**Écoutent-ils la musique?**
Elles finissent le match.	**Finissent-elles le match?**

This way of forming a question is called INVERSION because we invert, that is, we change the word order. Look carefully and tell how the word order is changed: _____

_____ .

> Inversion reverses the order of the subject pronoun and the verb.

NOTES:

1. We do not normally invert with **je**. Use **est-ce que** to form questions with **je**.

   Est-ce que **je danse bien?**

2. Inversion is usually more formal than the other ways of asking a question, except in some common expressions (**Quelle heure est-il? Comment allez-vous? Quel temps fait-il?**).

Activité

O. You are very curious today and ask many questions. Change these sentences to questions by changing the order of the subject and verb.

1. Tu gagnes la compétition. _____

2. Vous aimez le CD. _____

3. Nous jouons bien. _____

4. Ils cherchent un stylo. _____

5. Tu applaudis l'acteur. _____

6. Elles arrivent à sept heures. _____

7. Nous travaillons avec des amis. _____

8. Vous choisissez un crayon. _____

6 Now look at these examples.

Il danse.	Danse-*t*-il?
Elle travaille.	Travaille-*t*-elle?
Il parle.	Parle-*t*-il?
Elle a chaud.	A-*t*-elle chaud?

Did we invert with **il** and **elle**? _____ But we added an extra letter. Which letter did we add? _____ Where did we put it? _____

_____

How did we join the extra letter to the rest of the question? _____

Why did we do so? _____

Why don't we have to add the extra letter when **ils** or **elles** is the subject? _____

_____

Why don't we have to do so when **nous, vous,** or **tu** is the subject? _____

_____

For **-IR** verbs, no **-t-** is needed for inversion with **il** or **elle.**

Finit-il l'exercice?

Activités

P. Your friend tells you what's going on, but you like to make sure. Ask questions using inversion.

    EXAMPLE: Il joue.   **Joue-t-il?**

1. Elle marche dans le parc.

   _____

2. Il pense en français.

   _____

3. Elle habite une maison moderne.

   _____

4. Il punit l'élève.

   _____

5. Elle regarde un film français.

   _____

6. Il applaudit le gagnant (*the winner*).

   _____

Q. You and your friends ask each other in which sport you participate this year.

    EXAMPLE: ils / le base-ball   **Choisissent-ils le base-ball?**

1. il / le golf _____

2. tu / le football _____

3. nous / la natation _____

4. elle / le basket-ball _____

 There is still one more group of sentences to look at.

Marie danse.	Marie danse-*t-elle*?
Paul parle.	Paul parle-*t-il*?
Marie et Anne chantent.	Marie et Anne chantent-*elles*?
Les garçons regardent le match.	Les garçons regardent-*ils* le match?
Anne et Paul applaudissent.	Anne et Paul applaudissent-*ils*?
Les livres sont sur la table.	Les livres sont-*ils* sur la table?

In French, we cannot form a question by inverting with a person or a noun subject. We can invert only with a pronoun and a verb. To form a question with inversion if the subject is a person's name or a noun, we must add a pronoun and the order is:

SUBJECT NOUN + VERB + PRONOUN

Marie danse-*t-elle*?

Les livres sont-*ils* sur la table

Remember to use the pronoun that agrees in gender and number with the subject noun, and to add a -t- between the verb form (ending with a vowel) and the subject pronouns *il* or *elle*.

NOTE: This type of question is used mostly in written French.

Activité

R. Change these sentences to questions using inversion.

1. Marie écoute.

   _____

2. Les garçons parlent.

   _____

3. Paul et Anne dansent beaucoup.

   _____

4. La petite fille arrive à huit heures.

   _____

5. Le dîner est délicieux.

   _____

6. La robe est élégante.

   _____

Some basic question words will help you ask for most of the information you need. These question words may be used at the beginning of the sentence with **est-ce que** or with inversion. In informal speech, they can also be used in questions formed by intonation, usually at the end of the sentence, except **pourquoi** which is better at the beginning.

COMMENT { est-ce que tu chantes?   **Tu chantes comment?**
{ chantes-tu?

Comment means _____ .

OÙ { est-ce que vous habitez?   **Vous habitez où?**
{ habitez-vous?

Où means _____ .

POURQUOI } est-ce qu'il applaudit?   Pourquoi il applaudit?
         } applaudit-il?

Pourquoi means _____ .

QUAND } est-ce qu'ils finissent le match?   Ils finissent le match quand?
      } finissent-ils le match?

Quand means _____ .

QUI } est-ce qu'elle punit?   Elle punit qui?
    } punit-elle?

Qui means _____ .

QU' } est-ce qu'elles saisissent?   Elles saisissent quoi?
QUE } saisissent-elles?

Qu'est-ce que and **Que** mean _____ .

Note that the final **e** of **Que** is dropped. Why was it dropped?

_____

Que (Qu') becomes **quoi** at the end of a question using voice intonation.

Activités

S. Choose the best answers to the questions you hear. Write the letter of your answer next to the corresponding number of the question.

a. à midi	1. _____	
b. très bien	2. _____	
c. le champion	3. _____	
d. la natation	4. _____	
e. la balle	5. _____	

T. You didn't hear the question but you will hear the answers. Listen to the answers and choose what the question must have been.

1. Il arrive	a. pourquoi?	b. où?	c. quand?	_____
2. Ils travaillent	a. où?	b. quoi?	c. qui?	_____
3. Elles dansent	a. comment?	b. où?	c. à quelle heure?	_____
4. Elle regarde	a. qui?	b. quoi?	c. où?	_____
5. Il adore	a. comment?	b. quoi?	c. qui?	_____

U. You're being curious again. Form questions using **est-ce que** and inversion to get the latest news.

1. (Où) Tu joues au tennis.

    _____

    _____

2. (Comment) Pierre gagne le match.

    _____

    _____

3. (Pourquoi) Vous saisissez la balle.

    _____

    _____

4. (Quand) Elles finissent les devoirs.

    _____

    _____

5. (Qui) Nous applaudissons.

    _____

    _____

6. (Que) Ils choisissent comme sport.

    _____

    _____

Parlons français

With a partner, discuss what sports you play and when you play them. Follow the example.

EXAMPLE   You: **Tu fais quel sport?**
            Partner: **Je fais du football.**

            You: **Quand?**
            Partner: **En automne. Quel sport aimes-tu?**

CONVERSATION

Vocabulaire

le but the goal   **quel . . . !** what a . . . !

Page culturelle

Les sports

What is your favorite sport?

In France, soccer (**le football** or **le foot**) is the national sport. Many French cities have home teams. Each team can be identified by the distinctive colors of its uniform. The best soccer teams compete for the national championship, **la Coupe de France,** at the end of the season. There are also international matches between the best soccer teams in the world. Every two years, the Euro Cup alternates with **la Coupe du Monde** (the World Cup). France won the World Cup in 1998 and was runner-up in 2006. A new, large, modern stadium was built for the 1998 World Cup a few miles north of Paris. It is not only used for soccer, but also for concerts and rugby championships. Rugby is another favorite sport in France

Le Tour de France, which takes place annually in July, is the longest and best-known bicycle race in the world. Participants from many countries compete in this spectacular twenty-two-lap event, which covers more than 1,500 miles. Each year, a different French city is chosen as the starting point, with Paris always the final destination. The winner receives a large sum of money, but, more importantly, he becomes a national hero in his country. An American, Lance Armstrong, holds an impressive record. He has won the Tour de France seven consecutive years, from 1999 to 2005.

Most other sports are also practiced in France, even baseball, which is beginning to have fans. The French excel in winters sports, especially in alpine and free-style skiing.

Rappel

1. The national sport of France is _____ .

2. Each team can be identified by _____ of its uniforms.

3. _____ is the National Championship held at the end of the season.

4. The Tour de France is the longest and most famous _____ race.

5. This race has _____ laps and covers more

   than _____ miles. It always ends in _____ .

À Vous

1. Write a report on the rules of soccer.
2. Write a biography of a famous Tour de France winner.

La Chasse au trésor

 http://

Using your best Internet search skills, find the answers to the following questions:

1. What nickname do the French give to the Tour de France?
2. Approximately how many kilometers does this event cover?
3. What is "une ville étape?"
4. Approximately how many cyclists participate in this race each year?
5. What are the prizes for the winner?
6. Who are "lièvres?"
7. Who won the most recent Tour de France?
8. Is there a Tour de France for women?

C'est authentique!

Match the sport with the time the schedule says you can see it on television.

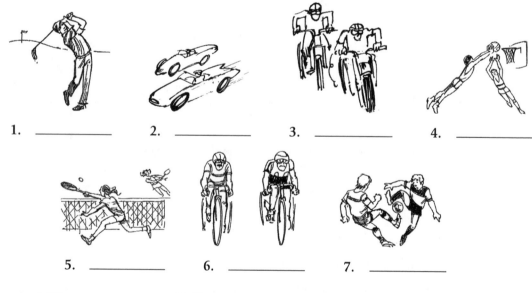

1. _____ 2. _____ 3. _____ 4. _____

5. _____ 6. _____ 7. _____

a. 6.55 P.M.	**c.** 11:00 A.M.	**e.** 11:00 P.M.	**g.** 10:00 P.M.
b. 3.20 P.M.	**d.** 12:00 midnight	**f.** 9:00 P.M.	

Samedi
CABLE/SATELLITES
Sélection des principales émissions

EUROSPORT FRANCE

11.00 : Automobile/ voitures de tourisme : 11e manche de la série GT BRP Endurance à Nogaro, en France (80803341).
15.20 : Motocyclisme : Grand Prix du Brésil à Rio de Janeiro. 125, 250 et 500 cc (73679341).

18.55 : Basket-ball : 5e journée du championnat. CSP Limoges/Pau-Orthez (6940254).
21.00 : Cyclisme : Coupe du monde. Paris/Tours (375438). demi-finale du Grand Prix de Lyon (867921).
22.00 : Football : matches qualificatifs pour la coupe du monde 98 : Ukraine/Portugal, Lettonie/Ecosse, Pays de Galles/Pays Bas, Moldavie/Italie, Irlande du Nord/Arménie (887785).

23.00 : Golf de la PGA européenne 1999 : le Linde German Masters à Berlin. 4e tour (388902).
0.00 : Tennis : demi-finale du tournoi de Marbella, en Espagne (118631).

MOTS NÉCESSAIRES

SPORTS
la **balle** ball (baseball, tennis, golf)
le **ballon** ball (soccer, basketball, football)
le **base-ball** baseball
le **basket-ball, basket** basketball
la **batte** bat
la **bicyclette** bicycle
le **casque** helmet
la **crosse** hockey stick
le **cyclisme** cycling
l'**équipe** f. team
le **football** soccer
le **football américain** football
le **gant de base-ball** mitt

le **golf** golf
la **gymnastique** gymnastics
le **hockey** hockey
la **natation** swimming
le **panier** basket
le **patin** skate
le **patinage** skating
la **raquette** racket
le **ski** ski, skiing
le **sport** sport
le **tennis** tennis
le **vélo** bicycle
la **voiture** car

VERBS
applaudir to applaud, clap
choisir to choose

faire + de + *def. art.* / jouer + à + *def. art.* (*sport*) to play
finir to finish
punir to punish
remplir to fill (out)
saisir to grab, seize

QUESTION WORDS
comment? how?
où where?
pourquoi? why?
qu'est-ce que? what?
quand? when?
que (qu') what?
qui? who? whom?
quoi? what?

Révision III
(LEÇONS 9–12)

Leçon 9

a. The verb **avoir** is an irregular verb that means *to have*. Memorize all its forms.

j'ai	nous avons
tu as	vous avez
il / elle a	ils / elles ont

b. The same rules as those for -ER verbs apply for making a sentence negative or for asking a question.

Je n'ai pas beaucoup de travail.
Est-ce que nous avons un bon professeur?

c. Learn the meanings of these special expressions with **avoir**. They may be used with any subject representing a person.

avoir chaud	*to be hot, warm*	avoir raison	*to be right*
avoir faim	*to be hungry*	avoir tort	*to be wrong*
avoir froid	*to be cold*	avoir sommeil	*to be sleepy*
avoir soif	*to be thirsty*	avoir _____ ans	*to be _____ years old*

J'ai chaud.	*I'm warm.*
Nous avons faim.	*We are hungry.*

If the subject is not a person or an animal, use the verb **être**.

La soupe *est* froide. *The soup is cold.*

Leçon 10

LES JOURS	LES MOIS	LES SAISONS
lundi	janvier	l'hiver
mardi	février	
mercredi	mars	
jeudi	avril	le printemps
vendredi	mai	
samedi	juin	
dimanche	juillet	l'été
	août	
	septembre	
	octobre	l'automne
	novembre	
	décembre	

216

Leçon 11

a. The verb **faire** is an irregular verb that means *to make, to do*. All its forms must be memorized.

je fais	nous faisons
tu fais	vous faites
il / elle fait	ils / elles font

b. Faire is used in expressions of weather.

Quel temps fait-il?	*What is the weather?*
Il fait froid.	*It's cold.*
Il fait chaud.	*It's warm.*
Il fait beau.	*It's beautiful.*
Il fait mauvais.	*It's bad.*
Il fait du vent.	*It's windy.*
Il fait du soleil.	*It's sunny.*

Leçon 12

a. Use **faire du** before the name of a masculine singular sport.

Use **faire de la** before the name of a feminine singular sport.

Use **jouer à** (+ article) before names of sports where you play matches.

b. To conjugate an **-IR** verb, drop **-ir** from the infinitive and add the appropriate endings.

EXAMPLE: **finir**

If the subject is		add		to the remaining stem:		
	je	is			je	fin*is*
	tu	is			tu	fin*is*
	il / elle	it			il / elle	fin*it*
	nous	issons			nous	fin*issons*
	vous	issez			vous	fin*issez*
	ils / elles	issent			ils / elles	fin*issent*

The same rules as those for **-ER** verbs apply for making a sentence negative or asking a question.

Nous *ne* **finissons** *pas* **la phrase.**
Est-ce que Jacques finit l'exercice?

c. Questions can be formed with inversion (changing the order of the subject pronoun and the verb). Put the verb first, followed by the subject pronoun. Do not invert with **je.**

Parlons - nous?

When there is inversion with **il** or **elle**, **-t-** is inserted between the verb and the subject if the verb ends in vowel.

Parle-t-il?   A-t-elle?

but   Est-il?   Finit-il?

To form a question with inversion if the subject is a person or a noun, the order is

SUBJECT NOUN	+ VERB		+ PRONOUN
Pierre	parle	-t-	**il?**
Les élèves	chantent	-	**ils?**

d. The following words form questions with **est-ce que** or with inversion:

Comment *(How)*
Où *(Where)*
Pourquoi *(Why)*   **est-ce-que** + subject + verb . . . ?
Quand *(When)*   or
Que [Qu'] *(What)*   Verb-Pronoun . . . ?
Qui *(Who)*

In informal familiar conversation, using voice intonation, the question word is usually at the end of the sentence. **Que** becomes **quoi** at the end of a sentence.

Tu reviens quand?

Activités

A. Each picture illustrates a situation. What is it? Use an expression with **avoir** in your answers.

1. _____   2. _____   3. _____

4. _____   5. _____   6. _____

B. Write the name in French of each body part shown beneath the amount of letters it contains. Then fit the words into the puzzle boxes accordingly.

3 LETTERS	4 LETTERS	5 LETTERS	6 LETTERS	7 LETTERS	8 LETTERS

C. Jumble. Unscramble the names of the months. Then unscramble the letters in the circles to find out the message.

B E T O R O C ⬤ ☐ ⬤ ☐ ☐ ☐ ☐

L U T I J E L ⬤ ⬤ ☐ ☐ ⬤ ☐ ☐

B E S T M E R P E ⬤ ☐ ☐ ☐ ☐ ☐ ☐ ☐ ⬤

E R R É V I F ☐ ☐ ☐ ☐ ⬤ ⬤ ☐

Jean dit à Sylvie: _____ _____ _____ .

D. After filling in all the horizontal boxes, look at the vertical box. You will find a mystery word that describes your French class.

1. le mois après janvier   — — — — — — — —
2. le mois après juillet   — — — — — —
3. le jour après mardi   — — — — — — — —
4. le jour après lundi   — — — — — —
5. le mois avant juin   — — —
6. le jour après samedi   — — — — — — — —
7. le mois après mars   — — — — — —
8. le mois après septembre — — — — — — —
9. le jour après dimanche   — — — — — —
10. le mois après août   — — — — — — — — —

E. Which holidays are suggested by the pictures? What season do they fall in? What's the weather like? What date is it?

1. _____ .
   _____ .
   _____ .
   _____ .

2. _____ .
   _____ .
   _____ .
   _____ .

3. _____ .

   _____ .

   _____ .

   _____ .

4. _____ .

   _____ .

   _____ .

   _____ .

F. Find 10 items of sport equipment in the puzzle and circle them.

B	A	S	C	P	E	V	R	E	P
L	I	O	L	L	U	S	N	G	A
A	T	C	L	C	N	B	R	N	T
B	C	A	Y	I	A	T	A	A	R
B	B	G	T	C	A	S	Q	U	E
A	O	A	L	N	L	R	U	P	I
L	P	A	T	O	Q	E	E	I	N
L	B	Y	L	T	A	U	T	V	A
O	V	E	T	A	E	B	T	T	P
N	V	S	G	A	N	T	E	R	E

1.

2.

3.

4.

5.

6.

7.

8.

9.

10.

G. After filling in all the letters, look at the vertical box to find the answer to this question:

Cécile est championne de quoi?
Elle est championne de _____ .

1. _____ _____ _____ _____ _____

2. _____ _____ _____ _____ _____-_____ _____ _____ _____

3. _____ _____ _____ _____ _____ _____

4. _____ _____ _____-_____ _____ _____ _____

5. _____ _____ _____ _____ _____ _____

6. _____ _____ _____ _____

7. _____ _____ _____

8. _____ _____ _____ _____ _____ _____ _____ _____ _____

The Cognate Connection

Write the meanings of the following French and English words.

FRENCH		ENGLISH COGNATE	
1. bras _____		embrace _____	
2. dent _____		dentist _____	
3. langue _____		linguist _____	
4. main _____		manual _____	
5. pied _____		pedestal _____	

H. Identify and give the correct verb form. Then write the indicated letters in the boxes below to reveal whom M. Rimbaud is punishing:

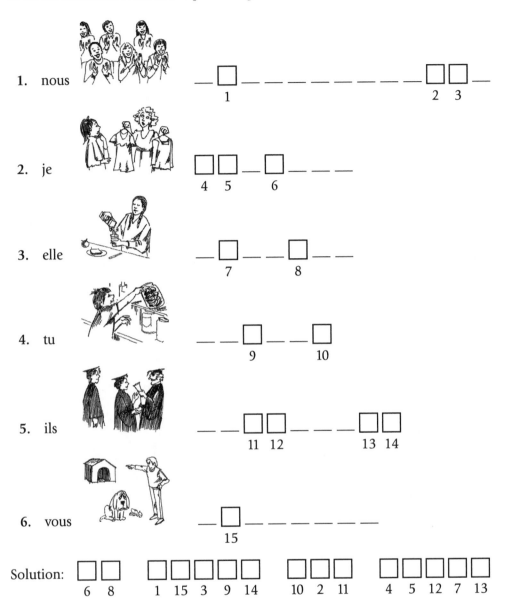

1. nous   _ ☐ _ _ _ _ _ _ _ _ _ ☐☐ _
                  1   2 3

2. je   ☐☐ _ ☐ _ _ _
              4 5   6

3. elle   _ ☐ _ _ ☐ _ _
                   7   8

4. tu   _ _ ☐ _ _ ☐
                  9   10

5. ils   _ _ ☐☐ _ _ _ ☐☐
                   11 12   13 14

6. vous   _ ☐ _ _ _ _ _ _
                    15

Solution: ☐☐ ☐☐☐☐☐ ☐☐☐ ☐☐☐☐☐
           6 8   1 15 3 9 14   10 2 11   4 5 12 7 13

4

quatrième partie

13
La musique

Using -RE Verbs

---

1   **Vocabulaire**

le violon   la guitare   la clarinette

la flûte   la trompette   le trombone

le piano   la batterie   le jazz

le concert   la musique classique   la musique folklorique

la musique populaire　　　**la musique rock**　　　**la fanfare**
　　　　　　　　　　　　　　　　le rock

Activités

A. Your friends go to concerts regularly. Listen to your teacher. Put the number under the picture being described.

a. _____　　　　　b. _____　　　　　c. _____

d. _____　　　　　e. _____

 Use the verb **jouer + de** to express that a person plays a musical instrument. Before the name of a masculine instrument, *de* contracts with *le* to become **du.**

> **Sophie joue de la guitare.**
> **Henri joue du piano.**

B. Express the instrument that each person plays.

EXAMPLE: **je/**
Je joue de la trompette.

1. nous/ *Jouons du violon* .

2. tu/ *joues* .

3. elle/ *joue de la batterie* .

4. vous/ *jouez du piano* .

5. ils/ *jouent du trombone*   *pronounce like joue* .

6. je/ *joue de la flute* .

The following new group of verbs belong to the **-RE** conjugation. See if you can guess their meanings.

attendre   *wait*

descendre

entendre   *hear*

répondre

vendre

~~ecouter~~ -to
ecouter   listen

Do you recall what you did with **-ER** and **-IR** verbs when you used them? You dropped the **-er** or **-ir** ending from the infinitive and added certain endings.

parle/r/	*to speak*	fini/r/	*to finish*
je	parle	je	finis
tu	parles	tu	finis
il / elle	parle	il / elle	finit
nous	parlons	nous	finissons
vous	parlez	vous	finissez
ils / elles	parlent	ils / elles	finissent

We do the same thing with **-RE** verbs. Let's see what happens. Read the following story; look for the **-RE** verbs, and see if you can spot the endings.

Samedi soir

C'est samedi. Il est onze heures du soir. Michelle et Anne sont chez leur amie Brigitte. Les parents de Brigitte ne sont pas à la maison. Ils sont au théâtre.

Les trois jeunes filles ont peur. Tout à coup Michelle dit:

— Vous **entendez** quelque chose?

ANNE ET BRIGITTE: Non, **nous n'entendons** rien. Et toi? **Tu entends** quelque chose?

MICHELLE: Oui, **j'entends** un bruit. Il y a quelqu'un dans la maison, Brigitte. J'ai peur.

Les trois jeunes filles **descendent** l'escalier. **Elles entendent** quelque chose. Tout à coup Brigitte rit. **Elle entend** un bruit.

BRIGITTE: Écoute! Michelle, **tu entends ?** C'est mon chat? Il joue avec mon chien.

(glosses)
ont peur are afraid
tout à coup suddenly
quelque chose something
ne . . . rien nothing
un bruit a noise
quelqu'un somebody
l'escalier *m.* stairs
rit laughs
Écoute listen

Activité

C. **Oui ou non?** If the sentence is incorrect, change it to make it correct.

1. C'est dimanche. _____

2. Il est huit heures du matin. _____

3. Il y a trois garçons à la maison. _____

4. Elles sont chez Anne. _____

5. Elles ont faim. _____

6. Les filles entendent le professeur. _____

7. Elles descendent d'un autobus. _____

8. Les filles entendent deux animaux. _____

4 Now complete the correct endings by looking at the story. To form the present tense of -RE verbs, take the infinitive, drop _____ , and add these endings:

j'entend _____   nous entend _____

tu entend _____   vous entend _____

il / elle entend _____   ils / elles entend _____

NOTE: j'entends. What happens to the **e** in **je**? _____

What do we put in place of the **e** in **je**? _____

Why did we do this? _____

D. Select the appropriate ending to the sentences you hear. Write the letter of the correct ending next to the number of the sentence.

a. ma voiture   b. mon ami   c. la musique

d. l'escalier   e. vos questions

1. _____   2. _____   3. _____   4. _____   5. _____

E. Select the correct answer to the question you hear.

1. a. le bus   b. à l'école   _____

2. a. sa voiture   b. le français   _____

3. a. à minuit   b. rapidement   _____

4. a. le professeur   b. un taxi   _____

5. a. en auto   b. après les classes _____

F. Let's practice with other -RE verbs. Fill in all the forms.

	attendre	descendre	répondre	vendre
je	_____	_____	_____	_____
tu	_____	_____	_____	_____
il / elle	_____	_____	_____	_____
nous	_____	_____	_____	_____
vous	_____	_____	_____	_____
ils / elles	_____	_____	_____	_____

G. Match the sentences with the pictures they describe.

Monsieur Lamont vend des fruits.   Il attend une amie.
Je réponds bien en classe.   Tu descends l'escalier.
Nous entendons la musique.   Vendez-vous la guitare?

1. _____ .   2. _____ .

3. _____ .   4. _____ .

5. _____ .   6. _____ .

H. Your mother asks you about the strange noises coming from musical instruments being played in the garage. Tell her what you hear.

EXAMPLE: **J'entends un violon.**

1.    J'entends un trombone _____ .

2.   J'entends une trompette _____ .

3.  _J'entends une clarinette_ .

4.  _J'entends une flute._ .

I. Work with a partner. Take turns being the customer in a store selling musical instruments. Ask the sales clerk in the store if he/she sells the following items. Then write the questions and answers.

EXAMPLE:

You: **Vendez-vous des trombones ?**
Partner: **Oui, nous vendons des trombones.**

1. _Vendez-vous le piano?_
   Oui, je vends le piano.

2. _Vendez-vous la flute?_
   Oui, je vends la flute.

3. _Vendez-vous la batterie?_
   Oui, je vends la batterie.

4. _Vendez-vous le violon?_
   Je vends le violon.

J. There is a lot of static. Say which kind of concert the following people cannot hear on the radio.

EXAMPLE: **Georges n'entend pas le concert de jazz.**

1. Nicole _____

2. Les garçons _____

_____

_____

3. Patrick _____

4. Michèle et Anne _____

_____

_____

K. Tell what these people are doing by completing the sentences with the correct forms of the verbs in parentheses.

1. (attendre) J' _attends_ mes parents.

2. (descendre) Nous _descendons_ à l'hôtel du Nord à Paris.

3. (entendre) Tu _entends_ la fanfare.

4. (répondre) Vous _répondez_ en classe.

5. (vendre) Il _vend_ son auto.

6. (attendre) Elles _attendent_ leurs amies.

7. (descendre) Marie _descend_ de l'autobus.

8. (entendre) Paul et Alain _entendent_ de la musique.

9. (répondre) Sylvie et Régine _répondent_ rapidement.

10. (vendre) Ils _vendent_ des billets.

L. Answer these questions about yourself.

1. Entendez-vous bien le professeur?

    Oui, j'entends bien le professor.

2. Répondez-vous aux questions?

    Oui, je réponds aux questions

3. Attendez-vous vos amis après l'école?

    Oui, j'attends mes amis.

4. Descendez-vous souvent en ville ?

Oui, je descends souvent en ville,

M. Complete these five sentences by writing something original about yourself.

1. J'attends _____ .
2. Je descends _____ .
3. J'entends _____ .
4. J'apprends _____ .
5. Je vends _____ .

CONVERSATION

Vocabulaire

alors so
il faut you must
chéri sweetie

Je ne veux pas I don't want
Pourquoi pas? Why not?
occupé busy

s'il te plaît please
lui to her/him

DIALOGUE

Complete the dialog with expressions chosen from the following list.

faut	pourquoi	sortir
le téléphone	veux	occupée
François	s'il te plait	parler
Sortir	entends	

Prononciation

- **j** always sounds like the *s* in *treasure*.

    je   **jour**   **jaune**   **jeune**   **joli**   **jupe**   **jeudi**

    Bonjour, Jacques. Jeudi, je joue au foot avec Jean chez Julien.
    J'adore cette jolie jupe jaune de Jacqueline.

Have a conversation with a partner in which you discuss the music you like and dislike. Follow the example.

EXAMPLE:	You:	**Tu aimes / tu n'aimes pas quel genre de musique?**
	Partner:	**J'aime / je n'aime pas la musique classique.**
	You:	**Pourquoi?**
	Partner:	**Elle est formidable (horrible).**

C'est authentique!

Read the listings and then match the answers to the questions

TELEVISION SAMEDI

C+

23.30: DISCO MACHINE (5234414). Concert animé en direct du Palais Omnisports de Bercy par Yves Noël et Philippe Corti, avec la participation d' LNA et Séverine Ferrer. Parents et enfants, fans des seventies, se retrouvent pour cette soirée qui réunit les nouveaux talents du disco et les plus grands interprètes des années paillettes.

France 2

0.00: WYNTON MARSALIS: I LOVE TO SWING (28761). Documentaire de Frank Cassenti. Portrait de la vedette mondiale de la trompette à travers son interview et les témoignages de trompettistes prestigieux, tels Clark Terry ou John Fadis.

France 3

23.45: MUSIQUES AU CŒUR (7679490). Magazine présenté par Eve Ruggieri. Portrait de la jeune et belle cantatrice Jennifer Larmore, mezzo-soprano américaine, devenue l'une des meilleures chanteuses rossiniennes au monde.

1. On which station would you see a documentary about a musician? _____

2. On which station would you learn about an opera singer? _____

3. On which station would you hear a concert with music from the 1970's? _____

Page culturelle

La Musique

French teens love music. Rock music in many moods, such as Blues rock, **Rock musette,** hip hop, is extremely popular. So is jazz, whether Dixieland, Ethno jazz, Afro jazz, or Jazz funk. French students also love the World Musique, which blends ethnic sounds and rhythms from around the world. Dance and pop music are also popular.

ASSEMBLÉE
NATIONALE

Le 21 juin à 20h30
Fête de la Musique

JACQUES HIGELIN

CHEB MAMI

En grand concert gratuit
sur les marches de
L'ASSEMBLÉE NATIONALE
(Pont de la Concorde)

In Paris, music is played all over town in cafés, clubs, parks, even on boats on the Seine. Concerts are given in the large halls of Bercy and the Zenith.

Every year on June 21, music of all kinds is played in free concerts throughout Paris, as well as in many other towns. The Fête de la Musique is very festive and exciting.

If you want to keep up-to-date with «**les derniers tubes**», the latest hits, just check a French website on the Internet.

If you prefer more traditional French music, you might listen to recordings of some older favorites sung by Edith Piaf, Charles Aznavour, Gilbert Bécaud, and Jacques Brel.

A famous love song made popular by Édith Piaf may help you understand why French, with its beautiful sounds, is often considered « **la langue de l'amour** », the language of love. Perhaps your teacher can help you learn to sing it.

La vie en rose

Quand il me prend dans ses bras,
Et me parle tout bas,
Je vois la vie en rose.
Il me dit des mots d'amour,
Des mots de tous les jours,
Et ça me fait quelque chose.
Il est entré dans mon cœur
Une part de bonheur,
Dont je connais la cause.
C'est lui pour moi,
Moi pour lui dans la vie.
Il me l'a dit,
L'a juré pour la vie.
Et dès que je l'aperçois,
Alors je sens en moi,
Mon cœur qui bat.

Rappel

1. French teenagers like to listen to _____ .

2. Music which blends ethnic sounds and rhythms from around the world is called _____ .

3. The Fête de la Musique takes place on _____ .

4. Charles Aznavour and Gilbert Bécaud are known for _____ songs.

5. _____ sang a beautiful love song called *La vie en rose.*

À Vous

1. Listen to a recording of *La vie en rose* and sing along.

2. Select a song sung by a French singer. Write a paragraph expressing your feelings about the performer and the song.

La Chasse au trésor

http://

Using your best Internet search skills, find the answers to the following questions.

1. What are the names of five popular French singers or musical groups?
2. What is Françoise Hardy's nickname?
3. Who is the French equivalent of Elvis Presley?
4. What is the name of a song written by Jean-Jacques Goldman?
5. What was Édith Piaf's nickname?

MOTS NÉCESSAIRES

NOUNS
la batterie drums
la clarinette clarinet
le concert concert
la fanfare band
la flûte flute
la guitare guitar
le jazz jazz
la musique classique classical music

la musique folklorique folk music
la musique populaire pop music
le piano piano
le rock rock (music)
la stéréo stereo
le violon violin

VERBS
attendre to wait (for)
avoir peur to be afraid
descendre to go down;
entendre to hear
répondre to answer
vendre to sell

14

Les animaux

Making Commands

1 Vocabulaire

le chat

le chien

le cheval

la vache

la chèvre

l'âne *(m.)*

le cochon

le poisson

le canard

le lion

l'éléphant *(m.)*

le tigre

le loup   le renard   le lapin

le mouton   le singe   l'oiseau *(m.)*

Activités

A. Match the animal with the description you hear.

a. l'éléphant ____   c. le singe ____   e. l'oiseau ____   g. l'âne ____

b. le poisson ____   d. le tigre ____   f. le cheval ____   h. le chien ____

B. You went to visit the zoo. Here are some of the animals you saw. Label the pictures.

1. _____   2. _____   3. _____

4. _____   5. _____   6. _____

C. Can you label all the animals on Pierre's farm?

Prononciation

• The French **r** is quite different from the **r** in English. In English it is pronounced at the front of the mouth with the lips rounded. In French it is pronounced at the back of the throat (as if you were clearing your throat) with your tongue against the lower teeth.

bonjour	sœur	rapide	ferme	grand	gros	très
au revoir	merci	arriver	rester	tigre	renard	peur

Robert travaille rapidement dans son garage.
Au revoir, Régine. Je vais rentrer à quatre heures.

Activités

D. Qui suis-je? Now that you know the French names of some animals, let's see if you can figure out who they are by their descriptions. Work with a partner. Take turns reading the descriptions and giving the answers. Then write the name of each animal.

1. Je suis un animal de la ferme. Je mange de l'herbe. Je suis grand et intelligent. Je transporte les gens et les objets. Je travaille. Je cours rapidement.

   la ferme the farm
   l'herbe grass
   les gens people
   travaille work   **cours** run

   Je suis _____.

Complete

2. Je suis petit. Je mange de la viande. Je suis le meilleur
   ami des hommes. Je n'aime pas les chats.

   Je suis ___le chien___ .

   de la viande meat
   le meilleur the best

3. Je suis grosse et stupide. J'habite la campagne. Je mange
   de l'herbe toute la journée. Je donne du lait.

   Je suis ___la vache___ .

   gros(se) big
   la campagne the country
   toute la journée all day
   du lait milk

4. Je suis un animal sauvage. Je suis comme un chien. Je
   mange de la viande. Quand les gens me voient, ils ont
   peur.

   Je suis ___le loup___ .

   sauvage wild
   voient see
   ont peur are afraid

5. Je suis un très grand animal. Je ne suis pas féroce. Je
   mange de l'herbe. J'ai un très long nez que j'emploie
   comme une main.

   Je suis ___l'éléphant___ .

   j'emploie I use

6. J'habite dans les maisons des gens. J'habite aussi dans
   les rues. Je n'aime pas les chiens. Je mange des souris.

   Je suis ___le chat___ .

   les rues the streets
   des souris mice

7. J'habite la campagne. Je suis une sorte d'oiseau. Je fais
   des œufs. Je mange du maïs.

   Je suis ___la poule___ .

   des œufs eggs
   du maïs corn

8. Je suis un animal très gros. Je suis souvent très sale. Je
   donne la viande de porc. Grâce à moi vous avez du
   jambon pour vos sandwichs.

   Je suis ___le cochon___ .

   souvent often   **sale** dirty
   grâce à moi thanks to me
   le jambon ham

9. Je suis un animal très intelligent. J'habite dans les arbres
   Je suis aussi au zoo et au cirque. J'aime les bananes.

   Je suis ___le singe___ .

   le cirque the circus
   la banane banana

10. Je suis un animal de la campagne. On fait des manteaux,
    des pull-overs et d'autres vêtements avec ma laine.

    Je suis ___le mouton___ .

    la laine the wool

E. There are ten animals hidden in this picture. Find them and list them below.

_____   _____

_____   _____

_____   _____

_____   _____

_____   _____

F. Put the animals in groups.

Animaux domestiques: _____

Animaux de la ferme: _____

_____

Animaux sauvages: _____

_____

G. Work with a partner. Ask each other the questions below. Then write your answers.

1. Quels *(which)* animaux aimez-vous?

   _____

2. Quels animaux n'aimez-vous pas?

   _____

3. Quels animaux sont féroces?

   _____

4. Quels animaux sont petits?

   _____

 Read this story and then answer the questions that follow.

Claude et l'hypnotiseur

Le samedi après-midi, Claude est au café avec des amis. Un hypnotiseur arrive. Il aime obliger les gens à faire des choses étranges. Les jeunes gens discutent de l'hypnotisme avant la présentation. Claude, un garçon pratique, dit:

— Seules les personnes sans intelligence sont susceptibles d'être hypnotisées.

Les amis de Claude ne partagent pas son opinion. Monsieur Henri, l'hypnotiseur, commence. Il choisit Claude. Il dit à Claude:

— **Regardez** ma montre. Vous avez sommeil. **Fermez** les yeux. **Dormez**.

Quand Claude est hypnotisé, Monsieur Henri dit:

— **Marchez** comme un éléphant. **Chantez** comme un oiseau. **Courez** comme un cheval. **Criez** comme un singe.

Devant ses amis surpris et amusés, Claude obéit sans embarras. Monsieur Henri continue:

— **Comptez** jusqu'à dix. **Ouvrez** les yeux et **parlez** de votre expérience.

Claude regarde les spectateurs et dit:

— Quelle expérience? Je ne suis pas sensible à l'hypnotisme. L'hypnotisme est pour les gens stupides.

la chose the thing
   étrange strange
discuter de to discuss
   avant before
pratique practical
   dit says
seules only   **sans** without
partager to share

dormez sleep

courez run   **criez** scream

devant in front of
   obéit obeys

comptez count
   jusqu'à up to

quel(le) what
   sensible à responsive to

Activité

H. Complete these sentences about Claude's experience.

1. Les jeunes gens sont dans un _____ .

2. Dans ce café, _____ arrive.

3. Il oblige les gens à faire _____ .

4. Claude pense que les personnes _____ sont susceptibles
   d'être hypnotisées.

5. L'hypnotiseur choisit _____ .

6. Il dit à Claude: — _____ comme un éléphant.
   _____ comme un oiseau _____ comme un singe.

7. Claude obéit sans _____ .

8. Ses amis sont _____ .

9. Claude pense qu'il n'est pas sensible _____ .

10. Il pense que l'hypnotisme est pour _____ .

2 Monsieur Henri gave a number of commands to Claude. Look at the words in bold
type in the story. These are verbs in the command or IMPERATIVE form. To practice the
imperative, play this little game.

Simon says:

> *Marchez.*
> *Chantez* «Frère Jacques».
> *Jouez* au basket-ball.
> *Fermez* le livre.
> *Applaudissez.*
> *Répondez:* «J'aime le français.»

All the commands above are lacking something. What are they lacking?

_____

If you answered "a subject" or "a subject pronoun," you are correct. Although French commands
do not use a subject pronoun, what is the subject of the command forms above understood to
be? _____ How did you know? _____

Activité

I. Work with a partner and take turns playing the role of teacher. The teacher gives the command and the student says what he/she is doing and acts it out.

EXAMPLE: fermer les fenêtres
            Teacher: **Fermez les fenêtres.**
            Student: **Je ferme les fenêtres.**

1. parler français

   _____   _____

2. regarder le tableau

   _____   _____

3. finir les devoirs

_____   _____

4. applaudir

_____   _____

5. descendre l'escalier

_____   _____

6. répondre au téléphone

_____   _____

 Let's play some more "Simon says".

> _Marche._
> _Chante_ «Frère Jacques».
> _Joue_ au basket-ball.
> _Ferme_ le livre.
> _Applaudis._
> _Réponds:_ «J'aime le français.»

How many ways are there to say "you" in French? _____ .

What are they? _____ and _____ .

We use **vous** when speaking to _____ .

We use **tu** when speaking to _____ .

What is the understood subject of the commands above? _____ .

Underline all the verbs that belong to the **-ER** family. What did we drop from the **tu** form of these verbs? _____ .

Did we do the same with verbs from the **-IR** or **-RE** family? _____

Activités

J. Your older sister is bossing you around. Listen to her commands and match them with the corresponding picture.

a.

b.

c.

d.   e.   f.

1. _____   2. _____   3. _____   4. _____   5. _____   6. _____

K. Work with a classmate. Tell him/her to do the following tasks. Then write out the command.

1. chanter avec le professeur

   _____

2. parler français en classe

   _____

3. regarder les jolies fleurs

   _____

4. finir le dîner à huit heures

   _____

5. applaudir l'orchestre

   _____

6. choisir un autre sport

   _____

7. descendre de l'autobus

   _____

8. répondre en français

   _____

 One more round of "Simon says"?

> *Marchons.*
> *Chantons* «Frère Jacques.»
> *Jouons* au basket-ball.
> *Fermons* les livres.
> *Applaudissons.*
> *Répondons:* «Nous aimons le français.»

What is the understood subject of the commands above? _____

How do we express these commands in English? _____

Let's look at another way to offer a suggestion.

> **On joue au football?**
> **On finit les devoirs?**
> **On descend en ville?**

Use the pronoun _____ *(one, we)* and conjugate the verb the same way you would for the subject pronouns _____ and _____ .

Activité

L. Ask your friends in two ways to join you in the following activities.

> EXAMPLE: parler français
> **Parlons français. On parle français?**

1. préparer la leçon

   _____   _____

2. fermer la porte

   _____   _____

3. visiter la France

   _____   _____

4. choisir un bon livre

   _____   _____

5. finir l'exercice

   _____   _____

6. applaudir les amis

   _____   _____

7. répondre au téléphone

   _____   _____

8. attendre le professeur

   _____   _____

 After all these games, Simon is a bit tired.

> **Simon dit à Pierre:** *Ne chante pas.*
> **Simon dit à Anne et Marie:** *N'applaudissez pas.*
> **Simon dit à la classe:** *Ne jouons pas.*

How do these commands differ from the others you have learned?

_____

To make a command negative, put **ne** _____ and **pas** _____ the verb.

How would you say the three commands above in English? _____

_____

_____

Subject pronouns are omitted in French commands (also called imperatives).

Formal or plural commands are expressed with the **vous** form of the verb.

Fermez la porte. Finissez le livre. Attendez ici.

Familiar commands are expressed with the **tu** form of the verb. **-ER** verbs drop the final **-s.**

Ferme la porte. Finis le livre. Attends ici.

Commands equivalent to *Let's* are expressed with the **nous** form of the verb.

Fermons la porte. Finissons le livre. Attendons ici.

Suggestions can be made using **on.**

On ferme la porte? On finit le livre? On attend ici?

To make a command negative, **ne** comes before the verb and **pas** after it.

**Ne ferme pas la porte. Ne finis pas le livre.
N'attendons pas ici.**

Activités

M. Tell the following people not to do the activities indicated.

EXAMPLE: André / jouer au base-ball
Ne joue pas au base-ball.

1. le professeur / chanter

    Ne chantez pas

2. Isabelle/ parler anglais

    Ne parle pas anglais

3. nous / regarder le tableau

    Ne regardons pas le tableau

4. Monsieur Rolland / finir la leçon

    Ne finissez pas la leçon.

5. Nicolas/ applaudir l'élève

    N'applaudis pas l'élève.

6. nous / punir l'enfant

    Ne punissons pas l'enfant

7. les amis / descendre l'escalier

   Ne descendez pas l'escalier.

8. une petite fille / répondre à la question

   Ne réponds pas à la question.

CONVERSATION

Vocabulaire

Je m'ennuie I'm bored
de la some
le transistor radio

Quoi faire alors? So what should we do?
ne marche pas doesn't work

finish

Parlons français

Work with a partner. Take turns playing the part of "le Grand Maître", the world's greatest hypnotist and the part of his "victim", acting out the various commands. Follow the example.

EXAMPLE: You: **Regardez ma montre!** (Student shows his watch or wrist.)
Partner: **Je regarde votre montre.** (Student looks at his watch.)

DIALOGUE

You are the first person in the dialog. What suggestions would you make to your friend?

Page culturelle

Les expressions sauvages *(Animal expressions)*

The names of animals are used in many French expressions. Here are some that you might find useful.

Être comme l'oiseau sur la branche.	Here today, gone tomorrow.
Son cheval de bataille.	His favorite subject.
Un remède de cheval.	A drastic remedy.
Un métier de chien.	A very difficult job.
Appeler un chat un chat.	To call a spade a spade.
Un tour de cochon.	A dirty trick.
Un vieux renard.	A sly old fox.
Poser un lapin à quelqu'un.	To stand someone up
Revenons à nos moutons.	Let's get back to our subject.
C'est un vrai mouton.	He's as mild as a lamb.
Laid comme un singe.	As ugly as sin.
Une faim de loup.	A ravenous hunger.
Quand les poules auront des dents.	When pigs fly.
Manger de la vache enragée.	To have a hard time of it.
Parler français comme une vache espagnole.	To speak very poor French.

Rappel

1. If you're extremely hungry you have _____ .

2. If someone's French accent is horrible and his grammar is poor, he is said to speak French like _____ .

3. When something is ugly, it is _____ .

4. When a job is quite hard it is said to be _____ .

5. Money often flies right through our fingers. One might say: "L'argent est _____ _____ ".

À Vous

1. Make a poster illustrating one of your favorite French animal expressions.

2. Make up five of your own original expressions using the names of animals.

La Chasse au trésor

http://

Using your best Internet search skills, find the answers to the following questions:
How would you say the following in French using the name of an animal:

a. "You have style"?
b. "I have goose pimples"?
c. "He has a frog in his throat"?
d. "You are as sly as a fox"?
e. "She has a raging fever."

C'est authentique!

LES DINOSAURES SONT DE RETOUR AU ZOO DE GRANBY

Jusqu'au 15 sept.

Les dinosaures sont fascinants! Laissez-vous envoûter et attrapez la DINOMANIE.

On vous attend!

À 45 minutes de Montréal

Sorties 68 ou 74 de l'autoroute 10

What does this ad tell you? _____

1. Dinosaurs will come back on September 15.

2. The dinosaurs are walking on Highway 10.

3. Dinosaurs will be on display for a while.

4. You must protect yourself against a serious illness.

MOTS NÉCESSAIRES

l'âne *m.* donkey
l'animal *m.* animal
l'animal domestique *m.* pet
le canard duck
le chat cat
le cheval horse
la chèvre goat
le chien dog

le cochon pig
l'éléphant *m.* elephant
le lapin rabbit
le lion lion
le loup wolf
le mouton sheep
l'oiseau *m.* bird
le poisson fish

le porc pork
le renard fox
le singe monkey
la souris mouse
le tigre tiger
la vache cow

15

Les lieux

*Forming Contractions with **de** and **à***

 1   Look at the pictures and try to guess the meanings of the words:

l'aéroport *(m.)*

l'appartement *(m.)*

la bibliothèque

le café

l'église *(f.)*

la gare

l'hôtel *(m.)*

le lycée

la maison

le restaurant

l'usine *(f.)*

la ville

Activités

A. Choose the correct completion to the sentences you hear.

a. une maison	**d.** la bibliothèque	**g.** un restaurant
b. l'hôtel	**e.** un lycée	**h.** l'aéroport
c. une usine	**f.** la gare	

1. _____ 3. _____ 5. _____ 7. _____

2. _____ 4. _____ 6. _____ 8. _____

B. Work with a partner. Take turns asking about and identifying the places. Then write your answers.

EXAMPLE: **Qu'est-ce que c'est?**
C'est l'appartement.

1. _____ 2. _____

3. _____ 4. _____ 5. _____

6. _____   7. _____   8. _____

9. _____   10. _____

 Now read this letter and see if you can answer the questions that follow.

Paris, le 11 juillet

Chère Maman,

J'adore Paris. La ville est très grande et très belle. L'aéroport Charles de Gaulle est magnifique. J'habite l'hôtel Saint-Germain. Ma chambre est petite. Je visite tous les monuments de Paris: l'Arc de Tríomphe, la tour Eiffel, la cathédrale Notre-Dame, le musée du Louvre. Je mange dans des cafés et des restaurants célèbres. Mes vacances sont fantastiques. S'il te plaît, maman, envoie-moi encore $150. Merci.

Ta fille, Lisette

la **chambre** the room
tous all
la **tour** the tower
le **musée** the museum
célèbre famous
s'il te plaît please
envoie-moi send me
encore more

Activité

C. Répondez aux questions.

1. Quelle est la date?

_____

2. Où est Lisette?

_____

3. Qu'est-ce qu'elle adore?

_____

4. Que pense-t-elle de Paris?

   _____

5. Comment s'appelle l'aéroport à Paris?

   _____

6. Quel hôtel Lisette habite-t-elle?

   _____

7. Qu'est-ce qu'elle visite?

   _____

8. Où mange-t-elle?

   _____

9. Comment sont ses vacances?

   _____

10. Qu'est-ce qu'elle demande à sa maman?

    _____ Elle demande de l'argent _____

2 Now let's learn about French contractions. Look carefully at these groups of sentences.

_J'm talking about ____._

I	**II**
J'arrive *à la* bibliothèque.	Je parle *de la* bibliothèque.
J'arrive *à la* chambre.	Je parle *de la* chambre.
J'arrive *à la* gare.	Je parle *de la* gare.
J'arrive *à la* maison.	Je parle *de la* maison.
J'arrive *à la* ville.	Je parle *de la* ville.

What is the gender of all the nouns in Groups I and II? _____

Are the nouns singular or plural? _____

How do you know? _____

Do the nouns start with consonants or vowels? _____

Which little word did we put before **la** in Group I? _____

What does **à la** mean? _____

Which little word did we put before **la** in Group II? _____

What does **de la** mean? _____

3

I voyelle	**II**
J'arrive *à l'*aéroport.	Je parle *de l'*aéroport.
J'arrive *à l'*appartement.	Je parle *de l'*appartement.
J'arrive *à l'*usine.	Je parle *de l'*usine.

Je vais au parc
(consonant)
consonne

What is the gender of all the nouns in Groups I and II? _____

Are the nouns singular or plural? _____

How do you know? _____

Do the nouns start with consonants or vowels? _____

Which little word did we put before l' in Group I? _____

What does **à l'** mean? _____

Which little word did we put before l' in Group II? _____

What does **de l'** mean? _____

4

I	II
J'arrive *au* café.	Je parle *du* café.
J'arrive *au* lycée.	Je parle *du* lycée.
J'arrive *au* musée.	Je parle *du* musée.
J'arrive *au* restaurant.	Je parle *du* restaurant.
J'arrive *au* village.	Je parle *du* village.

What is the gender of all the nouns in Groups I and II? _____

Are the nouns singular or plural? _____

How do you know? _____

Do the nouns start with consonants or vowels? _____

Which two little words did we combine to get **au**? _____

What does **au** mean? _____

Which two little words did we combine to get **du**? _____

What does **du** mean? _____

5

I	II
Ils arrivent *aux* aéroports.	Ils parlent *des* aéroports.
Ils arrivent *aux* lycées.	Ils parlent *des* lycées.
Ils arrivent *aux* maisons.	Ils parlent *des* maisons.

What is the gender of all of the nouns in Group I and II? _____

Are the nouns singular or plural? _____

How do you know? _____

Do the nouns start with consonants or vowels? _____

Which two little words did we combine to get **aux**? _____

What does **aux** mean? _____

au = à + le   *du = de + le*

Which two little words did we combine to get **des**? _____

What does **des** mean? _____

We call the combination of two words (like French **du, des, au, aux**) a _____

Activités

D. Listen to the places to which Pierre must go. Put a check in the correct box to express *to the.*

	AU	À LA	À L'	AUX
1.				
2.				
3.				
4.				
5.				
6.				

E. Pierre speaks about other places. Now put a check in the correct box to express *about the.*

	DU	DE LA	DE L'	DES
1.				
2.				
3.				
4.				
5.				
6.				

F. Mme Chenet is looking for her son Paul, who is writing an article about the city. Offer her suggestions where he might be.

EXAMPLE:  **Il est peut-être au lycée**

1. 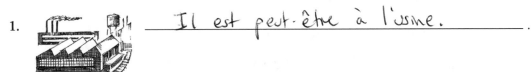 *Il est peut-être à l'usine.*

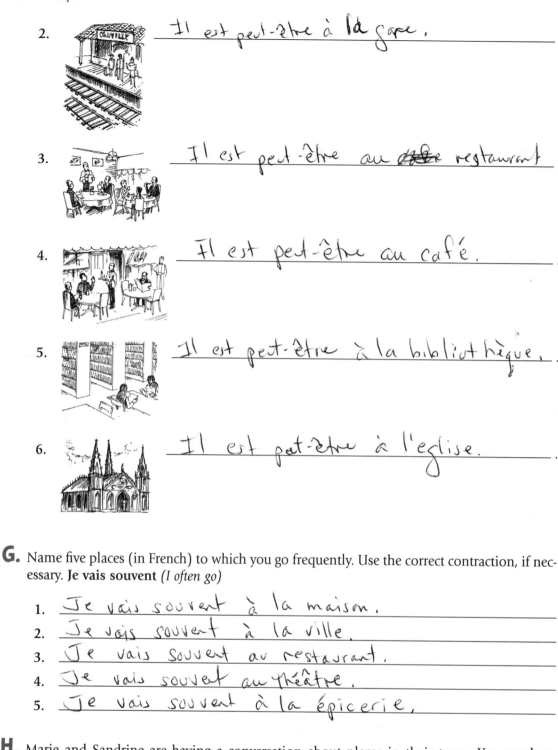

2. Il est peut-être à la gare.

3. Il est peut-être au ~~être~~ restaurant.

4. Il est peut-être au café.

5. Il est peut-être à la bibliothèque.

6. Il est pat-être à l'église.

G. Name five places (in French) to which you go frequently. Use the correct contraction, if necessary. **Je vais souvent** *(I often go)*

1. Je vais souvent à la maison.
2. Je vais souvent à la ville.
3. Je vais souvent au restaurant.
4. Je vais souvent au théâtre.
5. Je vais souvent à la épicerie.

H. Marie and Sandrine are having a conversation about places in their town. You overhear them. Tell what they are talking about.

EXAMPLE: (école) **Elles parlent de l'école.**

1. (café)   Elle parlent du café.
2. (lycée)   "   "   du lycée.

3. (usine)   *Elles parlent de l'usine.*
4. (maison)   " "   *de la maison.*
5. (restaurants)   " "   *des restaurants.*
6. (hôtels)   " "   *des hôtels.*
7. (gare)   " "   *de la gare.*
8. (appartement)   " "   *du appartement.*

How would you express in English that something belongs to someone? Instead of saying: "The house belongs to Paul," you could simply say, "That's _____ house." Instead of saying: "The apartment belongs to the girl," you could simply say: "That's _____ apartment." We show possession in English by using an apostrophe after the name or the noun referring to a person. Now look at these sentences to see how possession is expressed in French.

C'est la maison *de Paul.*
C'est le lycée *du garçon.*
C'est l'appartement *de la* fille.
C'est l'hôtel *de l'*homme.
C'est l'usine *des* Régnier.

Which little words are used in French to express that something belongs to someone?

_____

In our examples, what are the meanings of

de? _____   de l'? _____
du? _____   des? _____
de la? _____

What follows de? _____

du? _____

de la? _____

de l'? _____

_____

des? _____

De, du, de la, de l', des plus a name or a noun take the place of the apostrophe in English to express possession. The French word order is the reverse of English.

Activité

I. You have been asked to show some French visitors places in your town. Point them out in accordance with the pictures.

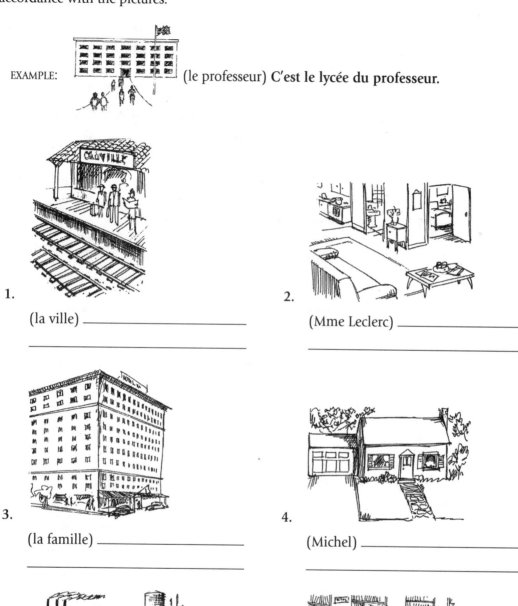

EXAMPLE: (le professeur) **C'est le lycée du professeur.**

1.
(la ville) _____

2.
(Mme Leclerc) _____

3.
(la famille) _____

4.
(Michel) _____

5.
(M. Robert) _____

6.
(le médecin) _____

How many ways are there to say *to the?* _____

What are they? _____

You use **à la** _____
_____
_____

à l' _____

au _____
_____

aux _____

How many ways are there to say *of/from/the ?* _____

What are they? _____

You use **de la** _____

de l' _____

du _____
_____

des _____

Prononciation

- **th** is always pronounced like the **t** in *to*. There is no sound in French similar to the English *th* sound.

  théâtre thé bibliothèque Catherine sympathique mathématiques

- Compare these English and French pronunciations:

ENGLISH	FRENCH	ENGLISH	FRENCH
Catherine	**Catherine**	math	**maths**
Matthew	**Mathieu**	theater	**théâtre**
sympathy	**sympathie**	thesis	**thèse**

Thomas et Thierry aiment les maths.
Catherine trouve Mathieu sympathique.
Thérèse va au théâtre avec Théo.

Parlons français

Have a conversation with a partner in which you discuss where you are going after school, at what time, with whom, and why. Follow the example.

EXAMPLES:
You: **Tu vas** *(You are going)* **où après les classes?**
Partner: **Je vais** *(I'm going)* **à la bibliothèque.**

You: **Tu vas à la bibliothèque à quelle heure?**
Partner: **À quatre heures.**

You: **Tu vas à la bibliothèque avec qui?**
Partner: **Avec des amis.**

CONVERSATION

Vocabulaire

seulement only
calme-toi calm down

alors so
occupé busy

aller to go

DIALOGUE

You are a member of the Arnaud family. Your parents are asking the whereabouts of your brothers and sisters. Respond with answers of your own choice.

Page culturelle

Allons visiter Paris

Paris is divided by the Seine River into two parts: **la rive gauche** (*the left bank*) and **la rive droite** (*the right bank*). In the middle of the river are two islands, **l'île Saint-Louis** and the more famous **île de la Cité**. Paris is an exciting city to visit. Every tourist wants to shop in the elegant boutiques and eat in the fabulous restaurants. But there is much more to see in Paris. Let's start on the left bank, **la rive gauche,** and discover some of the places of interest.

La Rive Gauche

1. Everyone thinks of **la tour Eiffel** when thinking of Paris. This famous tower, built in 1889 by the engineer Gustave Eiffel, is over 300 meters high. Tourists may visit the three levels of the tower. Admission fees vary with the level. There are two restaurants that afford a magnificent view of the city. Radio and television transmitters are located at the top of the Eiffel Tower.

2. **L'Hôtel des Invalides** is now a military museum containing the emperor Napoleon's tomb.

3. **Le Quartier Latin** is the center of student life. Here the important French institutions of higher education are located. **La Sorbonne** is the oldest part of the University of Paris. **Le boulevard Saint-Michel,** the principal street in the Latin Quarter, is lined with cafés frequented by students.

4. **Le Jardin du Luxembourg** is a large park where students like to meet. It has beautiful flower gardens and many activities for children.

L'Île de la Cité

1. The most famous church in Paris, **la cathédrale Notre-Dame,** is located on the **Île de la Cité.** Notre-Dame is a magnificent example of gothic architecture. Its stained-glass windows are among the most famous in the world.

2. **La Sainte-Chapelle** is another church in the gothic style, also famous for its magnificent stained-glass windows.

La Rive Droite

1. The most important museum in France is **le Louvre.** It houses the famous Mona Lisa (**La Joconde**), the Vénus de Milo, and the Winged Victory of Samothrace.

2. **Le Jardin des Tuileries** is a large park stretching from the Louvre to the Place de la Concorde. It contains many statues.

3. **Le Palais Garnier** is an opera house known for its sculptures and marble staircase.

4. **La Place Vendôme** is in a shopping area with many elegant shops. In the middle of this square is **la colonne Vendôme,** with a statue of Napoleon at the top, and scenes of his military victories along the sides.

5. **La Madeleine** is a famous church built like a Greek temple.

6. **La Place de la Concorde** is the square where many were guillotined during the French Revolution. In the center, there is a tall Egyptian obelisk surrounded by statues and fountains.

7. The former **Place de l'Étoile** derived its name from its position in the center of twelve avenues which form a star around **l'Arc de Triomphe,** the famous arch that straddles the Tomb of the Unknown Soldier. An eternal flame burns near the tomb. One avenue in the star is the **Champs-Élysées,** famous for its elegant stores. La Place de l'Étoile was renamed **Place Charles de Gaulle** in honor of France's former President.

8. **Montmartre** is the artists' quarter of Paris. It is a lively place with many restaurants.

9. **Le Sacré-Cœur** is a white church resembling a Turkish mosque. It is built on a hill in Montmartre, from which there is a beautiful view of the city.

10. **Le Bois de Boulogne** is a large public park on the west side of Paris, with race tracks, restaurants, lakes, and gardens.

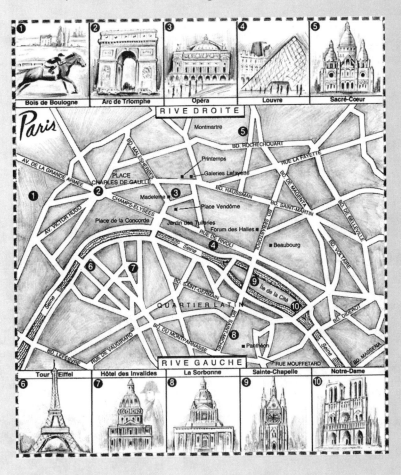

Rappel

1. Television and radio transmissions are emitted from the _la tour Eiffel_

2. Napoleon is buried in the military museum known as _l'Hôtel des Invalides._

3. The most famous church in Paris is _la cathédrale_ . Notre Dame

4. The *Mona Lisa* can be found in the _Louvre_ , the most famous museum in France.

5. The Sacré-Cœur is a white, mosque-like church that is built on a hill in _Montmartre_ .

À Vous

1. Draw a map of Paris on which you indicate the location of important places to visit.

2. Write a report about one famous place mentioned that you would like to visit.

La Chasse au trésor

http://

Using your best Internet search skills, find the names of two tourist attractions in:

a. Morocco.
b. Switzerland.
c. Guadeloupe.

d. Vietnam.
e. Gabon.
f. Monaco.

C'est authentique!

You are looking at souvenir ticket stubs that you collected while in France. Which was not an admission ticket to a tourist attraction? _____

1.

2.

3.

4.

MOTS NÉCESSAIRES

PLACES

l'aéroport *m.* airport
l'appartement *m.* apartment
la bibliothèque library
le café café
la cathédrale cathedral
l'église *f.* church

la gare train station
l'hôtel *m.* hotel
le lieu place
le lycée high school
le restaurant restaurant
l'usine *f.* factory
la ville city

CONTRACTIONS

à to
à l', à la, au, aux to the
de of, about, from
de l', de la, du, des of,
   about, from the

16
Les magasins

*Going Places in French; Using the Verb **aller***

la boucherie

la boulangerie

la boutique

l'épicerie *(f.)*

la librairie

le grand magasin

le marché

la pâtisserie

la pharmacie

le supermarché

272

Je vais à la pharmacie pour acheter de l'aspirine

Activités

A. Mme Legrand wants to buy many things. Match what she says she wants with where she has to go. Listen to your teacher.

a.　à la boulangerie　＿＿＿　　c.　à la pharmacie　＿＿＿　　e.　au marché　＿＿＿

b.　à la boucherie　＿＿＿　　d.　à la librairie　＿＿＿　　f.　à la boutique　＿＿＿

B. To which store would you go in order to buy the items in the left column? Write the matching letter.

1.　acheter un steak　　　　＿＿＿＿＿　　a.　à la pharmacie

2.　acheter un pull　　　　＿＿＿＿＿　　b.　à la boutique

3.　acheter des fruits　　　＿＿＿＿＿　　c.　à la pâtisserie

4.　acheter des croissants　＿＿＿＿＿　　d.　au marché

5.　acheter un livre　　　　＿＿＿＿＿　　e.　à la boulangerie

6.　acheter de l'aspirine　　＿＿＿＿＿　　f.　au grand magasin

7.　acheter un gâteau (*cake*)　＿＿＿＿＿　　g.　à la boucherie

8.　acheter des vêtements　＿＿＿＿＿　　h.　à la librarie

C. Work with a partner. Take turns asking and answering questions about the stores you are going to. Then write where you are going.

EXAMPLE:　　You:　**Où vas-tu ?**

Partner:　**Je vais à la pharmacie. Où vas-tu?**

1.　＿＿＿＿＿＿＿＿＿＿＿＿＿＿ .　　2.　＿＿＿＿＿＿＿＿＿＿＿＿＿＿ .

3.　＿＿＿＿＿＿＿＿＿＿＿＿＿＿ .　　4.　＿＿＿＿＿＿＿＿＿＿＿＿＿＿ .

5. _____ .   6. _____ .

Prononciation

- *ch* in French in pronounced *sh* like the *ch* in *machine*.

chez	cher	chance	acheter	chocolat	sandwich	choisir
chef	chic	chaud	chercher	toucher	chanter	Michel

- Compare the sound of *ch* in English and in French.

ENGLISH	FRENCH		ENGLISH	FRENCH
touch	**touche**		Charles	**Charles**
sandwich	**sandwich**		chocolate	**chocolat**
champion	**champion**			

Chantal choisit du chocolat chic pour le chef.
Charles a chaud à Cherbourg.

 In the letter that follows are all the forms of the irregular French verb **aller** *(to go)*. See if you can find them all.

la Martinique, le 7 août

Chère Marie,

Comment **vas-tu?** Moi, **je vais** bien. Je suis très contente parce que **je vais** tous les jours à la plage. Cet après-midi, mon amie Danielle et moi, **nous allons** faire les magasins de Fort-de-France. **Danielle va** être mon guide parce qu'elle connaît bien la ville. **Ses parents vont** acheter une maison à Fort-de-France. (C'est la capitale de la Martinique.)

Marie, **vas-tu** aller en vacances avec ta famille? Tes parents et toi, **allez-vous** visiter la France? Quelle chance tu as! Envoie-moi une carte postale.

Ton amie, Monique

Comment vas-tu? How are you?
cet this
faire les magasins to go shopping
connaît knows

Quelle chance! What luck!
Envoie-moi Send me

Did you find the forms of the irregular verb **aller** in the story? Fill in the proper verb forms for each subject. MEMORIZE them.

je _____   nous _____

tu _____   vous _____

il / elle _____   ils / elles _____

Look carefully at these sentences from the letter:

Comment vas-tu?   Je vais bien.

The verb **aller** is used to express a person's _____ .

Je vais bien.   I am well.
Je vais mal.   I am not well.

Activités

D. Répondez aux questions.

1. Où Monique est-elle en vacances?

   _____

2. Comment va-t-elle?

   _____

3. Où va-t-elle tous les jours?

   _____

4. Avec qui va-t-elle cet après-midi?

   _____

5. Qu'est-ce qu'elles vont faire?

   _____

6. Qui va être le guide?

   _____

7. Pourquoi?

   _____

8. Qu'est-ce que les parents de Danielle vont acheter?

   _____

9. Quelle est la capitale de la Martinique?

_____

10. Où est-ce que Marie va en vacances?

_____

E. Choose the correct answer to the questions your friend asks about you and your plans.

1. **a.** très bien
   b. au magasin
   c. avec Charles

2. **a.** au marché
   b. pas mal
   c. à midi

3. **a.** en avion
   b. en retard
   c. en bus

4. **a.** Je désire de l'aspirine.
   b. Je désire des éclairs et un gâteau au chocolat.
   c. Je désire un chemisier.

5. **a.** la voiture
   b. Marie
   c. le supermarché

6. **a.** après le dîner
   b. avec Robert
   c. en taxi

F. You and your friends have to run some errands. Where do you go?

EXAMPLE: **Je vais à l'épicerie.**

1. Jean _____ .

2. Marie et Nicole _____ .

3. Je _____ . 4. Vous _____ .

5. Claire _____ . 6. Tu _____ .

7. Ils _____ . 8. Nous _____ .

G. You are talking to some friends about places to go to or not to go to. Complete the sentences with the correct forms of **aller**.

1. Je ne _____ pas à l'école.

2. Nous _____ à l'aéroport.

3. _____ vous à la boum *(party)*?

4. Pierre _____ au supermarché.

5. Elle ne _____ pas à Paris.

6. Tu _____ au cinéma.

7. _____ ils à la Martinique?

8. Je _____ au magasin.

9. Paul et Anne ne _____ pas à la boucherie.

10. Où _____ t-il?

H. **Où allez-vous pendant la semaine?** Write five sentences about different places you go to.

EXAMPLE: **Le samedi, je vais au cinéma avec des amis.**

1. _____

2. _____

3. _____

4. _____

5. _____

3 Now look at these sentences from the story.

> **Nous *allons* faire les magasins.**   *We are going to the stores.*
> **Danielle *va* être mon guide.**   *Danielle is going to be my guide.*
> **Ses parents *vont* acheter une maison.**   *Her parents are going to buy a house.*

When are these actions taking place? In the past? present? future? _____

How do you know? _____

Underline the subject of each sentence. Now underline the verbs.

How many subjects are there in each sentence? _____

How many verbs are there? _____

Which verb is conjugated? _____

In what form is the second verb? _____

As you have seen, **aller** is a very important verb. Here is another reason for its importance.

> **Aller** can be used with an infinitive to express what is going to happen in the near future.

Why is it called the near future? _____

_____

4 Look at these sentences.

> **Nous *n'allons pas* faire les magasins.**
> **Elle *ne va pas* être mon guide.**
> **Ils *ne vont pas* acheter de maison.**

How do you make a sentence containing a CONJUGATED VERB + an INFINITIVE negative?

_____

J'ai le livre
Je n'ai pas du livre

Je mange le croissant.
Je n'ai pas mange du croissat

Now look at these sentences:

> *Allons-nous* faire les magasins?
> *Va-t-elle* être mon guide?
> *Vont-ils* acheter une maison?

How do you make a sentence containing a SUBJECT PRONOUN + a CONJUGATED VERB + an INFINITIVE into a question using inversion? _____

_____

Activités

I. Listen to Madeleine's plans and decide whether she is doing them today or will do them in the near future. Put a check in the appropriate box.

	PRESENT	NEAR FUTURE		PRESENT	NEAR FUTURE
1.	___	___	4.	___	___
2.	___	___	5.	___	___
3.	___	___	6.	___	___

J. You and your friends are making plans for tomorrow. What are you going to do? Complete the sentences with the correct forms of **aller** + infinitive and a closing of your choice.

1. Charles et Marie _vont marcher dans le parc._
2. Je _vais acheter des vetèments._
3. Vous _allez attendre pour moi_
4. Tu _vas_
5. Jacqueline _va_
6. Nous _allons_

K. You've had a change of plans. Make the sentences in Activité J negative.

1. _Ils ne vont pas marcher dans le parc._
2. _Je ne vais pas acheter_
3. _Vous n'allez pas attendre_
4. _Tu ne vas pas_
5. _Elle ne va pas_
6. _Nous n'allons pas_

CONVERSATION

Vocabulaire

le palmier palm tree
la mer des Antilles
   the Caribbean sea

le prix price
l'endroit *m.* place
prendre to take

l'avion *m.* plane
prochain next

Parlons français

Your friends have made a list of things to buy for a class picnic. Work with a partner and discuss where you are going shopping, what day you are going, and at what time you are going.

EXAMPLES: You: **Tu vas où?**
            Partner: **Je vais à la boucherie.**

You: **Quand vas-tu à la boucherie?**
Partner: **Je vais à la boucherie lundi.**

You: **Tu vas à la boucherie à quelle heure?**
Partner: **À cinq heures du soir.**

DIALOGUE

You are the second person in the dialog. Complete it with answers of your own choice.

C'est authentique!

Match the store with the product it sells.

a.

b.

c.

d.

e.

f.

fleurs Domaine de Valombreuse

1. _____

Le charcutier des Antilles

Jean Caby

2. _____

LE CONFISEUR DE PROVENCE

PRODUITS DU TERROIR

Nougats, Chocolats, Calissons, Tourons.

FRANCE NOUGAT S.A - BP 25 -
26201 MONTELIMAR Cedex

3. _____

Le Fournil de Jimmy

Votre boulanger

• Centre commercial de Grand-Camp
• Rue Peynier
• Marina - Pointe-à-Pitre
• Bourg de Sainte Anne

Pour vos commandes tél. : 83 75 72

4. _____

PARFUMERIE JG ODELIE

Section William - Saint-François - 97118 **Guadeloupe** - Tél.: 05 90 88 55 77
414 Squadra E - Quartier Dillon - 97200 **Martinique** - Tél.: 05 96 71 49 50
Appt N°3 - Agrément - 97150 **Saint-Martin** - Tél.: 05 90 87 99 39

*Toute une ligne de produits cosmétiques et de parfumerie
élaborée aux Antilles*

5. _____

BASTÉ

Votre Pâtisserie

**PRODUITS
ALIMENTAIRES**

16 Route de la Schlucht
STOSSWIHR
B.P. 63
68140 MUNSTER
Tél. : 03 89 78 35 00

6. _____

Page culturelle

On fait les courses *(Shopping)*

Most Americans do their weekly food shopping in supermarkets. The French also go to a **supermarché** or a **hypermarché** (large shopping center), if there is one near their residence. Many, however, still prefer the small, individualized neighborhood stores which are everywhere in towns and villages. There they feel sure of the quality and freshness of the products they buy. In the course of a day, a French person might visit these stores:

Pharmacie   *Poissonnerie*

Boucherie   *Fruiterie*

Épicerie   *Charcuterie*

Boulangerie   *Marchand de Vins*

Pâtisserie   *Bureau de Tabac*

What would you buy in each of these stores?

The French use the metric system when they go shopping.

WHEN YOU WEIGH FOODS	WHEN YOU MEASURE LIQUIDS
1 kilo(gram)= 2.2 pounds (lbs)	1 liter = 1.06 quart
1 pound = 0.45 kilo (kg)	4 liters = 1.06 gallon
100 grams = 0.22 lb	
500 grams = 1.1 lb	

For quick approximate conversions, multiply the number of liters by four to get gallons. Divide the number of gallons by four to get liters.

Rappel

1. Many French shoppers prefer to buy goods in individualized neighborhood stores because _____ .

2. In a charcuterie you'd expect to buy _____ .

3. To buy fresh bread, go to a _____ .

4. To buy about a pound of fresh fruit, you'd have to ask for _____ .

5. One gallon is equal to approximately _____ liters.

À Vous

1. Make a diorama of a French specialty store.

2. Go to your local supermarket and drugstore. Make a chart of products from France and the specialty stores in a French city where you might expect to purchase these items.

La Chasse au trésor

http://

Imagine you'll be taking a trip to Paris. Using your best Internet search skills, find the name and address of:

a. A supermarket.
b. A bakery.
c. A department store.
d. A bookstore.
e. A drugstore.

M O T S   N É C E S S A I R E S

STORES
la boucherie butcher shop
la boulangerie bakery
la boutique store
l'épicerie f. grocery store
le grand magasin
   department store
la librairie bookstore
le magasin store
le marché market

la pâtisserie pastry shop
la pharmacie drugstore
le supermarché supermarket

ALLER: TO GO
je vais I go
tu vas you go
il va he goes
elle va she goes
nous allons we go

vous allez you go
ils/elles vont they go

EXPRESSIONS
Comment vas-tu? How are
   you?
Comment allez-vous? How
   are you?
aller bien/mal to be
   well/not well

Révision IV
(LEÇONS 13–16)

Leçon 13

a. To conjugate an **-RE** verb, drop **-re** from the infinitive and add the appropriate endings.

EXAMPLE: **vendre**

If the subject is **je**   add **s**   to the remaining stem: **je vends**
               tu   **s**   **tu vends**
               il/elle   **–**   **il/elle vend**
               nous   **ons**   **nous vendons**
               vous   **ez**   **vous vendez**
               ils/elles   **ent**   **ils/elles vendent**

b. The same rules as those for **-ER** verbs apply to making a sentence negative or asking a question, except that no **-t-** is needed for inversion with **il** or **elle.**

> Elle *n'*attend *pas* l'autobus.
> *Attend-il* le professeur?

Leçon 14

a. Subject pronouns are omitted in French commands (imperatives).

Familiar imperatives are expressed with the **tu** form; **-ER** verbs drop final **-s.**

> **Parle français.**

Formal and plural imperatives are expressed with the **vous** form.

> **Finissez vos devoirs.**

Nous form imperatives are equivalent to *Let's.*

> **Répondons au téléphone.**   *Let's answer the phone.*

Negative commands are preceded by **ne** and followed by **pas.**

> *Ne* parle *pas* anglais.

b. Suggestions can be made by using the pronoun **on.**

> **On va au parc?**   *Shall we go to the park?*

Leçon 15

a. Contractions in French:

à + le = au	Use **au** before masculine singular nouns beginning with a consonant: **au restaurant.**
à + les = aux	Use **aux** before all plural nouns: **aux restaurants.**
de + le = du	Use **du** before masculine singular nouns beginning with a consonant: **du restaurant.**
de + les = des	Use **des** before all plural nouns: **des restaurants.**

b. To express possession and relationship:

Use **de** before the name of one person: **la bicyclette** *de* **Paul**
Use **des** before the name of more than one person: **le chien** *des* **Marchand**
Use **du, de la, de l'**, or **des** before nouns, following the rules above:

la lettre *du* professeur   les devoirs *de l'*étudiant
la fin *de la* semaine   les vêtements *des* enfants

Leçon 16

a. The verb **aller** *(to go)* is irregular. Memorize all its forms.

je vais	nous allons
tu vas	vous allez
il / elle va	ils / elles vont

b. **Aller** is used in expressions of health.

Comment allez-vous?	*How are you?*
Je vais bien.	*I am well.*
Je vais mal.	*I am not well.*

c. **Aller** is used to express the near future.

Nous allons finir **le dîner à huit heures.**	*We are going to finish dinner at eight o'clock.*

Activités

A. Identify the animals. Then write the letters in the boxes below to reveal what Jean-Paul keeps as a pet.

1.   ☐☐☐☐
1

2. ☐☐☐☐☐
   2   3

3. ☐☐☐☐☐☐
             4

4. ☐☐☐☐☐
   5   6   7

5. ☐☐☐☐☐☐
     8 9

6. ☐☐☐☐☐☐
     10

7. ☐☐☐☐
    11

8. ☐☐☐☐☐
 12 13

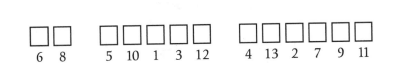

☐☐ ☐☐☐☐☐ ☐☐☐☐☐☐
6 8   5 10 1 3 12   4 13 2 7 9 11

B. Write the French words under the pictures. Then circle the words in the puzzle.

1. _____

2. _____

3. _____

4. _____

5. _____

6. _____

7. _____

8. _____

9. _____

10. _____

11. _____

12. _____

13. _____   14. _____   15. _____

```
S   N   G   M   A   R   C   H   É   E   R
L   U   E   M   S   E   N   I   S   U   E
P   É   P   C   R   S   G   L   A   Q   S
I   H   V   E   I   R   L   U   O   I   T
B   E   A   É   R   O   P   O   R   T   A
O   L   F   R   G   M   M   E   F   U   U
U   A   V   N   M   L   A   S   V   O   R
C   M   T   I   U   A   I   R   M   B   A
H   Ô   T   E   L   E   C   S   C   L   N
E   P   R   S   R   L   A   I   E   H   T
R   E   P   A   C   N   E   V   E   R   É
I   E   G   E   I   R   E   C   I   P   É
E   I   S   M   A   I   S   O   N   A   S
```

C. Mots croisés.

HORIZONTALEMENT

1. (answer) nous ＿＿
5. (ask) vous ＿＿
10. (have) j' ＿＿
12. one
13. the
14. in
16. (is) il ＿＿
17. gray ＿＿
18. to sell
20. he
21. (hear) vous ＿＿
22. (are) tu ＿＿
24. (have) elles ＿＿
25. of
26. (find) tu ＿＿
29. (dance) ils ＿＿
30. the
31. (seize) je ＿＿
32. (are) tu ＿＿
33. (have) tu ＿＿
34. (to) like
39. if

40. (to) play
42. (works) elle ＿＿
43. from
44. one
45. (close) tu ＿＿
46. I
47. (gives) il ＿＿
50. (chooses) elle ＿＿
53. the
54. (have) vous ＿＿
57. one
59. (are) vous ＿＿
60. (prepare) je ＿＿
63. (enters) elle ＿＿
64. (have) vous ＿＿
67. one
68. the
69. of
71. (give) ils ＿＿
72. (invite) nous ＿＿
74. (taste) tu ＿＿

VERTICALEMENT

1. (arrange) elles ＿＿
2. (punish) nous ＿＿
3. one
4. (ask) tu ＿＿
5. (descend) je ＿＿
6. (is) elle ＿＿
7. (likes) il ＿＿
8. of
9. (enter) ils ＿＿
11. (invite) tu ＿＿
13. the
15. (have) vous ＿＿
19. (is) il ＿＿
23. one
24. one (pronoun)
25. (descend) nous ＿＿
27. (seize) elles ＿＿
28. (are) tu ＿＿
30. the
33. (waits for) elle ＿＿
34. (arrive) j' ＿＿
35. (walks) il ＿＿
36. (look at) vous ＿＿

37. (sing) vous ＿＿
38. (speak) je ＿＿
39. he
40. I
41. one
43. (descend) ils ＿＿
46. (plays) il ＿＿
48. (listen) vous ＿＿
49. (have) tu ＿＿
51. they
52. he
54. (applaud) j' ＿＿
55. (enter) tu ＿＿
56. (look for) elles ＿＿
58. (win) tu ＿＿
60. (think) tu ＿＿
61. (listens) elle ＿＿
62. (like) ils ＿＿
65. (have) elles ＿＿
66. (have) ils ＿＿
70. in
73. he

D. Every morning, Pierre leaves his house and walks to his high school, taking the shortest route. On his way, he passes many places. Figure out the shortest way to school and list the places he passes.

_____

_____

_____

_____

E. Jumble: Unscramble the words. Then unscramble the circled letters to complete the message.

Q E S M U I U   _ ◯ _ _ _ _ ◯

O E M T O R B N   ◯ _ _ _ ◯ _ ◯ _

T E A R I U G   _ _ _ ◯ ◯ _ _

E N T A R L C I E T   _ _ _ _ ◯ _ _ _ _ ◯

T P R E M T O T E   _ ◯ _ _ _ ◯ _ _ _

Pour son anniversaire, Michel désire _____

The Cognate Connection

Write the meanings of the following French and English words.

FRENCH		ENGLISH COGNATE	
1. bibliothèque	_____	bibliography	_____
2. descendre	_____	descendant	_____
3. mouton	_____	mutton	_____
4. musique	_____	musical	_____
5. vendre	_____	vendor	_____

5

cinquième partie

17

La maison

Expressing Location; Using Prepositions

Vocabulaire

la maison

l'immeuble *(m.)*

l'appartement *(m.)*

l'entrée *(f.)*

la cuisine

la salle à manger

le séjour/le living

le salon

la chambre

la salle de bains

les toilettes *(f.)*

le sous-sol

le grenier

le garage

le jardin

Activités

A. Roland is having a phone conversation with a friend about his rich cousin's house. Choose the correct word to describe each thing he is talking about.

1. **a.** grands **b.** grande **c.** grandes
2. **a.** charmant **b.** charmante **c.** charmants
3. **a.** élégantes **b.** élégant **c.** élégante
4. **a.** parfaites **b.** parfait **c.** parfaite
5. **a.** jolis **b.** joli **c.** jolie

B. **Qu'est-ce que c'est?** Work with a partner. Take turns identifying the rooms. Then write your answers.

EXAMPLE:

You: **Qu'est-ce que c'est?**
Partner: **C'est le sous-sol.**

1. _____

2. _____

3. _____

4. _____

5. _____   6. _____

C. You are writing a composition about your house. Complete these sentences.

1. J'habite _ma maison_ .
2. Ma mère prépare les repas dans _la cuisine_ .
3. Je mange dans _la salle à manger_ .
4. Je regarde la télé dans _le living_ .
5. Je dors (*sleep*) dans _la chambre_ .
6. Je plante des fleurs dans _le jardin_ .

2 Les meubles

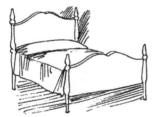

le lit   le canapé   la table

le miroir, la glace   l'armoire (*f.*)   l'étagère (*f.*)

la chaise   la lampe   le lampadaire   le réfrigérateur

Activités

D. Odette just moved into a new house. Match what she describes with the place you'd expect to find it.

    a. le garage   _____   **d.** la salle à manger   _____

    b. le jardin   _____   **e.** le salon   _____

    c. la chambre   _____

E. The Dufour family just moved into a new house. Tell where the movers must have put these items.

    EXAMPLE: **L'armoire est dans la chambre.**

    1. Le réfrigérateur _____ .

    2. L'auto _____ .

    3. Le lit _____ .

    4. Le lampadaire _____ .

    5. La table _____ .

    6. Le canapé _____ .

F. Answer these questions about yourself.

    1. Où est votre lit?

          _____ dans ma Chambre _____

    2. Où préparez-vous le dîner?

          _____ dans la cuisine _____

    3. Où regardez-vous la télévision?

          _____ dans le living _____

    4. Comment est votre maison (appartement)?

          _____ Ma maison n'est pas grande. _____

    5. Combien d'étages (*floors*) a votre maison (appartement)?

          _____ Il y a trois d'étags à ma maison _____

G. On a separate sheet of paper, draw your house, especially your room. Label the rooms in your house and the objects in your room.

Prononciation

- The letter combination **gn** is pronounced like the *ni* in the English word *onion*.

montagne	signe	Espagne	Bretagne	gagner	accompagner
campagne	ligne	Allemagne	Champagne	Agnès	magnifique

C'est magnifique. J'accompagne Agnès en Bretagne.
À la campagne, en Espagne, Mme Dagneau signe sur la ligne.

 Read this story about two girls trying to impress each other.

JEANNE: Bonjour, Sylvie. Ça va?

SYLVIE: Ça va. J'ai beaucoup de travail.

JEANNE: Beaucoup de travail? Pourquoi?

SYLVIE: Notre famille habite une grande maison. Il y a beau-coup de chambres et j'aide ma mère à faire le ménage.   **faire le ménage** to do the housework

JEANNE: Oui, moi aussi. Ma maison est énorme. Nous avons dix pièces. Mes parents ont une grande chambre. Ma sœur et moi, nous avons chacune une grande chambre et mon frère a aussi une grande chambre pour lui   **la pièce** room
chacune each (one)
pour lui for himself

SYLVIE: Combien de salles de bains avez-vous?

JEANNE: Trois. Nous avons aussi un grand salon, une salle à manger et une cuisine où notre bonne prépare les repas.   **la bonne** the maid
le repas the meal
sert serves

SYLVIE: Oui, notre bonne prépare et sert aussi les repas. Ils sont magnifiques.

(À ce moment-là, la mère de Sylvie entre.)

MAMAN (à sa fille):   Sylvie, pourquoi dis-tu que nous avons une bonne? Tu sais bien que ce n'est pas vrai.   **dis-tu** do you say
tu sais bien you know well
ce n'est pas vrai it's not true

SYLVIE: Oui, maman. Ce sont des mots en l'air. Nous rêvons! Jeanne habite comme nous un petit appartement.   **des mots en l'air** idle talk, just words
nous rêvons we are dreaming

Activité

H. Complete the sentences based on the story.

1. Selon Sylvie, sa famille habite _____ .

2. Dans la maison, il y a beaucoup de _____ .

3. Sylvie aide sa mère à _____ .

4. Selon Jeanne, sa maison est _____ .

5. La maison de Jeanne a _____ pièces.

6. Ses parents ont _____ .

7. La maison de Jeanne a trois _____ .

8. _____ prépare les repas.

9. Elle prépare les repas dans _____ .

10. À vrai dire (*In fact*), Sylvie et Jeanne habitent _____ .

 Où est tout le monde? (*Where is everybody?*)

Read the following story and look at the picture. The expressions in bold type are prepositions. Many prepositions tell us where people and things are. Other prepositions show the relationship between words. Can you figure it out?

C'est aujourd'hui l'anniversaire de Georges. Il a quinze ans. Ses amis donnent une boum **pour** cette occasion spéciale. Georges ne sait pas que tous ses amis sont **chez** lui ce soir. Il va être très surpris. Où sont ses amis? Voyons:

boum party
sait knows **que** that
voyons let's see

Richard est **sous** la table.
Marie est **sur** le canapé.
Paul est **devant** la télévision.
Annette est **derrière** les rideaux.
Marc est **à côté de** Paul.
Sylvie est **près de** la fenêtre.
Louis est **loin de** la porte.
Régine et Henri sont **autour de** la table.
Claire est **en face de** la cuisine.
André est **avec** Marthe.
Renée est **dans** la cuisine.

rideaux *m.* curtains

Georges arrive **chez** lui. Il est triste parce qu'il est **sans** amis. Généralement, ses amis sont très gentils **envers** lui. Il ne comprend pas. Georges arrive **avant** sept heures. Il ouvre la porte. Tous ses amis crient: «Bon anniversaire, Georges!» **Après** cela, Georges est très content.

cela this

PREPOSITIONS

à *at/to*	**avec** *with*	**devant** *in front of*	**pour** *for, in order to*
à côté de *next to*	**chez** *at (the house of)*	**en face de** *facing, opposite of*	**près de** *near*
après *after*	**dans** *in*		**sans** *without*
autour de *around*	**de** *of, from*	**envers** *toward*	**sous** *under*
avant *before*	**derrière** *behind*	**loin de** *far from*	**sur** *on*

Activités

I. **Où sont les amis de Georges?** Match the person with the location. Write the matching letter.

1.	Richard	_____	a.	derrière les rideaux
2.	Marie	_____	b.	près de la fenêtre
3.	Paul	_____	c.	avec Marthe
4.	Annette	_____	d.	sur le canapé
5.	Marc	_____	e.	autour de la table
6.	Sylvie	_____	f.	à côté de Paul
7.	Louis	_____	g.	dans la cuisine
8.	Régine et Henri	_____	h.	sous la table
9.	Claire	_____	i.	en face de la cuisine
10.	André	_____	j.	loin de la porte
11.	Renée	_____	k.	devant la télévision

J. Répondez aux questions.

1. Quel âge a Georges aujourd'hui?

   _____

2. Qu'est-ce que ses amis donnent?

   _____

3. Où sont les amis de Georges ce soir?

   _____

4. Pourquoi Georges est-il triste?

   _____

5.   Comment sont ses amis généralement?

_____

6.   À quelle heure arrive-t-il chez lui?

_____

7.   Qu'est-ce que ses amis crient?

_____

8.   Comment est Georges après?

_____

CONVERSATION

Vocabulaire

tard late
mon chéri my darling

mon amour my love
à tout à l'heure see you later

Parlons français

You have misplaced something you need and you are discussing this with a parent. Work with a partner and take turns pretending to be the parent and the child. Have a dialog about where your lost item may be.

EXAMPLES: You: **Je ne trouve pas mon classeur.**
Partner: **Cherche sous ton lit.**
You: **Il n'est pas là.**
Partner: **Tant pis.** (*too bad*) **Regarde dans la cuisine.**
You: **Ah! voilà mon classeur! Il est sur le réfrigérateur.**

Page culturelle

Chez soi *(At home)*

Many French families own their own home. Some also own a vacation home, called **une résidence secondaire.** They can escape there on weekends and vacations and indulge in their love of gardens.

French homes are quite comfortable and well-equipped. Most kitchens contain modern appliances (**les robots ménagers**), such as a refrigerator (**un réfrigérateur** or **un frigo**), a dishwasher (**un lave-vaisselle**), and a microwave oven (**un four à micro-ondes**). French people do not usually eat in the kitchen, so there is no dining area in that room.

You might be surprised to find no toilet in the bathroom. That's because the **toilettes** are in a separate washroom, along with a small sink and a mirror.

Bedrooms rarely have built-in closets, so the French hang their clothes in wardrobes.

Houses also have a washing machine (**une machine à laver**), but they usually do not have a dryer (**un sèche-linge**). The wash is hung on lines in the basement or the garden. It may be dried in a small room equipped with a ceiling rack, called **un séchoir.**

There are no shades or blinds on the windows, but wood or metal shutters (**les volets**) are pulled over the windows outside at night, or during the day when there is too much sun. These shutters keep the rooms cool and dark at night, and protect against burglars, as well.

Many French families also live in an apartment building (**un immeuble**), which is maintained by **un concierge** or **un gardien.** The **concierge** or **gardien** usually lives in a ground-floor apartment and is responsible for building security, mail distribution, and cleaning of stairs and entryways. In many buildings nowadays, a resident or visitor must input a private code on an electronic keypad to unlock the front door. The hall lights are often controlled by a timer (**une minuterie**) that turns the light off automatically after one minute. You must press the switch again to get the light back on.

Note how the floors in a French building are designated:

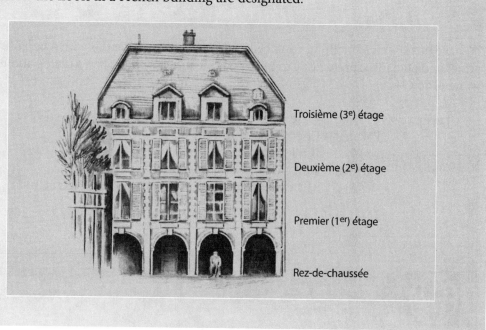

Troisième (3e) étage

Deuxième (2e) étage

Premier (1er) étage

Rez-de-chaussée

Rappel

1. Many French families own _____ .

2. _____ is a home where people go to spend weekends or vacations.

3. Les **robots ménagers** are _____ .

4. The person who maintains a French apartment building is called the _____ .

5. The ground floor of a French building is called _____ .

À Vous

1. Make a floor plan of a French house.

2. Make a drawing of your favorite room in the house and label everything in it.

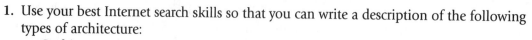

La Chasse au trésor   http://

1. Use your best Internet search skills so that you can write a description of the following types of architecture:
   a. Gothic.   **c.** Beaux arts.   **e.** Art deco.
   b. Baroque.   **d.** Art nouveau.

2. Write a short biography of these two famous French architects:
   a. Charles Garnier.   **b.** Le Corbusier.

C'est authentique!

Which ad offers a house that

1. has a large entrance? _____

2. is close to Paris? _____

3. has 6 bedrooms? _____

4. is in a quiet area? _____

> 378 000€
> **GRANDE MAISON**
> au coeur du village
> 1h Paris par A6 gare
> SNCF Montargis 45
> **8 PCES**
> + dépendances
> **TERR. 1000M2**
> clos LOCATION VENTE
> 3700F/MS CONSTANT
> 16/38 85. 22. 92. 24h/24

a.

> – 6 km Malesherbes (45) part vend MAISON sur 1 300 m² boisés, grande en- trée, cuis., salle à manger, 2 chb., salle de bns, w.-c., gd sous-sol, chauf. central, gar., cave, appentis. 280 000€ à débattre. (16) 38.39.18.67.

b.

> **DINARD marché:** bonne maison centrale et calme, séj., 4 ch., 2 s.d.b., gge, jard. 300 000€ A1.

c.

> **DINARD Centre:** maison bour- geoise, vaste séjour, 6 ch., garage, beau jardin clos et planté. 550 000€ A1.

d.

M O T S   N É C E S S A I R E S

MAISON

l'appartement *m.* apartment
l'armoire *f.* wardrobe
le canapé sofa
la chaise chair
la chambre bedroom
la cuisine kitchen
l'entrée *f.* entrance
l'étage *m.* floor, story
l'étagère *f.* bookcase
le garage garage
la glace mirror
le grenier attic
l'immeuble *m.* apartment building
le lampadaire floor lamp
la lampe lamp
le lit bed
le living living room

la maison house
le miroir mirror
la pièce room
le réfrigérateur refrigerator
le repas meal
le rideau curtain
la salle à manger dining room
la salle de bains bathroom
le salon living room
le séjour living room, great room
le sofa sofa
le sous-sol basement
la table table
les toilettes *f./pl.;* bathroom

PREPOSITIONS

à at; to
à côté de next to
après after
autour de around
avant before
avec with
chez at (the house) of
dans in
de of; from
derrière behind
devant in front of
en face de facing, opposite
envers toward
loin de far from
pour for; in order to
près de near
sans without
sous under
sur on

18

Les nouveautés

Saying "This, That, These", and "Those"

 Vocabulaire

Can you figure out the meanings of these modern-day technological marvels?

l'ordinateur *(m.)*

le four à micro-ondes

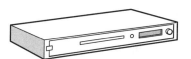

le lecteur de DVD

le téléphone sans fil

l'ordinateur *(m.)*
de poche

l'iPod *(m.)*

la mini-console
de jeux vidéo

l'ordinateur portable /
le portable

l'appareil-photo *(m.)* numérique

le caméscope

la télévision à écran plat

le (téléphone) mobile
(au Canada, le cellulaire)

le calculateur solaire

Activités

A. Choose the letter of what you would use in the situations mentioned by your teacher.

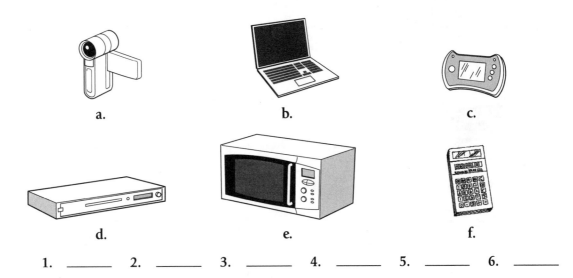

a.

b.

c.

d.

e.

f.

1. _____   2. _____   3. _____   4. _____   5. _____   6. _____

B. M. et Mme Armand are shopping for a birthday present for their teenager. Tell what they are looking for.

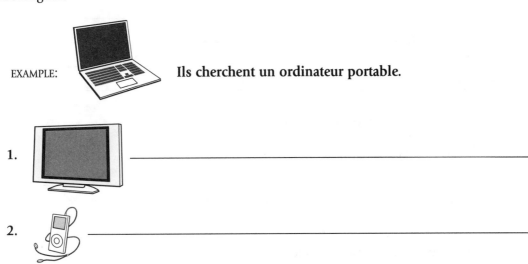

EXAMPLE: **Ils cherchent un ordinateur portable.**

1. _____

2. _____

3. _____

4. _____

C. Martin is going to college. Work with a partner. Take turns asking and telling what he has with him. Then write your answer.

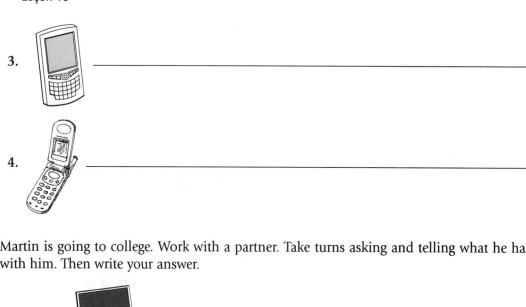

EXAMPLE: Qu'est-ce qu'il a?
Il a un portable.

1. _____   **2.** _____

_____   _____

3. _____   **4.** _____

_____   _____

D. List five electronic items you have or you would like to have in your room.

1. _____
2. _____
3. _____
4. _____
5. _____

E. Answer the questions in complete sentences.

1. Combien de télévisions votre famille a-t-elle?

_____

2. Combien de téléphones votre famille a-t-elle?

_____

3. De quelle couleur est votre téléphone?

_____

4. Quel ordinateur est le meilleur *(the best)*?

_____

5. Qu'est-ce qu'on fait avec un four à micro-ondes?

_____

Prononciation

- In **-tion** the *t* has the sound of *s*.

action	nation	disposition	attention
relation	collection	information	prononciation

- In **-sion** the *s* has the sound of *z* when it follows a vowel.

télévision	révision	occasion	division

- *s* sounds like *z* when it occurs between two vowels.

mademoiselle	raison	musée	cousin
prestigieuse	musique	visiter	lisons

C'est l'occasion de faire une révision de la prononciation.
Ma cousine Rose présente les informations à la télévision.

 Read this story about an overeager young woman. See if you can find the demonstrative adjectives **ce, cet, cette** *(this, that)*, and **ces** *(these, those)*.

La peau de l'ours

Brigitte finit ses études à l'université. Elle trouve un poste de rédactrice dans une grande société prestigieuse. Afin de se préparer à l'avance pour son travail, elle va dans un magasin où elle dépense beaucoup d'argent pour toutes les machines nécessaires à une femme d'affaires moderne. Elle met tout dans sa chambre. Elle explique à son amie que **cet** ordinateur, **ce** fax, **cette** imprimante, **ce** calculateur et **ce** téléphone sans fil vont être très utiles quand elle va travailler à la maison. Brigitte pense qu'elle est très intelligente.

la peau skin
l'ours *m.* bear

la rédactrice editor
prestigieuse influential
afin de in order to
dépenser to spend
femme d'affaires business woman
met *puts*
le fax fax
l'imprimante *f* printer
utile useful

Le premier jour de travail arrive. Brigitte entre dans son bureau où elle parle avec son chef:

le chef the boss

BRIGITTE: Pardon, mais où est mon ordinateur?

LE CHEF: Nous n'utilisons pas **ces** machines dangereuses. Nous avons peur des rayons qui s'en échappent!

le rayon ray
s'échapper to escape
la machine à écrire typewriter

BRIGITTE: D'accord. Mais alors où est ma machine à écrire électrique?

LE CHEF: Mais **cette** machine coûte trop cher. Notre slogan est: «Ne gaspillez pas d'argent!»

coûte trop cher is too expensive
gaspiller to waste

BRIGITTE: J'ai sans doute un fax à ma disposition.

LE CHEF: Non, mademoiselle. Les fax ne sont pas utiles.

utile useful

BRIGITTE: Mais vous allez au moins me donner une machine à écrire manuelle?

au moins at least
manuel(le) manual

LE CHEF: Je regrette. La machine à écrire est hors de service et le technicien qui la répare est en vacances en Europe pour trois mois.

hors de out of

BRIGITTE: Hélas! **Cette** compagnie est prestigieuse, mais elle n'est pas du tout moderne. Je n'aurais pas dû dépenser tout **cet** argent. Mon amie a raison quand elle dit: «Ne vendez pas la peau de l'ours avant de l'avoir tué!»*

Je n'aurais pas dû I shouldn't have

Activité

F.   Complétez les phrases.

1.   Brigitte finit _____ .

2.   Elle trouve un poste de _____ .

3.   Au magasin Brigitte achète _____ .

4.   Elle pense que ces machines vont être _____ .

5.   Brigitte pense qu'elle est très _____ .

6.   La compagnie n'utilise pas d'ordinateurs parce que _____ _____ .

7.   Les employés ont peur des _____ .

8.   La compagnie n'utilise pas de machine à écrire électrique parce que _____ _____ .

9.   Le slogan de la compagnie est _____ .

10.   La compagnie n'utilise pas de fax parce que _____ .

11.   La machine à écrire manuelle est _____ .

12.   Le technicien qui répare cette machine est _____ .

13.   La compagnie est prestigieuse, mais elle n'est pas _____ .

14.   Brigitte aurait dû écouter son amie qui dit souvent: _____ _____ .

* "Don't count your chickens before they are hatched." (Literally, "Don't sell the bearskin before you have killed the bear.")

In French there are many kinds of adjectives. Now you are going to learn about demonstrative adjectives. Look at the two groups of words.

I	II
la machine	*cette* machine
la famille	*cette* famille
la télévision	*cette* télévision
la chambre	*cette* chambre
la maison	*cette* maison
l'amie	*cette* amie

What is the gender of all these nouns? _____

Are they singular or plural? _____

How do you know? _____

Which word in Group II replaces **la** from Group I? _____

What does **cette** mean? _____

Is **cette** used with nouns that start with consonants or vowels? _____

3

I	II
le mobile	*ce* mobile
le programme	*ce* programme
le portable	*ce* portable
le calculateur	*ce* calculateur
le téléphone	*ce* téléphone

What is the gender of all these nouns? _____

Are they singular or plural? _____

How do you know? _____

Which word in Group II replaces **le** from Group I? _____

What does **ce** mean? _____

Is **ce** used with nouns that start with consonants or vowels? _____

4

masc.

(screen)

I	II
l'ordinateur	*cet* ordinateur
l'écran	*cet* écran
l'iPod	*cet* iPod
l'appareil-photo	*cet* appareil-photo
l'homme	*cet* homme

What is the gender of all these nouns? _____

Are they singular or plural? _____

How do you know? _____

Which word in Group II replaces **l'** from Group I? _____

What does **cet** mean? _____

Is **cet** used with nouns that start with consonants or vowels? _____

5

	I	II
	les machines	*ces* machines
	les fours	*ces* fours
	les ordinateurs	*ces* ordinateurs
	les télévisions	*ces* télévisions
	les programmes	*ces* programmes
	les écrans	*ces* écrans

What is the gender of all these nouns? _____

Are they singular or plural? _____

How do you know? _____

Which word in Group II replaces **les** from Group I? _____

What does **ces** mean? _____

Is **ces** used with nouns that start with consonants or vowels? _____

Cette, cet, ce all mean _____. **Ces** means _____.
Use **cette** before _____
   cet before _____
   ce before _____
   ces before _____

Activités

G. Check the demonstrative adjective you would use to describe the nouns in the sentences you hear:

	CE	CET	CETTE	CES
1.	____	____	____	____
2.	____	____	____	____
3.	____	____	____	____
4.	____	____	____	____
5.	____	____	____	____
6.	____	____	____	____

H. You are in a department store with a friend. Describe what you see.

> EXAMPLE: four / petit
> **Ce four est petit.**

1. ordinateur / moderne

   Cet _____

2. télévision / grande

   Cette _____

3. calculateur / utile

   Ce _____

4. téléphone sans fil / formidable

   Ce _____

5. écrans / immenses

   Cet _____

6. caméscope / splendide

   Cet _____

7. lecteurs de DVD / chers

   Ce _____

8. ordinateur de poche / élégant

   Cet _____

Parlons français

You are looking for a graduation gift in an electronics store. You are speaking to a salesperson who is trying to convince you to make a purchase. Work with a partner and create a dialog about possible options and cost.

> EXAMPLE: Partner: **Bonjour. Je peux vous aider?**
> You: **Oui. Je cherche un cadeau.**
> Partner: **Regardez ce caméscope.**
> You: **Il coûte combien?**
> Partner: **Cinq cents dollars.**
> You: **Oh là là. Je préfère un appareil-photo numérique . C'est combien?**
> Partner: **Cent cinquante dollars.**
> You: **Parfait. Donnez-moi cet appareil-photo, s'il vous plaît.**

CONVERSATION

le lecteur de disques compacts CD player

La Chasse au trésor

http://

Using your best Internet search skills, find the answers to the following questions:

How much do the following items cost in France:
   a. A flat screen TV?
   b. An iPod?
   c. A cell phone?
   d. A digital camera?
   e. A laptop?

Page culturelle

Passe-temps modernes *(Modern Pastimes)*

French teenagers do many of the same things during their spare time as their American contemporaries. Playing games on a computer is one pastime they share.

Computers play a major role in today's education. Many schools have clubs in which students are taught how to operate computers and run and write programs. Students communicate via e-mail and do research on the Internet, just as American students do. Many French youths gain experience on a personal computer at home.

Both American and French teens enjoy playing video games. They talk about them and trade them with friends. Video games **(les jeux vidéo)** and game stations **(les consoles vidéo)** have created a very active and profitable business. Far from being just characters in a story, the heroes of video games earn a lot of money for their designers and manufacturers. In France, as well as in the United States, video games have become a popular gift item.

New game stations are very popular. The next generation of video games will have high-quality pictures equal to those of the best films made today. **"Un grand hit"** is an extremely popular game.

Rappel

1. One pastime that French and American teens share is _____ .
2. Students can attend _____ to learn programming.
3. French and American students can communicate via _____ .
4. In French, video games are called _____ .
5. The French word for "game station" is _____ .

À Vous

1. Write a review of a French film or video game with which you are familiar.
2. Write an advertisement, in French, for a **"nouveauté."**

C'est authentique!

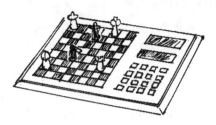

UN NOUVEAU GADGET ÉLECTRONIQUE

Il confirme à haute voix le coup joué et annonce les résultats. Un programme de 46 ouvertures classiques lui permet de réagir instantanément.

C'est un jeu d'échecs qui parle comme vous et moi.

How would you use this device? _____

1. Dictate a report for school.

2. Listen to music.

3. Tape conversations.

4. Play a game with a "friend."

MOTS NÉCESSAIRES

ELECTRONICS

l'appareil-photo numérique *m.* digital camera

le calculateur solaire solar calculator

le caméscope camcorder

le (téléphone) cellulaire cell phone (au Canada)

la mini-console de jeux vidéo handheld game station

le fax fax machine

le four à micro-ondes microwave oven

l'iPod *m.* iPod

le lecteur de DVD DVD player

la nouveauté novelty, new item,

l'ordinateur *m.* computer

l'ordinateur de poche *m.* handheld computer

l'ordinateur portable, le portable laptop

le téléphone mobile, le mobile, cell phone

le téléphone sans fil cordless phone

la télévision à écran plat flat screen TV

DEMONSTRATIVES

ce, cet *m.* this, that

cette *f.* this, that

ces *m./f.* these, those

19
Les aliments

Expressing the Partitive

 Les repas du jour

LE PETIT DÉJEUNER

le verre de jus d'orange   les céréales *(f. pl.)* avec du lait   les œufs *(m.)* au bacon

le pain grillé avec du beurre   la tasse de café   le sucre

Activité

A. Au menu aujourd'hui. Our chef today, **Charles le Cuisinier** (*Charles the Cook*), has prepared three meals for us. Here is the first: breakfast. Can you describe in French what it consists of? Label each picture.

le petit déjeuner

LE DÉJEUNER

**le sandwich au jambon
et au fromage**

le beurre

la salade de laitue *(f.)*
avec des tomates

la mayonnaise

la moutarde

le sel

le poivre

les frites *(f. pl.)*

la pomme

la poire

le raisin

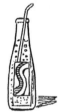

le soda

Activités

B. Here is Charles the Cook's menu for our lunch. Label each picture.

le déjeuner

C. You are having lunch with several friends at a cafeteria and you need certain items.

EXAMPLE:  **Donne-moi le sel, s'il te plaît.**

1. _____

2. _____

3. _____

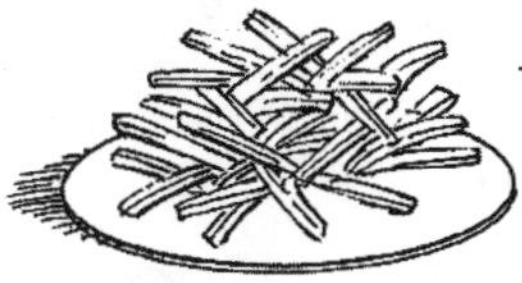

4. _____

5. _____

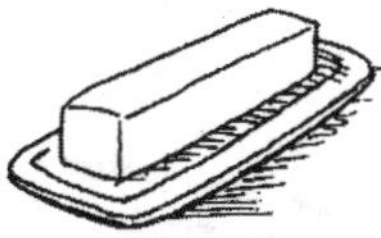

6. _____

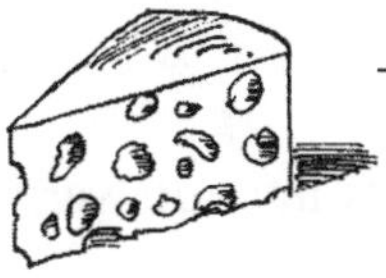

7. _____

8. _____

LE DÎNER

le pain

la soupe

le poulet

le bifteck

la viande

le poisson

les pommes *(f.)* de terre

les légumes *(m.)*

les épinards *(m.)*

les carottes *(f.)*

les petits pois *(m.)*

les haricots verts *(m.)*

la glace (à la vanille)

le gâteau au chocolat

l'eau *(f.)* minérale

Activités

D. You're preparing a menu. Check under which heading you'd put the items you hear.

1. _____	_____	_____	_____
2. _____	_____	_____	_____
3. _____	_____	_____	_____
4. _____	_____	_____	_____
5. _____	_____	_____	_____
6. _____	_____	_____	_____
7. _____	_____	_____	_____
8. _____	_____	_____	_____

E. And here is our dinner menu. Label the pictures.

le dîner

F. Your mother asks you what you would like for dinner tonight. Using the pictures below, tell her what you like.

EXAMPLE:  **J'aime le poulet.**

1. _____ .

2. _____ .

3. _____ .

4. _____ .

5. _____ .

6. _____ .

7. _____ .

8. _____ .

9. _____ .

10. _____ .

G. You are shopping for your family. Make a shopping list of the things you would buy.

SUPERMARCHÉ

1. _____
2. _____
3. _____
4. _____
5. _____
6. _____
7. _____
8. _____
9. _____
10. _____

Now read this story and look for the phrases in bold type beginning with **du,**
de la, de l', and **des.** In this story, all these words mean *some.*

Le dîner français

La classe de français prépare un dîner. Les élèves apportent **des** | apportent bring
spécialités françaises.

Alain apporte **de la bouillabaisse.** La bouillabaisse est une
soupe faite avec **du poisson.** C'est la spécialité de Marseille. | **faite** made

Monique apporte une quiche. La quiche est faite avec **du jam-**
bon, du fromage, du lait, des œufs et **des épices.** La quiche | **les épices** *f.* spices
est un plat typique de la Lorraine.

Marie apporte **de la viande (du bifteck** et **du porc), des to-**
mates et **de la laitue.** Elle apporte aussi une salade niçoise. | **niçoise** from Nice
Cette salade est faite avec **du thon, des radis** et **des légumes.** | **le thon** the tuna (fish)
C'est la spécialité de Nice, une grande ville dans le Midi de la | **le radis.** the radish
France. | **le Midi** the South

Jacques apporte le dessert. C'est **de la mousse au chocolat.**
Tous les élèves adorent la mousse parce qu'elle est faite avec **du**
chocolat, de la crème et **des œufs.** C'est la spécialité du pro- | **la crème** the cream
fesseur de français.

Activités

H. Complete the sentences.

1. Les élèves préparent _____ françaises.

2. La bouillabaisse est _____ faite

   avec _____ .

3. La bouillabaisse est la spécialité de _____ .

4. La quiche est faite avec _____

   _____ .

5. La quiche est la spécialité de _____ .

6. Marie fait une salade niçoise avec _____

   _____ .

7. La salade niçoise est la spécialité de _____ .

8. Le professeur fait de la mousse avec _____

   _____ .

1. Répondez aux questions.

1. Que fait la classe?

   _____

2. Qu'est-ce qu'Alain apporte au dîner?

   _____

3. Quel est le plat typique de la Lorraine?

   _____

4. Qui apporte la quiche?

   _____

5. Qu'est-ce que Marie apporte au dîner?

   _____

6. Quelle sorte de viande apporte-t-elle?

   _____

7. Qui apporte le dessert?

   _____

8. Quel dessert apporte-t-il?

   _____

2   Let's take a closer look at the **partitive**. Study the following groups of phrases.

I	II	III	IV
de la viande	*de l'*eau	*du* café	*des* sandwiches
de la salade	*de l'*orangeade	*du* lait	*des* pommes
de la soupe	*de l'*argent	*du* fromage	*des* fruits

In Group I, what is the gender of all the nouns? _____

How do you know? _____

Which little word did we put before **la**? _____

What does **de la** mean? _____

In Group II, is the gender of the nouns important? _____ If you answered "No," you were correct. If the gender is not important in Group II, then something else must be important. Look at all the nouns in Group II. They all have something in common. Look carefully at their beginnings. How are the nouns similar?

_____

Which little word did we put before **l'**? _____

What does **de l'** mean? _____

In Group III, what is the gender of all the nouns? _____

How do you know? _____

Which little word did we put before all the nouns? _____

Which two little words did we combine to get **du**? _____

What does **du** mean? _____

In Group IV, is the gender of the nouns important? _____ If the gender is not important in Group IV, then something else must be important. Look at all the nouns in Group IV. They all have something in common. Look carefully at their endings. How are the nouns similar?

_____

Which little word did we put before all the nouns? _____

Which two little words did we combine to get **des**? _____

What does **des** mean? _____

> **de la, du, de l′**, and **des** express the partitive.

Why do you think they are called "partitive"? _____

Activités

J. Check the box of the partitive you would need to ask a waiter for some of the following.

	DU	DE LA	DE L′	DES
1.	_____	_____	_____	_____
2.	_____	_____	_____	_____
3.	_____	_____	_____	_____
4.	_____	_____	_____	_____
5.	_____	_____	_____	_____
6.	_____	_____	_____	_____
7.	_____	_____	_____	_____
8.	_____	_____	_____	_____

K. Jean-Philippe's brother Laurent comes home hungry and asks what there is in the house to eat. Work with a partner. Take turns playing the part of Jean-Philippe and Laurent. Then write your answer.

EXAMPLE: Laurent: **Qu′est-ce qu′il y a à manger?**
                     Jean-Philippe: **Il y a du jambon.**

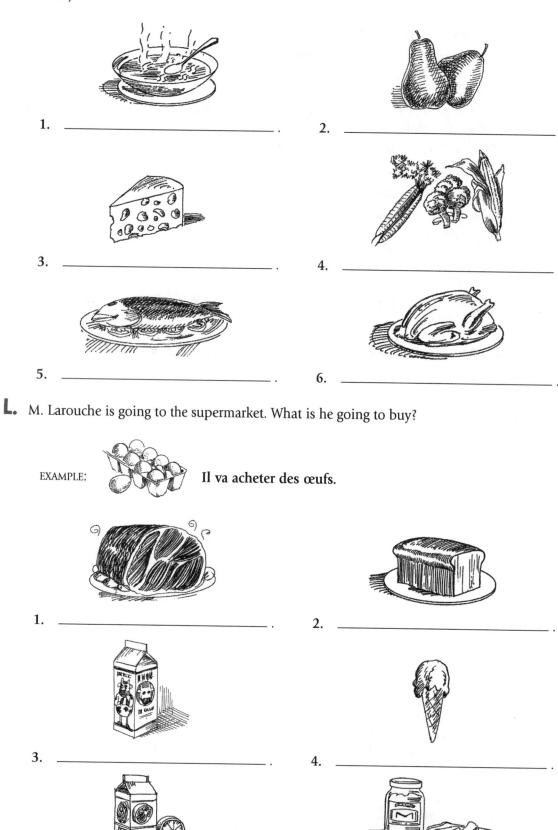

1. _____ .

2. _____ .

3. _____ .

4. _____ .

5. _____ .

6. _____ .

L. M. Larouche is going to the supermarket. What is he going to buy?

EXAMPLE: **Il va acheter des œufs.**

1. _____ .

2. _____ .

3. _____ .

4. _____ .

5. _____ .

6. _____ .

M. Qu'est-ce-que vous apportez à l'école pour votre déjeuner?

1. J'apporte _____
2. _____
3. _____
4. _____
5. _____

3 Now look carefully at the following sentences.

> Je **n**'apporte <u>pas</u> de sandwiches.
> Elle **n**'a <u>pas</u> de salade.
> Vous <u>ne</u> mangez <u>pas</u> de jambon.
> Nous <u>ne</u> préparons <u>pas</u> d'orangeade.

What do the underlined words tell you about each sentence? _____

Circle the word in each sentence that stands for "any" or "some." What happens to the partitive article (**du, de la, de l', des**) in a negative sentence?

_____

What happens to **de** before a vowel? _____

Activités

N. You are planning a party. You look into the refrigerator and find that it's practically empty. Have a conversation with your mother. Take turns with a partner playing the different roles. Then write your negative answer.

EXAMPLE: You: **Il y a de la salade?**
Partner: **Non, il n'y a pas de salade.**

1. _____

2. _____

3. _____

4. _____

5. _____

6. _____

O. Say what these people are not bringing to the picnic.

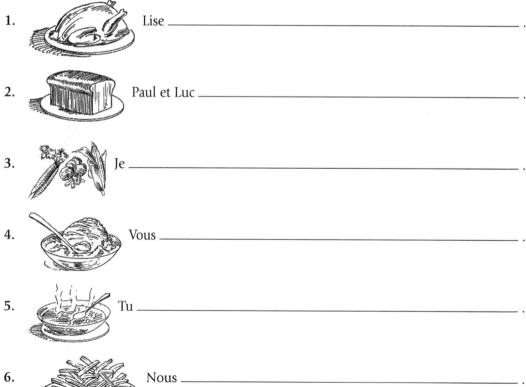

EXAMPLE: **Il n'apporte pas d'eau minérale.**

1. Lise _____ .

2. Paul et Luc _____ .

3. Je _____ .

4. Vous _____ .

5. Tu _____ .

6. Nous _____ .

CONVERSATION

Vocabulaire

bonsoir good evening
la serveuse the waitress
voici here is

j'ai très faim I'm very hungry
boire to drink

Prononciation

- **x** is pronounced *ks,* like the *xc* letter combination in *excellent.*

exact	excellent	exquis	texte	mixte
extra	exprimer	expérience	maximum	saxophone

- At the end of a word, **x** is usually not pronounced.

délicieux   vieux   toux

Maxime fait une explication de texte.
C'est excellent. M. Saxon joue du saxophone.

You are in a restaurant. Work with a partner and have a dialog with a waiter about what to order.

EXAMPLES:

	You:	**Oui, monsieur.**
	Partner:	**Qu'est-ce que vous avez comme viande?**
	You:	**Nous avons du poulet. Il est excellent.**
	Partner:	**Il y a de bons légumes?**
	You:	**Oui, les haricots verts sont délicieux.**
	Partner:	**Et pour finir?**
	You:	**Il y a de la glace. Elle est exquise.**

 # Page culturelle

Les spécialités françaises

Many regions in France are noted for their specialty dishes. Look at the map to see what to order in different parts of France.

Bretagne: This province on the English Channel is known for its seafood, particularly lobster **(le homard)** and mussels **(les moules);** apple cider **(le cidre);** and **crêpes,** thin pancakes sometimes filled with a variety of meat, vegetables, or dessert fillings. (1)

Normandie: The products for which this province is famous are cheese, butter, fish, apples, and a particularly good lamb, often served as a roasted leg: le **gigot.** (2) .

From the **Champagne** region, we get the famous sparkling wine, **le champagne.** (3)

The provinces of **Alsace and Lorraine** are on the border of France and Germany. Specialties here include **choucroute garnie,** a mixture of sauerkraut, sausage, and pork; and **quiche lorraine,** a mixture of egg, milk, cheese, and bacon or ham baked in a pie crust. (4)

The city of **Paris** has a special dish called **bœuf à la mode,** a type of pot roast with carrots. **Brie** cheese is a popular cheese. (5)

The **Bourgogne** region is known for its wine, beef, and snails **(les escargots).** (6)

Savoie is on the border of France and Switzerland. Here **fondues** are popular. **Gruyère** cheese is melted in a special **fondue** pot and bread is dipped into the cheese before it is eaten. Certain meat and dessert dishes may also be prepared as **fondues.** (7)

Aquitaine: This province in southwestern France is famous for **foie gras** made from goose liver; **pâté,** a paste of chopped liver and meat; and a dish made with potted goose called **confit d'oie.** Its principal city, **Bordeaux,** is noted for its wine and for seafood dishes made with oysters. (8)

Provence is famous for its **bouillabaisse,** a thick soup made with various types of fish. **Salade niçoise** is popular in the city of Nice. It is made with lettuce, tuna, hard-boiled eggs, olives, and anchovies. **Pissaladière** is a type of pizza made with onions, anchovies, and without tomatoes. (9)

Rappel

1. Thin pancakes, sometimes stuffed with meat, vegetables, or a dessert filling, are called _____ .

2. Gigot is a special dish often served in Normandy. It is made from _____ .

3. Bourgogne is known for its escargots which we call _____ .

4. Goose liver is an hors d'œuvre called _____ .

5. Bouillabaisse is a type of _____ soup.

À Vous

1. Find a crêpe, quiche, or bouillabaisse recipe. Write in your own words the necessary ingredients and how to prepare the dish.

2. Draw a map labeling the French regions and their specialties.

3. Write an authentic looking French menu.

La Chasse au trésor

http://

Using your best Internet search skills, find the answers to the following questions.
What is a typical dish in the following francophone countries? Describe the dish.

  a. Morocco?
  b. Haiti?
  c. Cambodia?
  d. Madagascar?
  e. Tahiti?
  f. Louisiana Cajun cuisine?

C'est authentique!

Match the restaurant with what it offers.

a.

b.

c.

d.

e.

f.

Vieux-Québec, **Restaurant du Bateau-Mouche de Québec**, *p. R11*
132, rue Saint-Pierre G1K 4A7 (418) 692-4949

Superbe bateau ultra-moderne, climatisé. Dîners-croisières pour savourer un repas raffiné dans un cadre spectaculaire. Tous les soirs à 19h départ du Bassin Louise. Prière de réserver. Tarifs de groupe disponibles.

1. _____

Vieux-Québec, **Voûtes du Cavour (Les)**
38, rue Saint-Pierre G1R 3Z6 (418) 694-1294

Bistro italien et salle de réception. Depuis 1984, nous sommes des spécialistes dans le service de groupe. Situé au coeur de la Place-Royale. Le site le plus ancien en Amérique du Nord.

2. _____

Vieux-Québec, **Cochon Dingue (Le)**, *p. R2*
46, boul. René-Lévesque Ouest G1R 2A4
(418) 523-2013

Réputé pour ses petits déjeuners, son steak frites et ses desserts cochons. Maison datant de 1911. Parmi les plus belles terrasses jardins à Québec.

3. _____

Sainte-Foy, **Au Petit Coin Breton**
2620, boul. Laurier G1V 2L1 (418) 653-6051

Atmosphère typique, un coin de Bretagne à Québec. Spécialités de crêpes bretonnes, salades, soupe à l'oignon. Personnel costumé à l'ancienne.

4. _____

Québec, **Saint-Hubert**
605, boulevard Hamel G1M 2T4 (418) 527-1234

Familial, économique, table d'hôte, menus pour enfants.
Dans un décor agréable et confortable.

Sainte-Foy, **Tyrolienne (La)**
2846, chemin Gomin G1V 2J8 (418) 651-6905

Architecture unique. Ambiance de chalet suisse.
Spécialités : fondues, grillades et fruits de mer.
Stationnement 80 espaces. Près de Place Laurier.

5. _____

6. _____

MOTS NÉCESSAIRES

FOOD
l'aliment *m.* food
le bacon bacon
le beurre butter
le bifteck steak
le café coffee
la carotte carrot
les céréales *f. pl.* cereal
le chocolat chocolate
la crème cream
le déjeuner lunch
le dessert dessert
le dîner dinner
l'eau *f.* water; **eau minérale** mineral water
les épinards *m. pl.* spinach
les frites *f. pl.* French fries
le fromage cheese
le gâteau cake
la glace ice cream

les haricots verts *m. pl.* string beans
le jambon ham
le jus juice
le lait milk
la laitue lettuce
le légume vegetable
la mayonnaise mayonnaise
la moutarde mustard
l'œuf *m.* egg
l'orange *f.* orange
le pain bread; **pain grillé** toast
le petit déjeuner breakfast
les petits pois *m. pl.* peas
le plat dish
la poire pear
le poisson fish
le poivre pepper
la pomme apple

la pomme de terre potato
le poulet chicken
le raisin grapes
la salade salad
le sandwich sandwich
le sel salt
la soupe soup
le sucre sugar
la tasse cup
la tomate tomato
la vanille vanilla
le verre glass
la viande meat

PARTITIVE ARTICLES
de some/any [of; from]
de l', de la some
des some
du some

20
Le pique-nique
Using **vouloir** *and* **pouvoir; tout**

Vocabulaire : **le couvert** (*the table setting*), **le pique-nique**

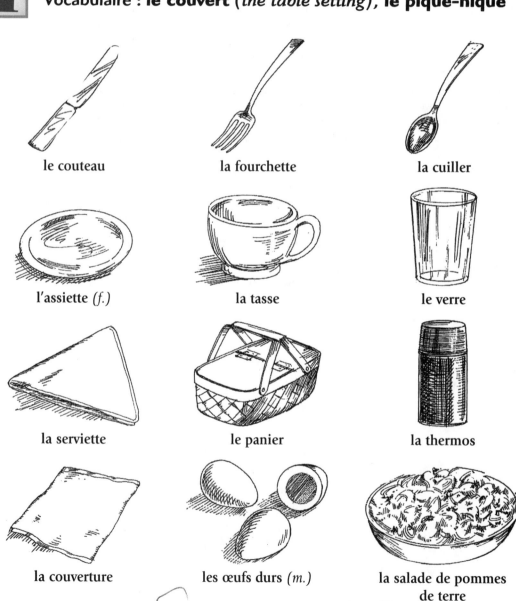

le couteau

la fourchette

la cuiller

l'assiette (*f.*)

la tasse

le verre

la serviette

le panier

la thermos

la couverture

les œufs durs (*m.*)

la salade de pommes
de terre

plural pronounce the "f"

singular - do not pronounce the "f"

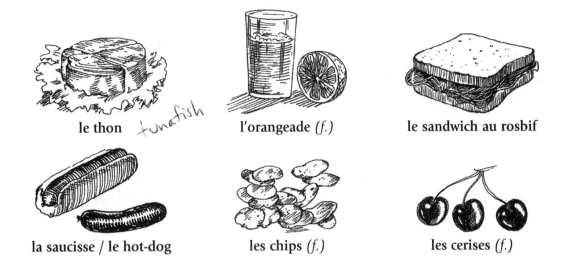

le thon *tunafish*   l'orangeade *(f.)*   le sandwich au rosbif

la saucisse / le hot-dog   les chips *(f.)*   les cerises *(f.)*

Activités

A. You're learning to set the table (*mettre le couvert*) in French. Write the letter of the item you hear next to the appropriate number.

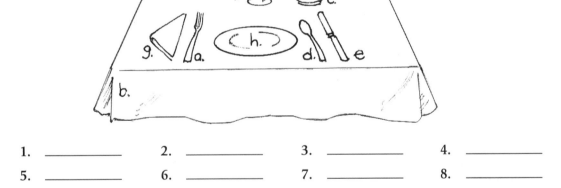

1. _____   2. _____   3. _____   4. _____
5. _____   6. _____   7. _____   8. _____

B. You are going to a picnic. Take turns working with a partner asking and answering what you are taking along. Then write your answer.

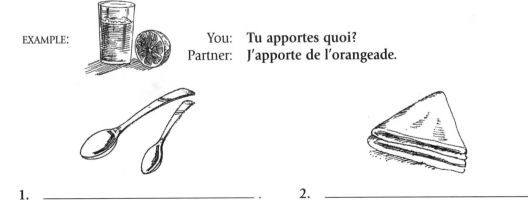

EXAMPLE: You: **Tu apportes quoi?**
                  Partner: **J'apporte de l'orangeade.**

1. _____ .   2. _____ .

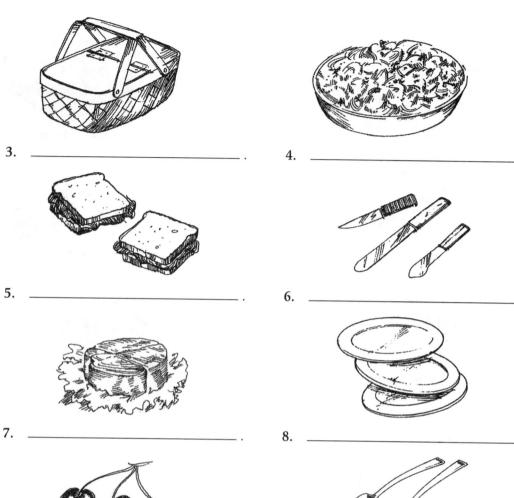

3. _____ .   4. _____ .

5. _____ .   6. _____ .

7. _____ .   8. _____ .

9. _____ .   10. _____ .

C. What kinds of foods do you like or dislike? Use the scale to tell how you feel about the following.

EXAMPLE: J'adore la glace.

j'adore
j'aime beaucoup
j'aime
je n'aime pas
je déteste

1. _____ .   2. _____ .

3. _____ .   4. _____ .

5. _____ .   6. _____ .

7. _____ .   8. _____ .

D. What do you eat at a picnic? Identify the foods you eat or don't eat.

EXAMPLE: **Je mange du pain.**
Je ne mange pas de pain.

1.  _____

2. _____

3.  _____

4.  _____

5. _____

6.  _____

7.  _____

8.  _____

9.  _____

10.  _____

Prononciation

- Nasal sounds are sounds that are made when air passes through your nose and your mouth at the same time.

  -an (-am) and **-en (-em)** are the same nasal sound when they are at the end of a word or followed by a consonant except *n* or *m*.

dans	manger	jambon	parent	en	temps
grand	sandwich	maman	enfant	encore	décembre
France	lampe	ambulance	enfin	souvent	employé

  Henriette attend Bertrand tout le temps.
  En décembre les employés ambitieux vont souvent en France.

You already know how to say that you like something. Now you will learn how to say that you want something. Read the following conversation and see if you can find all the forms of the irregular verb **vouloir** (*to wish, to want*).

Le pique-nique

Michel, 5 ans, et Eric, 8 ans, vont faire un pique-nique avec leurs parents.

MAMAN: **Papa veut** manger des hamburgers. Les hamburgers sont délicieux. Ils donnent des muscles!

ÉRIC: Moi, je déteste les hamburgers. **Papa veut** peut-être manger des hamburgers, mais moi, **je veux** manger des hot-dogs.

MICHEL: **Tu veux** manger des saucisses? Oh! Moi, **je veux** manger des sandwiches au jambon, s'il te plaît, maman.

MAMAN: **Mes enfants veulent** toujours manger des plats différents. Ils ne sont jamais d'accord. Bon. J'apporte des hamburgers, des hot-dogs et des sandwiches au jambon. Alors, mes enfants, **vous voulez** de l'orangeade ou de l'eau minérale?

> les plats *m. pl.* dishes
> ne . . . jamais never
> d'accord in agreement

ÉRIC: De l'orangeade, maman!

MICHEL: De l'eau minérale, maman!

MAMAN: Quel désastre! Bon. J'apporte de la limonade.

> le désastre disaster

ÉRIC ET MICHEL: Ah non! Pas de limonade!

MAMAN: Êtes-vous d'accord pour le dessert au moins?

> au moins at least

ÉRIC ET MICHEL (après une longue conversation animée):   Oui, maman. **Nous voulons** un gâteau au chocolat et des fruits.

> animée animated

MAMAN: Enfin!

> enfin finally

Activité

E. Complétez les phrases.

1. Michel a _____ ans.

2. Éric a _____ ans.

3. Michel, Éric, maman et papa vont faire _____.

4. Papa veut manger _____.

5. Éric veut manger _____.

6. Michel veut manger _____.

7. Comme boisson (*drink*) Éric veut _____.

8. Mais Michel préfère _____.

9. Alors, maman finit par choisir _____.

10. Comme dessert les deux garçons veulent _____.

2 Did you find the forms of the irregular verb **vouloir** (*to wish, to want*) in the story? Fill in the proper forms for each subject. Memorize them.

je _____   nous _____

tu _____   vous _____

il / elle _____   ils / elles _____

Activités

F. What do these people want? Complete the sentences with the correct forms of **vouloir**.

1. Tu / une glace _____
2. Il / une pomme _____
3. Vous / un œuf dur _____
4. Marguerite / une orange _____
5. Nous / des saucisses _____
6. Je / un sandwich au thon _____
7. Charles et Chantal / de l'orangeade _____
8. Mes grands-parents/ un sandwich au rosbif _____
   _____

G. Work with a partner. You are in a coffee shop. The waitress asks you what you want. Answer the questions.

EXAMPLE: Partner: **Voulez-vous de l'eau?**
             You: **Oui, je veux de l'eau.**

1. Voulez-vous un sandwich au thon ou au poulet?
   _____

2. Voulez-vous un sandwich au rosbif avec de la moutarde ou de la mayonnaise?
   _____

3. Voulez-vous de la salade de pommes de terre ou des frites?
   _____

4. Voulez-vous un verre de lait ou une orangeade?
   _____

5. Voulez-vous de la glace à la vanille ou au chocolat?
   _____

H. You and your friends are discussing what you want to do this weekend. Complete the sentences with the correct forms of **vouloir**.

1. Nous / jouer au tennis

   _____

2. Guillaume / aller au cinéma

   _____

3. Tu / regarder la télévision

   _____

4. Je / faire un pique-nique

   _____

5. Anne et Louise / aller à une discothèque

   _____

3 There is another French verb that resembles **vouloir** when it is conjugated. That verb is **pouvoir** (*to be able, can*). Note the two spelling differences:

je **peux**	nous **pouvons**
tu **peux**	vous **pouvez**
il / elle **peut**	ils / elles **peuvent**

I. Use the verb **pouvoir** to tell what these people can do.

1. Janine _____ préparer une mousse excellente.
2. Tu _____ jouer au tennis.
3. Nous _____ parler français.
4. Ils _____ aller en France.
5. Vous _____ bien danser.
6. Je _____ chanter.

4 Now look at these sentences:

Je ne veux pas manger de légumes.   *I don't want to eat any vegetables.*
Danielle *ne* peut *pas* aller au match.   *Danielle can't go to the game.*

To make a sentence containing a conjugated verb plus an infinitive negative, put **ne** _____ and **pas** _____ .

Observe these sentences:

> **_Veux-tu_ aller au cinéma?**   _Do you want to go to the movies?_
> **_Peuvent-ils_ jouer au football?**   _Can they play football?_

To form a question using inversion, when a subject pronoun and a conjugated verb are followed by an infinitive, invert _____ .

Activités

J. Say that you don't want to eat any of the following.

 EXAMPLE: **Je ne veux pas manger de porc.**

1. _____ .

2. _____ .

3. _____ .

4. _____ .

5. _____ .

6. _____ .

K. Say that these people can't do the following.

> EXAMPLE: **tu / aller au cinéma**
> **Tu ne peux pas aller au cinéma.**

1. je / jouer au tennis

   Je ne peux pas jouer au tennis

2. vous / manger au restaurant

   Vous ne pouvez pas manger au restaurant

3. elles / aller à la plage

   Elles ne peuvent pas aller à la plage.

4. il / faire une promenade dans le parc

   Il ne peut pas faire une promenade dans le parc.

5. nous / travailler à la bibliothèque

   Nous ne pouvons pas travailler à la bibliothèque.

L. You are a talented and clever person applying for a job. Make a list of all the things you can do and that you want included in your résumé.

> EXAMPLE: **Je peux travailler comme secrétaire.**

1. _____
2. _____
3. _____
4. _____
5. _____

M. Ask if the following people want to do the activities indicated.

> EXAMPLE: il / aller au parc
> **Veut-il aller au parc ?**

1. elle/aller au match de tennis

   Veut-elle aller au match de tennis ?

2. vous/faire un pique-nique

   Voulez-vous faire une pique-nique ?

3. tu/acheter une bicyclette

   Veux-tu acheter une bicyclette ?

4. nous/écouter la radio

   Voulons-nous écouter la radio ?

5. ils/jouer au basket-ball

   Veulent-ils jouer au basket ball ?

Now look at these sentences.

> Il mange *tout le gâteau.*
> Elle mange *tout le sandwich.*
> Ils mangent *tout le fromage.*

In each sentence, all the food is being eaten.

What is the gender (masculine or feminine) of each food being eaten? _____

How do you know? _____

How many of each item are being eaten? _____

Which word expresses "all"? _____

Here's another group of sentences.

> Il mange *tous les gâteaux.*
> Elle mange *tous les sandwiches.*
> Ils mangent *tous les fromages.*

In each sentence, how much of the food is being eaten? _____

How do you know? _____

What is the gender of each food? _____

How many of each item are being eaten? _____

Which word expresses "all"? _____

 Now look at these sentences.

> Il mange *toute la salade.*
> Elle mange *toute la carotte.*
> Ils mangent *toute la pomme.*

In each sentence, how much of the food is being eaten? _____

What is the gender of each food being eaten? _____

How do you know? _____

How many of each item are being eaten? _____

Which word expresses "all"? _____

Here's our last group of sentences.

> Il mange *toutes les salades.*
> Elle mange *toutes les carottes.*
> Ils mangent *toutes les pommes.*

In each sentence, how much of the food is being eaten? _____

How do you know? _____

What is the gender of each food being eaten? _____

How many of each item are being eaten? _____

Which word expresses "all"? _____

There are four ways to express "all".

Use **tout** before _____ .

Use **tous** before _____ .

Use **toute** before _____ .

Use **toutes** before _____ .

Activités

N. Gérard ate too much. Check the appropriate box as he tells you what he consumed.

	TOUT	TOUS	TOUTE	TOUTES
1.	_____	_____	_____	_____
2.	_____	_____	_____	_____
3.	_____	_____	_____	_____
4.	_____	_____	_____	_____
5.	_____	_____	_____	_____
6.	_____	_____	_____	_____
7.	_____	_____	_____	_____
8.	_____	_____	_____	_____

O. A friend says to you at a dinner party, "I bet you can't eat the whole thing." Tell him that you are going to eat all of what you see.

EXAMPLE: **Je vais manger toutes les carottes.**

1. _____

2. _____

3. _____

4. _____

5.  _____

6.  _____

7.  _____

8.  _____

P. The manager of this supermarket forgot to label some items. Can you do it?

bananes	haricots verts	oranges	poulet
carottes	jambon	pommes	raisin
cerises	lait	tomates	pommes de terre
fromages	laitue	viandes	
glaces	œufs		

Q. You are having a **boum** (*a party*). Make a list of all the foods you would (and would not) include on the menu.

Oui   Non

1. _____ .   1. _____ .
2. _____ .   2. _____ .
3. _____ .   3. _____ .
4. _____ .   4. _____ .
5. _____ .   5. _____ .

 # CONVERSATION

Vocabulaire

la nourriture the food
je grossis I get fat

tu maigris you get thin
il n'y a pas there isn't

avoir mal à l'estomac to have a stomach ache

Parlons français

Work with a partner. Make plans for a class picnic. Discuss the date, the location, and who will bring what.

EXAMPLES:

You:	**Quand est notre pique-nique?**
Partner:	**Dimanche, le neuf juin.**
You:	**Où est le pique-nique?**
Partner:	**Au parc.**
You:	**Qui va au pique-nique?**
Partner:	**Tous les élèves de la classe.**
You:	**Qu'est-ce qu'on apporte?**
Partner:	**Moi, j'apporte des sandwiches.**

Page culturelle

Un pique-nique français

If you were going on a picnic in France, you would pack a different basket than you would for an American picnic. Compare the scenes below and point out the differences you see.

Rappel

1. At an American picnic you'd expect to eat _____
   _____ .

2. At a French picnic you'd expect to eat _____
   _____ .

3. You'd be more likely to eat on the ground at a(n) _____ picnic.

4. You'd be more likely to eat at a table at a(n) _____ picnic.

5. Cooking would probably be done at a picnic in _____ .

À Vous

1. Find the names of five places in and around Paris where you might have a picnic and explain why you selected them.

2. Make a list in French of the French specialty stores you'd have to visit and the products you'd have to buy in order to have an ideal picnic.

3. Have a French picnic in class.

La Chasse au trésor

http://

Using your best Internet search skills, find one dish that a French restaurant would serve for each of these courses:

a. Hors d'œuvre.
b. Fish course.
c. Main course.

d. Salad course.
e. Cheese plate.
f. Dessert.

C'est authentique!

You're looking for a place to enjoy a nice summer day. Read this ad for a beach near Paris and answer the question.

What type of food is not available at this beach? _____

1. picnic
2. pizza
3. crêpes
4. gourmet specialties

PLAGE DE VILLENNES. A 27 km de Paris, autoroute A13 ou A14 direction Rouen, sortie Poissy Villennes. 01.39.75.82.03/83. Dans une île, traversée permanente de la Seine par bateau, piscines, toboggan aquatique jeux, aires de pique-nique, restaurations (crêperie, pizzeria, self-service), croisières sur la Seine. Ouvert tlj de 10h à 19h. Tarifs semaine: 8 et 6 €, week-ends et jours fériés: 10 et 8 €. Parking gratuit.

M O T S   N É C E S S A I R E S

LE COUVERT
l'assiette *f.* plate
le couteau knife
le couvert table setting
la couverture blanket
la cuiller spoon
la fourchette fork
la nappe tablecloth
la serviette napkin
la tasse cup
la thermos thermos
le verre glass

LE PIQUE-NIQUE
la cerise cherry
les chips *f. pl.* chips

le hot-dog hot dog
l'œuf dur *m.* hard-boiled
   egg
l'orangeade *f.* orange soda
le panier basket
le pique-nique picnic
le rosbif roast beef
la saucisse sausage
le thon tunafish

WORD TO REMEMBER
tout, toute, tous, toutes all

IMPORTANT VERBS
vouloir to want
je veux I want

tu veux you want
il/elle veut he/she wants
nous voulons we want
vous voulez you want
ils/elles veulent they want

pouvoir can, to be able to
je peux I can
tu peux you can
il/elle peut he/she can
nous pouvons we can
vous pouvez you can
ils/elles peuvent they can

Révision V
(LEÇONS 17–20)

Leçon 17

Prepositions are words that connect two elements of a sentence (noun to noun, verb to noun, pronoun, or another verb).

COMMON FRENCH PREPOSITIONS

à *to, at*

à côté de *next to*

après *after*

autour de *around*

avant *before*

avec *with*

chez *at the house of*

dans *in*

de *of, from*

derrière *behind*

devant *in front of*

en face de *facing, opposite*

envers *toward*

loin de *far from*

pour *for, in order to*

près de *near*

sans *without*

sous *under*

sur *on*

Leçon 18

Demonstrative adjectives are used to point out people and things. Use :

ce	before masculine singular nouns beginning with a consonant to express *this / that*.
cet	before masculine singular nouns beginning with a vowel to express *this / that*.
cette	before all feminine singular nouns to express *this / that*.
ces	before all plural nouns to express *these / those*.

Leçon 19

The partitive is used to express *some* (part of a thing). Use :

du	before masculine singular nouns beginning with a consonant.
de la	before feminine singular nouns beginning with a consonant.
de l'	before masculine and feminine singular nouns beginning with a vowel.
des	before all plural nouns.
de (d')	before all nouns in a negative sentence.

Leçon 20

a. The verbs **vouloir** (*to wish, to want*) and **pouvoir** (*to be able to, can*) are irregular verbs. Memorize all forms.

VOULOIR	POUVOIR
je veux	je peux
tu veux	tu peux
il / elle veut	il / elle peut
nous voulons	nous pouvons
vous voulez	vous pouvez
ils / elles veulent	ils / elles peuvent

b. To express *all* in French, use :

tout	before a masculine singular noun;
tous	before a masculine plural noun;
toute	before a feminine singular noun;
toutes	before a feminine plural noun.

Activités

A. **Où est le chat?** Identify the places. Then write the indicated letters in the boxes below to reveal where Minou, the cat, is hiding.

1. □□ _ _ □ _ _
   1 2   3

2. _ □□ _ _ _
     4 5

3. _ □ _ □ _   _ □   _ _ _ _ □
     6   7   8   9

4. □ _ _ _ -□□ _
   10   11 12

Solution □□□□ □□ □□□□□□
         11 12 2 10 7 5 1 4 6 3 9 8

B. JUMBLE. To answer the question below, unscramble the words. Then unscramble the circled letters.

O C M E P A É S C   _ _ Ⓞ _ _ _ _ _ _

U L A C C L T U A E R   _ _ _ _ Ⓞ _ _ _ _ _

N P T O É É L H E   _ _ Ⓞ _ _ _ _ Ⓞ

E N O R T A D I R U   Ⓞ _ _ Ⓞ Ⓞ _ _ _ _

O T P A B E R L   _ _ _ _ _ Ⓞ _ _

Qu'est-ce que Michel désire comme cadeau?   _ _   _ _ _ _ _

C. You are preparing a meal. The guests will arrive soon. See what's on the table. You may have forgotten a few things. Here's a check list.

	Oui	Non			Oui	Non
1. les œufs			11. le jambon			
2. le poisson			12. le café			
3. la glace			13. le sucre			
4. la soupe			14. le pain			
5. le beurre			15. le poivre			
6. la salade			16. les pommes			
7. les sandwiches			17. les fruits			
8. le fromage			18. la viande			
9. le sel			19. l'eau			
10. le poulet			20. le gâteau			

D. JUMBLE. Unscramble these words. Then unscramble the circled letters to complete the message.

A D L A S E

S P É N I D R A

D E O G A R E N A

U T E I L A

M E O T A T

Quand il a très soif, François boit __ __   __   __ __ __   __ __ __ __ __ __ __ __

E. Mots croisés

HORIZONTALEMENT

1. salad
4. steak
7. ice creams
11. year
12. milk
13. in order to
14. your
15. fish
16. summer
18. soup
20. tomato
22. water
23. fruit
25. my
28. the
30. to the
31. and
33. juice
35. money
36. grapes
38. egg
40. in
42. he
43. peas: **petits** ___
45. juice
46. the
47. pork
48. and
50. they
52. juice
55. string bean: ___ (vert)
57. the
58. I have: (J') ___
60. one (pronoun)
61. orangeade
64. he
65. in
66. ham
67. tuna

VERTICALEMENT

1. salt
2. lettuce
3. of, from
5. tuna
6. carrot
7. cake
8. coffee
9. in
10. spinach
13. why
15. few, a little
17. tomatoes
19. breads
21. she
24. he
26. to the
27. cherry
29. water
32. your
34. salt
37. they
39. cheese
41. milk
43. chicken
44. he
49. tuna
51. on
53. his
54. bread
56. year
59. he
61. one (pronoun)
62. to the
63. I have: (J') ___

F. After filling in all letters, look at the vertical box to see what Martine ordered for dessert.

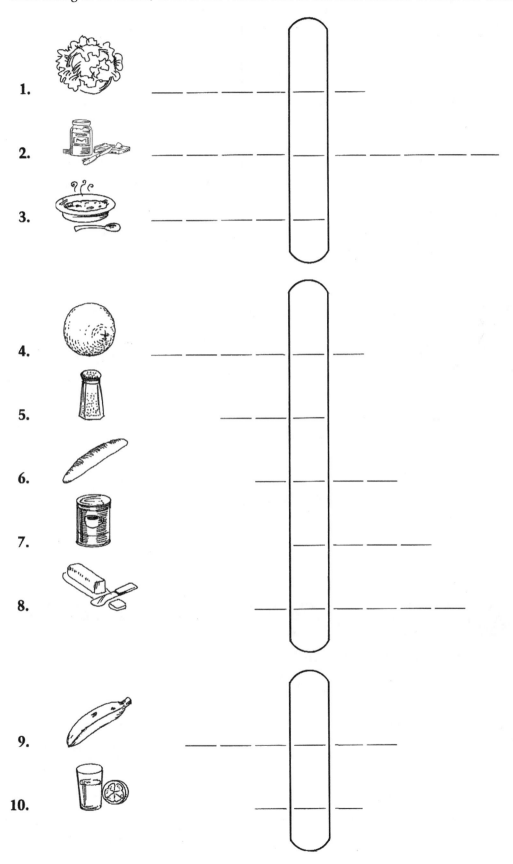

1.

2.

3.

4.

5.

6.

7.

8.

9.

10.

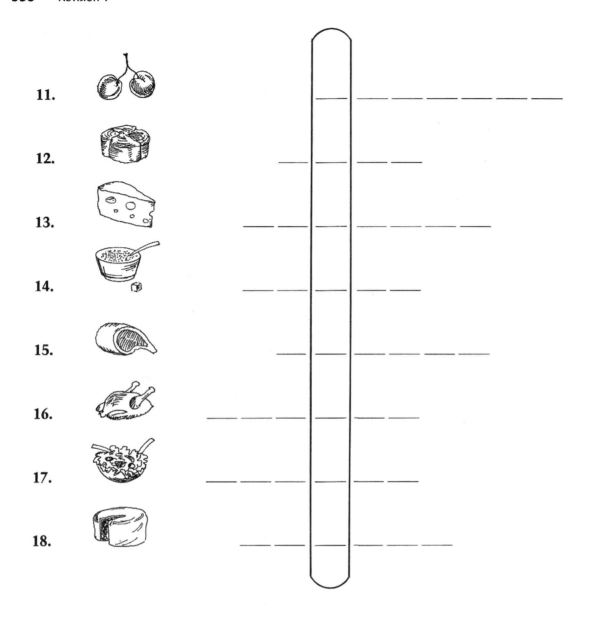

11.

12.

13.

14.

15.

16.

17.

18.

The Cognate Connection

Write the meanings of the following French and English words.

FRENCH	ENGLISH COGNATE
1. repas _____	repast _____
2. sel _____	saline _____
3. servir _____	servitude _____
4. utile _____	utilize _____
5. vouloir _____	voluntary _____

6

sixième partie

21
Le monde est petit

Talking About Countries, Nationalities, Languages

PAYS	NATIONALITÉ	LANGUE
les États-Unis *m. pl.*	américain(e)	anglais
l'Angleterre *f.*	anglais(e)	anglais
le Canada	canadien(ne)	français, anglais
l'Espagne *f.*	espagnol(e)	espagnol
la France	français(e)	français
Haïti *f.*	haïtien(ne)	français, créole
l'Italie *f.*	italien(ne)	italien
l'Allemagne *f.*	allemand(e)	allemand
la Russie	russe	russe
la Chine	chinois(e)	chinois
le Japon	japonais(e)	japonais

Activités

A. Give the name of the country that each person comes from.

1. Pablo _____

2. Mario _____

3. François _____

4. Mary _____

5. Natasha _____

6. Hans _____

7. Han-Ling _____

8. Noriko _____

B. Match the food with the country it comes from and write the matching letter in the space provided.

1.	la Russie	_____	**a.**	pizza
2.	le Japon	_____	**b.**	borscht
3.	l'Angleterre	_____	**c.**	sukiyaki
4.	Haïti	_____	**d.**	wonton soup
5.	l'Italie	_____	**e.**	crêpes Suzette
6.	la France	_____	**f.**	paella
7.	la Chine	_____	**g.**	kidney pie
8.	l'Espagne	_____	**h.**	riz créole

2 Look carefully at the following sentences.

I	**II**
J'aime la France.	**Je vais aller *en* France.**
J'aime la Chine.	**Je vais voyager *en* Chine.**
J'aime la Russie.	**Je vais travailler *en* Russie.**

In Group I, what is the gender of the names of the countries? _____

How do you know? _____

In Group II, which word is used to say TO or IN the country? _____

3 Now compare these sentences.

I	**II**
J'aime le Canada.	**Je vais aller *au* Canada.**
J'aime le Japon.	**Je vais voyager *au* Japon.**

In Group I, what is the gender of the names of the countries? _____

How do you know? _____

In Group II, which word is used to say TO or IN the country? _____

4

I	**II**
J'aime les États-Unis.	**Je vais travailler *aux* États-Unis.**

Is **États-Unis** a singular or plural noun? _____

How do you know? _____

In Group II, which word is used to say TO or IN the country? _____

NOTE: When referring to small islands, **à**, **à la** or **aux** is used instead of **en**.

Je vais *à* Cuba.   Je suis *à la* Martinique.
Je vais *aux* îles Caraïbes.

To say *TO* or *IN* a specific country, use

en before _____

au before _____

aux before _____

à, à la, or **aux** before _____

Activités

C. You are taking a trip around the world. Check how you would say that you are going "to the" countries you hear.

	EN	AU	AUX	À
1.	___	___	___	___
2.	___	___	___	___
3.	___	___	___	___
4.	___	___	___	___
5.	___	___	___	___
6.	___	___	___	___

D. The Montard family is taking a trip around the world. Tell which countries they go to.

EXAMPLE: France   **Ils vont en France.**

1. Italie _____

2. Japon _____

3. États-Unis _____

4. Espagne _____

5. Chine _____

6. Haïti _____

7. Russie _____

8. Canada _____

E. Express where these people are or where they are going by completing the sentences with **à, en, au,** or **aux.**

1. Nous travaillons _____ Allemagne.

2. Vous êtes _____ Japon.

3. Elle voyage _____ États-Unis.

4. Tu arrives _____ France.

5. Il travaille _____ Canada.

6. Je suis _____ Haïti.

7. Vous voyagez _____ Chine.

8. Il arrive _____ Italie.

5 Compare these sentences.

J'aime la France.	Je suis français.	Je suis *de* France.
J'aime l'Italie.	Je suis italien.	Je suis *d'*Italie.
J'aime le Canada.	Je suis canadien.	Je suis *du* Canada.
J'aime les États-Unis.	Je suis américain.	Je suis *des* États-Unis.

When do you use **de, d', du,** or **des?**

Use **de** before _____

Use **d'** before _____

Use **du** before _____

Use **des** before _____ .

Activité

F. Where are these new students from? Introduce them by telling the class where they are from.

EXAMPLE: Pablo / Espagne
        Pablo est d'Espagne.

1. Anne / États-Unis _____

2. Claude / Canada _____

3. Mariko / Japon _____

4. Fritz / Allemagne _____

5. Sung / Chine _____

6. Olga / Russie _____

7. Jean-Louis / France _____

8. Leslie / Angleterre _____

Prononciation

- **in (im)** and **ain (aim)**, at the end of a word or followed by a consonant (except *n* or *m*), have the same nasal sound.

international	cinq	important	main	demain	faim
cousin	simple	impatient	certain	américain	daim

  Alain invite Martin, son important cousin américain.

- **ien** is a nasal sound in which the *i* has the sound of *y* in *you*, when it is at the end of a word or followed by a consonant except *n*.

bien	canadien	italien	rien	viens	combien

  Lucien, un Canadien, parle bien l'italien.

- **oi** represents the sound *wa* like the *wa* in *watch*. In **oy**, the *y* is pronounced.

moi	froid	trois	voyage	voyelle	pourquoi

  Moi, je vais en voyage trois fois par mois quand il fait froid.

- **oin** is a nasal sound that represents the *w* (as in *wag*) + the sound of **in**, as in **fin**.

coin	loin	moins	point	soin

- Compare **oi** and **oin**.

loi	loin	soi	soin
moi	moins	pois	point

  Quoi? Il a moins de points que toi?

Let's read something about our world, its countries, and its languages.

Dans le monde, il y a beaucoup de pays et beaucoup de langues. Savez-vous qu'il y a plus de mille langues dans le monde aujourd'hui? Généralement chaque pays a sa langue officielle. En France, c'est le français; en Espagne, c'est l'espagnol; en Italie, c'est l'italien; en Allemagne, c'est l'allemand.

le monde the world
les pays *m. pl.* countries
savez-vous do you know
mille one thousand
chaque each

Mais certains pays ont au moins deux langues officielles. En Suisse, par exemple, on parle français, allemand et italien. Au Canada les langues officielles sont le français et l'anglais. Aux

au moins at least

États-Unis, à la Nouvelle-Orléans, le français est une langue semi-officielle. Il y a des journaux, des magazines, des films, des programmes de radio et de télévision en français. Beaucoup de personnes parlent français dans leur vie quotidienne.

la vie quotidienne daily life

Le français est aussi une langue internationale. On parle français à la Martinique, en Haïti, en Afrique et partout dans le monde.

on one

partout everywhere

Aux Nations Unies, il y a six langues officielles. Savez-vous quelles sont ces langues? Les six langues officielles des Nations Unies sont: le français, l'anglais, le russe, le chinois, l'arabe et l'espagnol.

les Nations *f. pl.* **Unies** the United Nations

Et maintenant, comprenez-vous pourquoi la langue française est si importante pour vous?

si so

Activité

G. Répondez aux questions.

1. Combien de langues y a-t-il dans le monde?

2. Généralement, chaque pays a combien de langues officielles ?

3. Quelles sont les langues officielles de la Suisse?

4. Quelles sont les langues officielles du Canada?

5. Quelles langues parlez-vous?

6. Où y a-t-il des programmes de radio et de télévision en français?

7. Où parle-t-on français?

8. Combien de langues officielles y a-t-il aux Nations Unies?

9. Quelles sont ces langues officielles?

10. Pourquoi la langue française est-elle importante?

Look at the following sentences carefully.

Hans est *allemand*.	Greta est *allemande*.
François est *français*.	Françoise est *française*.
John est *américain*.	Jane est *américaine*.
Mark est *anglais*.	Ann est *anglaise*.
Hiro est *japonais*.	Michiko est *japonaise*.
Chang est *chinois*.	Lin est *chinoise*.
Raul est *espagnol*.	Maria est *espagnole*.
Ivan est *russe*.	Olga est *russe*.

How are the feminine adjectives different from the masculine adjectives? _____
_____

Repeat the sentences after your teacher. How is the sound different for the feminine adjectives?
_____

Which adjectives do not have a sound change? _____
Which is the only adjective that does not have a spelling change? _____
Why? _____

Activités

H. Circle the correct way to express the nationality of the foreign friends you hear about.

1. a. japonais   b. japonaises   c. japonaise
2. a. français   b. française   c. françaises
3. a. espagnoles   b. espagnols   c. espagnole
4. a. chinois   b. chinoise   c. chinoises
5. a. allemand   b. allemande   c. allemands
6. a. italien   b. italienne   c. italiens

I. Discuss boys and girls around the world by making these adjectives plural.

1. Ils sont allemand _____ .   Elles sont allemande _____ .
2. Ils sont américain _____ .   Elles sont américaine _____ .
3. Ils sont espagnol _____ .   Elles sont espagnole _____ .
4. Ils sont russe _____ .   Elles sont russe _____ .
5. Ils sont anglais _____ .   Elles sont anglaise _____ .
6. Ils sont français _____ .   Elles sont française _____ .
7. Ils sont japonais _____ .   Elles sont japonaise _____ .
8. Ils sont chinois _____ .   Elles sont chinoise _____ .

J. There are people of many nationalities in your neighborhood. Describe them.

EXAMPLE: Marie / France **Marie est française.**

1. Chang et Lin / Chine _____ .
2. Mariko et Michiko / Japon _____ .
3. Ludwig et Hans / Allemagne _____ .
4. Olga et Ivan / Russie _____ .
5. Paul et Richard / Angleterre _____ .
6. Nancy / États-Unis _____ .
7. Roger et Marie / France _____ .
8. Maria / Espagne _____ .

Now look at these sentences.

Jean-Pierre est _haïtien._   Marie-Hélène est _haïtienne._
Mario est _italien._   Marie est _italienne._
Jean est _canadien._   Jeanne est _canadienne._

If a masculine adjective ends in **-ien**, how do you form the feminine of the adjective? _____

_____

How would you form the masculine plural? _____

The feminine plural? _____

When describing the nationality of a person, is the name of the nationality written with a capital or small letter? _____

Activité

K. Complete the descriptions by using the correct adjectives.

1. (Haïti) Jean-Pierre et Henri sont _____ .
2. (Haïti) Marie-Hélène et Carine sont _____ .
3. (Italie) Mario et Giuseppe sont _____ .
4. (Italie) Maria et Carla sont _____ .
5. (Canada) Jean et Marc sont _____ .
6. (Canada) Jeanne et Sylvie sont _____ .

Look carefully at these sentences.

Les _Canadiens_ parlent anglais et français.
L'_Italienne_ prépare des dîners délicieux.

When speaking about the people of a country, is the noun referring to their nationality written with a capital or a small letter? _____

Activité

L. Complete the sentences with the correct information.

1. Nous sommes aux _____ .
   Ici habitent les _____ .
   Ils parlent _____ .

2. Nous sommes en _____ .
   Ici habitent les _____ .
   Ils parlent _____ .

3. Nous sommes en _____ .
   Ici habitent les _____ .
   Ils parlent _____ .

4. Nous sommes en _____ .
   Ici habitent les _____ .
   Ils parlent _____ .

5. Nous sommes au _____ .
   Ici habitent les _____ .
   Ils parlent _____ .

6. Nous sommes en _____ .
   Ici habitent les _____ .
   Ils parlent _____ .

7. Nous sommes en _____ .

    Ici habitent les _____ .

    Ils parlent _____ .

8. Nous sommes en _____ .

    Ici habitent les _____ .

    Ils parlent _____ .

CONVERSATION

Vocabulaire

le **pays** the country
se **trouve** is (located)
l'**édifice** *m.* the building

vous savez you know
beaucoup de choses a lot (of things)
ambassadeur *m.* ambassador

Parlons français

Pretend that you are taking a trip to a foreign country and that you need some advice from a travel agent. Create an appropriate dialog with a partner.

EXAMPLES:

You:	**Où allez-vous?**
Partner:	**Je vais en France. Je veux un bon hôtel à Paris.**
You:	**L'hôtel Dufour est excellent.**
Partner:	**Où est-il dans Paris?**
You:	**Près de la tour Eiffel.**
Partner:	**Combien coûte une chambre pour deux personnes?**
You:	**Cent euros la nuit.**

C'est authentique!

Tell in which countries the cities shown are located. Then give the expected weather for that city for the day.

Genève
Mini 8
EXAMPLE: Maxi 13   Genève est en Suisse. À Genève, il pleut.

Berlin
Mini 8
1.   Maxi 14   _____ .

Londres
Mini 8
2.   Maxi 13   _____ .

Madrid
Mini 7
3.   Maxi 22   _____ .

Moscou
Mini 4
4. Maxi 10 _____ .

Paris
Mini 10
5. Maxi 14 _____ .

Rome
Mini 14
6. Maxi 22 _____ .

Page culturelle

Vive la différence!

How is life in France different from life in the United States?

UNITED STATES

We carry credit cards, a driver's license, and money.

American apartment buildings typically start on the first floor. Sometimes, they don't have a 13th floor.

American hotels have bellmen, porters, doormen, receptionists, and telephones with numbers for housekeeping, room service, and so on.

In most of our large buildings, the lights stay on all day long.

FRANCE

The French carry not only these items but also an official I.D. card.

French apartment buildings start with the **rez-de-chaussée,** the ground floor. The first floor is really the second floor of the building.

In French hotels, call the concierge, who will take care of everything, including restaurant reservations.

In France, some lights are time-controlled by a wall switch called **une minuterie.** Lights are turned off automatically to save electricity and expense. In some public places (restrooms, for example), the lights will go on only when the door is closed or locked.

UNITED STATES	FRANCE
To buy stamps, we normally go to a post office.	In France, you can buy stamps at a **bureau de tabac.** This type of store also sells tobacco products, matches, and chocolate. A **bureau de tabac** is easily identified by a red cone, and there is usually a mail box in front of the store.
Our drugstores sell prescription drugs, toiletries, cosmetics, over the-counter medicines, paper goods, candy, and the like.	French pharmacies sell mainly prescription and over-the-counter medicine. A green cross identifies a French drugstore.
American youths spend their free time almost anywhere.	In France, adults and adolescents often meet in cafés where they sit and relax, gossip, watch passers-by, play pinball, read, eat, or drink sodas. Prices for foods and drinks served at the tables are higher than those charged for the same items at the counter. The higher prices are charged because you may sit at a table as long as you like.
To use a subway, you may have to read a map in the station or on the train, or ask for directions to find out where you want to go. The train doors open and close automatically.	In France, some stations have electronic wall maps. Push the button for your destination, and lights will indicate which **métro** line to take. A métro stop is often identified by an M. You must lift the lock to open the train doors.

Rappel

1. French light switches may be controlled by an energy-saving device known as _____ .

2. In France, a **bureau de tabac** sells not only tobacco but _____ as well.

3. If you need a pharmacy in France, look for the _____ that identifies it.

4. In France, people may meet at _____ to sit and relax.

5. A _____ is identified by an M.

À Vous

1. Write a short report telling how life and customs are different in another French-speaking country.

2. Draw a poster entitled "Vive la différence" showing three differences in life in America and in France.

La Chasse au trésor

http:// ▶

Using your best Internet search skills, identify one custom that is practiced in:

a. Egypt.
b. Algeria.
c. Cambodia.
d. Sénégal.
e. Haiti.

MOTS NÉCESSAIRES

COUNTRIES
l'Allemagne *f.* Germany
l'Angleterre *f.* England
le Canada Canada
la Chine China
l'Espagne *f.* Spain
les États-Unis *m. pl.*
  United States
la France France
Haïti *f.* Haiti
l'Italie *f.* Italy
le Japon Japan

le Mexique Mexico
la Russie Russia
la langue language
le monde world
la nationalité nationality
le pays country

NATIONALITIES
allemand(e) German
américain(e) American
anglais(e) English
canadien(ne) Canadian

chinois(e) Chinese
espagnol(e) Spanish
français(e) French
haïtien(ne) Haitian
italien(ne) Italian
japonais(e) Japanese
mexicain(e) Mexican
russe Russian

IMPORTANT WORD
en in; to

22

Les moyens de transport

Using the Verb **prendre**

 Vocabulaire

la voiture

l'autobus *(m.)*

le taxi

le vélo / la bicyclette

le scooter

la motocyclette / la moto

l'avion *(m.)*

le bateau

le train

le métro

le guichet

la gare

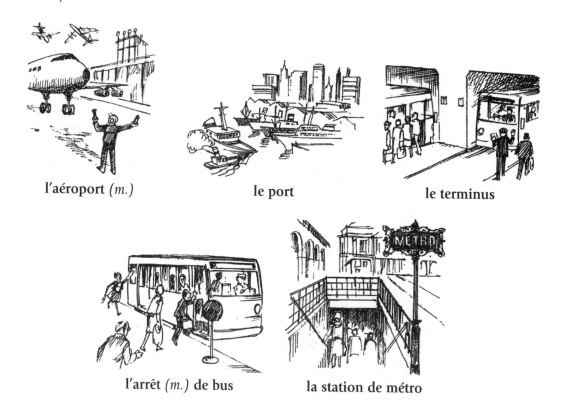

l'aéroport *(m.)*   le port   le terminus

l'arrêt *(m.)* de bus   la station de métro

Activités

A. Write the letter of the means of transportation each person says he/she will be taking.

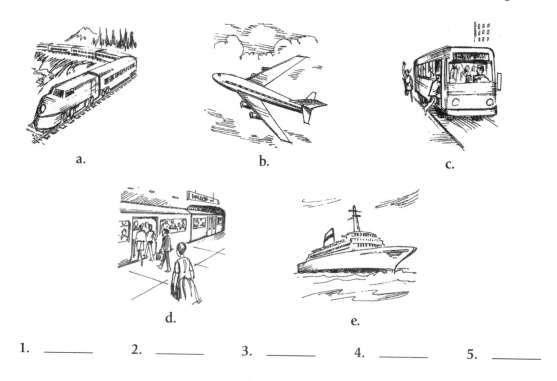

a.   b.   c.

d.   e.

1. _____   2. _____   3. _____   4. _____   5. _____

B. These people are going on a trip. How are they going?

EXAMPLE: **Michel va en scooter.**

1. M. Rochard _____   2. Je _____

_____ .   _____ .

3. Vous _____   4. Mes amis _____

_____ .   _____ .

5. Nous _____   6. Les agents de police _____

_____ .   _____ .

C. Can you identify the places you'd have to go to in order to take a trip?

1. _____ .   2. _____ .

3. _____ .   4. _____ .

5. _____ .   6. _____ .

You are a reporter for your school newspaper. You are taking a survey about which means of transportation students take to get to school. Read the dialog and see if you can find all the forms of the verb **prendre** (*to take*).

Vous: Quel moyen de transport est-ce que **vous prenez** pour aller à l'école?	**le moyen** the means
Alice et Sylvie: Notre père est chauffeur de taxi, alors **nous prenons** son taxi. Janine, **tu prends** ton vélo?	**le chauffeur** driver
Janine: Non, parce que **mon petit ami prend** sa moto. Alors **je prends** la moto avec lui.	**lui** him
André: **Les garçons** sportifs comme moi ne **prennent** ni le bus ni le train. Nous marchons.	**moi** I, me , myself **ni . . . ni** neither . . . nor

2 Did you find all the forms of the verb **prendre?** Fill in the correct form for each subject:

je _____   nous _____

tu _____   vous _____

il / elle _____   ils / elles _____

Activités

D. Some of your friends are taking trips by various means of transportation. Check if one or several persons are going. Listen to your teacher.

	ONE	SEVERAL		ONE	SEVERAL		ONE	SEVERAL
1.	_____	_____	4.	_____	_____	7.	_____	_____
2.	_____	_____	5.	_____	_____	8.	_____	_____
3.	_____	_____	6.	_____	_____			

E. Work with a partner. Take turns telling your friend what means of transportation you take on different days to get to school. Then write your answer.

EXAMPLE:

You: **Quel moyen de transport prends-tu?**
Partner: **Je prends le scooter.**

1. _____ .

2. _____ .

3. _____ .

4. _____ .

F. How are these people traveling?

EXAMPLE: il / scooter
Il prend le scooter.

1. nous / avion

_____

2. Claire et Anne / bateau

_____

3. Suzanne / voiture

_____

4. vous / train

_____

5. les Caron / métro

_____

6. tu / taxi

_____

Two other important verbs are conjugated like **prendre**.

apprendre	*to learn*
comprendre	*to understand*

Look again at the forms of **prendre** and conjugate **apprendre** and **comprendre**

	apprendre		comprendre
j′	_____	je	_____
tu	_____	tu	_____
il / elle	_____	il / elle	_____
nous	_____	nous	_____
vous	_____	vous	_____
ils / elles	_____	ils / elles	_____

Activités

G. Who is learning what?

EXAMPLE: je / l'histoire
J'apprends l'histoire.

1. Anne / les verbes français

    _____

2. tu / le vocabulaire

    _____

3. la classe de français / une chanson populaire

    _____

4. Richard et Jean / leurs leçons

    _____

5. vous / les noms des jours en français

    _____

6. nous / le poème

    _____

H. Ask if the following people understand the topics indicated.

EXAMPLE: tu / l'histoire
Comprends-tu l'histoire?

1. il / la leçon

    _____

2. nous / les devoirs

_____

3. tu / le vocabulaire

_____

4. ils / la question

_____

5. vous / la réponse

_____

6. elle / la solution

_____

CONVERSATION

Vocabulaire

flotter to float   **blaguer** to joke   **traverser** to cross

DIALOGUE

Pretend you are the second person in this dialog and you are going to France, this summer. How would you respond?

Parlons français

You want to take a trip into the city. Take turns with a partner asking for the best way to get to your destination.

EXAMPLE: You: **Je vais en ville.**
            Partner: **Comment vas-tu en ville?**
            You: **Je prends le bus.**
            Partner: **Mais non, prends le train.**
            You: **Pourquoi?**
            Partner: **Parce que le train va plus vite.**

Prononciation

- **-on (-om)** is a nasal sound when at the end of a word or followed by a consonant except *n* or *m*. However, the *n* or *m* is pronounced and not nasal when it is followed by a vowel or another *n* or *m*.

non	on	mon	garçon	onze	combien	tomber
bon	oncle	sont	confortable	pardon	compter	comprendre

but:

téléphone	comment	mayonnaise	bonne	fromage	pomme

Pardon! Le téléphone sonne. Je réponds: c'est mon bon oncle Raymond. Bonjour!

Page culturelle

Les transports

Two passenger airports near Paris serve as the main aviation hubs for travel to and within France. Charles de Gaulle airport is used primarily for international flights, while Orly airport is used primarily for domestic, European, and overseas charter flights. The supersonic plane, the Concorde, was developed through joint efforts by France and Great Britain. It began commercial service in the mid-1970s. With a speed of 1550 mph, it could fly from Paris to New York in three hours. It was taken out of service in 2003 because it would have required expensive maintenance, and fuel costs were rising.

Travelers can also take advantage of the extensive French railroad system. One can choose a first or second class seat, or can reserve sleeping space in a **couchette** (*bunk*) of a **wagon-lit** (*sleeping car*), either in a four-bunk compartment or in a private first-class compartment. Trains also have a **wagon-restaurant,** where you can have anything from a light snack to a complete meal. The **T.G.V. (Train à Grande Vitesse)** is among the fastest trains in the world, speeding along at 260 kilometers per hour. The TGV links all the major cities in France, allowing people to travel across the country in a few hours.

To travel around Paris, look for an above-ground "M," indicating a subway stop. **Le métro** is known for its clean, inexpensive, and efficient system. The new subway trains have linked cars so you can walk from one end of the train to the other. New stations have, along the edge of the platform, a glass wall which slides open in front of the metro doors when the train comes in. For economy or convenience, you can buy a book of ten tickets

(un carnet) or a pass **(une carte orange),** which entitles you to ride for one month or one year. These tickets are also good on buses, whose routes are clearly marked on signs at every stop and inside the bus.

Since French teenagers cannot drive until they are eighteen years old, many ride a bicycle **(un vélo)** to school. Fourteen-year-olds may also ride a moped **(une mobylette, un vélomoteur).**

Rappel

1. The two airports near Paris are _____ and _____ .

2. France and Great Britain developed the _____ , a supersonic airplane.

3. Among the fastest trains (260km/hr) in the world is France's _____ .

4. Paris' subway is called _____ .

5. Many French teenagers get to school by _____ .

À Vous

1. Write a biography of Charles de Gaulle, the French president for whom the airport was named.

2. Write a news story on the Chunnel, the tunnel under the English Channel that links England and France.

La Chasse au trésor

http://   ▶

Using your best Internet search skills, find the answers to the following questions:

1. What is a Eurail Pass?
2. How many different types of passes are there?
3. What is the price of each type of pass?
4. What are the benefits of each type of pass?

C'est authentique!

Where was this ticket used? _____

1. On a train.

2. On a boat.

3. On a plane.

4. In a taxi.

COMPAGNIE MARITIME CANNOISE
Quai Albert Edouard - 06400 Cannes - Tél 93 99 62 01

CIRCUIT DES DEUX ILES

Ste MARGUERITE - St HONORAT

ALLER RETOUR   A PRESENTER AU CONTRÔLE

PLEIN TARIF

Vu le caractère maritime, la Direction se réserve le droit d'annuler
ou de modifier les horaires, sans avis préalable
Billet valable pour l'Aller, le jour de la vente

MOTS NÉCESSAIRES

TRANSPORTATION
l'aéroport *m.* airport
l'arrêt *m.* stop
l'autobus, bus *m.* bus
l'avion *m.* plane
le bateau boat
la bicyclette bicycle
la gare train station
le guichet ticket window
le métro subway
la moto, motocyclette
    motorcycle

le moyen means
le port port
le scooter scooter
la station stop, station
le taxi taxi
le terminus terminal
le train train
le transport
    transportation
le vélo bicycle
la voiture car

VERBS
prendre to take
je prends I take
tu prends you take
il prend he takes
elle prend she takes
nous prenons we take
vous prenez you take
ils prennent they take
elles prennent they take
apprendre to learn
comprendre to understand

23
Les divertissements

*Having Fun; Using the Verb **voir**; Using Stress Pronouns*

 Vocabulaire

Can you guess the meanings of these words?

le cirque

la discothèque

le jardin

le match

le musée

la piscine

la plage

le stade

la boum

le jardin zoologique, le zoo

Do you recognize these fun places that you have already learned? Identify them.

_____   _____   _____

Activités

A. Indicate where you are. Put the appropriate number next to the places you hear.

    a. au cirque _____
    c. à la discothèque _____
    e. au stade _____

    b. à la plage _____
    d. au musée _____
    f. au jardin _____

B. You are traveling in France with a tour group. Work with a partner. Take turns asking about the places to which you are going. Then write your answers.

EXAMPLE:

        Nous
You: **Où allons-nous?**
Partner: **Nous allons au jardin.**

1. Il _____
2. Ils _____

3. Vous _____

4. Nous _____

5. Elles _____

6. Vous _____

7. Nous _____

8. Tu _____

9. Je _____

10. Elle _____

Prononciation

- **-un (-um)** is a nasal sound.

  un   brun   lundi   emprunter   parfum

- Nasal sounds occur in the combination vowel + *n* or *m*, unless followed by a vowel or another *n* or *m*.

NASAL	NON-NASAL	NASAL	NON-NASAL
Jean	Jeanne	banc	banane
prend	prennent	italien	italienne
cousin	cousine	américain	américaine
bon	bonne	pompier	pomme
un	une	parfum	parfumerie

Madame Lebrun emprunte du parfum italien à sa cousine américaine.
Lundi, Jeanne vient avec Martine et Jean pour camper sous la lune.

 When you take a trip, there is much to see. Read the story and look at the forms of the irregular verb **voir** (*to see*).

Je m'appelle Georges. J'ai un petit appartement. De ma fenêtre, **je vois** les gens qui passent. **Les gens** me **voient** aussi. Ils pensent que je suis drôle. Un jour, un jeune garçon arrive chez moi. **Il** me **voit.** Il me regarde pendant une demi-heure. Il me demande: «**Tu me vois ?**» Mais je ne réponds pas.

me me

pendant for

Ce gentil garçon me donne une banane à manger. J'adore les bananes. Mon ami et moi, quand **nous voyons** des gens avec des bananes, nous sommes très excités et nous sautons partout. Après ma banane, je suis très content. Je lance une cacahouète au garçon pour lui dire «merci». Le garçon n'est pas surpris. Pourquoi? Mais parce que, **vous voyez,** je suis un singe!

gentil nice

sautons jump
  partout everywhere
Après after   lance throw
  une cacahouète a peanut
lui him

Activité

C. Répondez aux questions.

1. Quel est le nom (*name*) du narrateur?

   _____

2. Comment est l'appartement de Georges?

   _____

3. Que voit-il de sa fenêtre?

   _____

4. Qu'est-ce que les gens pensent de Georges?

   _____

5. Qui arrive un jour?

   _____

6. Qu'est-ce qu'il donne à Georges?

   _____

7. Que font Georges et son ami quand ils voient des bananes?

   _____

8. Qu'est-ce qu'il lance au garçon?

   _____

9. Comment est le garçon?

   _____

10. Qui est Georges?

   _____

2 Did you find all the forms of the irregular verb **voir** in the story? Fill in the proper forms for each subject. MEMORIZE them!

je _____ nous _____

tu _____ vous _____

il / elle _____ ils / elles _____

Activités

D. Your French pen pal is visiting you. You take a bus ride to show him/her some of the sights. Ask if he/she sees the things you point out and then write down your pen pal's answers.

EXAMPLE:

Tu vois le musée?
Oui, je vois le musée.

1. _____
   _____ .

2. _____
   _____ .

3. _____
   _____ .

4. _____
   _____ .

E. Some tourists are looking from the third floor of the Eiffel Tower. What do these people see?

EXAMPLE: **Je vois une cathédrale.**

1.    Nous _____

2.    Tu _____

3.    Je _____

4.    Elles _____

5.    Vous _____

6.    Ils _____

F. These people are looking for some places on a map of Paris, but can't find them. Complete the sentences with the correct forms of **voir** in the negative.

> EXAMPLE: Je / le jardin des Plantes
> **Je ne vois pas le Jardin des Plantes.**

1. Paul _____ la piscine Molitor.

2. Nathalie and Suzanne _____ le zoo.

3. Vous _____ la gare Montparnasse.

4. Nous _____ le musée Grévin.

5. Tu _____ le théâtre des Champs-Élysées.

6. Je _____ la cathédrale Notre-Dame.

There are special pronouns in French that are used for emphasis or stress. You have already seen some stress pronouns in earlier lessons. Read this story and see if you can identify the stress pronouns.

Alice Latour, 16 ans, et son frère, Pierre, sont en vacances à Paris. Alice écrit une lettre à ses parents aux États-Unis.

Paris, le 29 juillet

Chers Parents,

Pierre et **moi,** nous sommes très contents d'être à Paris chez tante Lise et oncle Henri. Nous visitons tout Paris avec **eux** et ils sont très généreux envers **nous.** Nos vacances sont formidables.

Mais, Maman et Papa, j'ai un problème avec Pierre. Il veut être avec **moi** tout le temps. Je n'ai pas un moment de libre, **moi.** Il est toujours à côté de **moi.** C'est vraiment embarrassant. De plus, **lui,** il est insupportable. Il laisse ses vêtements partout. Il ne range pas sa chambre. Nous avons beaucoup de disputes, **lui** et **moi.** Qui est toujours égoïste et paresseux? **Lui.** Qui prend toujours toutes les décisions pour **nous** deux? **Moi.** J'en ai assez. Je veux le renvoyer chez **vous** et rester ici avec mes cousines. Je m'amuse beaucoup plus avec **elles** qu'avec **lui.**

Maman, j'ai un cadeau spécial pour **toi** et un aussi pour Papa. Dis à mon amie Rose que je vais acheter un souvenir pour **elle.**

Votre fille, Alice

de libre free

vraiment really
  de plus furthermore
insupportable unbearable
  il laisse he leaves
ranger to straighten
égoïste selfish
  paresseux lazy
j'en ai assez I've had enough
renvoyer to send back
je m'amuse I have a good
  time

Activité

G. Complete the sentences based on the story.

1. Pierre et Alice sont à _____ .

2. Ils sont chez _____ .

3. Les vacances sont _____ .

4. Alice a un problème avec _____ .

5. Il veut être avec Alice _____ .

6. Il laisse _____ partout.

7. Il ne range pas _____ .

8. Lui et Alice ont beaucoup de _____ .

9. Pierre est _____ et _____ .

10. Alice a _____ pour sa mère et _____ et pour

    son amie Rose.

	The stress pronouns are:		
moi	*I, me*	**nous**	*we, us*
toi	*you* (familiar)	**vous**	*you* (formal or plural)
lui	*he, him*	**eux**	*they, them (m)*
elle	*she, her*	**elles**	*they, them (f)*

 Look at these examples.

> *Lui,* il est insupportable.
> Je n'ai jamais un moment de libre, *moi.*

A pronoun is a small word used in place of a noun. Use stress pronouns before or after the subject when you want to _____ the subject pronoun.

 Now look at these examples and complete the explanation that follows.

> **Nous visitons tout Paris avec *eux.***
> **Ils sont très généreux envers *nous.***

A stress pronoun is used after _____ , words that connect nouns and pronouns to other words in the sentence.

Here's another group of examples.

> Qui est paresseux? — *Lui.*
> Qui prend toutes les décisions? — *Moi.*

Use a stress pronoun when the pronoun stands alone.

Now look at this last group of examples.

> Pierre et *moi, nous* sommes très contents.
> Nous avons beaucoup de disputes, *lui* et *moi.*

A stress pronoun is used when there is a compound subject with a noun and a pronoun, or two pronouns.

What is a compound subject? _____

_____ .

Notice that the compound subject may come before or after a subject pronoun, which may be expressed along with the compound.

> *Pierre et moi, nous* sommes. . .   *Pierre and I are . . .*
> *Nous* avons. . ., *lui et moi.*   *He and I have . . .*

Activités

H. Complete the sentences you hear using the appropriate stress pronoun.

   a. moi _____   b. toi _____   c. lui _____

   d. elle _____   e. elles _____   f. eux _____

I. Your friends are talking about where they want to go. Tell what they are saying, stressing the subject pronoun.

   EXAMPLE: Guy veut aller au cinéma.
   Lui, il veut aller au cinéma.

   1. Marcel veut aller au match.

   _____

   2. Je veux aller à la plage.

   _____

   3. Francine et Henri veulent aller au stade.

   _____

4. Tu veux aller à la piscine.

_____

5. Marie veut aller au cirque.

_____

J. Your teacher has given you the class seating plan. Tell the students where everyone is.

EXAMPLE: (him)   **Je suis à côté de lui.**

1. (you, familiar)   Pierre est devant _____ .
2. (them, _f._)   Richard est derrière _____ .
3. (us)   Vous êtes loin de _____ .
4. (her)   Ils sont près d' _____ .
5. (me)   Françoise est à côtè de _____ .
6. (him)   Nous sommes en face de _____ .
7. (you, formal)   Elles sont devant _____ .
8. (them, _m._)   Tu es derrière _____ .

K. All your friends have plans for tonight. Tell what they are by completing the statements.

EXAMPLE: (I)   Pierre et _____ , nous allons au cinéma.
Pierre et moi, nous allons au cinéma.

1. (he)   Jean et _____ , ils vont au théâtre.
2. (we)   Hubert et _____ , nous allons au stade.
3. (they, _f._)   Marie et _____ , elles vont à une boum.
4. (I)   André et _____ , nous allons à une discothèque.
5. (she)   Paul et _____ , ils vont au musée.
6. (you, formal)   Sylvie et _____ , vous allez à la piscine.
7. (they, _m._)   Alice et _____ , ils vont au cirque.
8. (you, familiar)   Michelle et _____ , vous allez au parc.

L. Your little brother and sister are asking a lot of questions. Give them a one-word answer in French.

EXAMPLE: Qui parle?   (he)
Lui.

1. Qui arrive?   (I) _____ .
2. Qui danse?   (they, _f._) _____ .
3. Qui chante?   (we) _____ .
4. Qui travaille?   (he) _____ .

5. Qui téléphone?   (you, familiar) _____ .

6. Qui prépare le dîner?   (they, *m.*) _____ .

7. Qui finit les devoirs?   (she) _____ .

8. Qui est curieux?   (you, formal) _____ .

CONVERSATION

Vocabulaire

avec plaisir with pleasure
nager to swim

Ça ne fait rien. It doesn't matter.
le maître-nageur lifeguard

DIALOGUE

You are the second person in the dialog. Respond in accordance with the instructions.

Veux-tu aller au parc avec moi?

(Ask why YOU, then respond positively.)

Toi et moi, nous pouvons faire un pique-nique.

(Say what YOU can bring to eat.)

Toi et moi, nous pouvons jouer au tennis.

(Say that YOU don't want to play tennis.)

Nous pouvons nager dans la piscine, toi et moi.

(Say that YOU can't swim.)

Parlons français

Work with a partner and make plans to go somewhere amusing. Discuss what you are going to do there.

EXAMPLES:

You:	**Qu'est-ce qu'on fait?**
Partner:	**Allons au cinéma!**
You:	**Oui, j'adore le cinéma. Allons voir** (title of film)
Partner:	**Tu veux aller au cinéma à quelle heure?**
You:	**À une heure de l'après-midi.**
Partner:	**D'accord.**

Page culturelle

Les loisirs (Leisure time)

School is taken very seriously in France. Classes usually begin at 8:30 AM and end at 5 PM, except on Wednesdays and Saturdays when they end at 12:30 PM. There is always a lot of homework to do after school, at least two hours every day.

French family life is also very important. French teenagers, therefore, must attend to various chores and family obligations.

Because French schools do not normally sponsor activities like dances or sports, many French students belong to sports clubs where they may practice many different sports. Some towns provide free after-school activities for 8- to 16-year-old students. There are also inexpensive vacation groups at holiday times that are devoted to such sports as kayaking or rock-climbing. Students can call **Allô-Sport** in Paris for information on all these programs. There are also youth centers, called **Maisons des Jeunes et de la Culture (MJC)**, where young people may attend classes in music, dance, drama, photography, or computer science. Movies and weekend excursions are often planned.

Other favorite distractions include, of course, dancing. A **boum** is a party organized in someone's house or in a rented place. Teens gather to celebrate birthdays or other events, and listen to music, dance, and talk while snacking on chips, small sandwiches, and soft drinks.

Rappel

1. Classes in a French school generally start at _____ and end at _____ .

2. Unlike American students, French students attend school for a half day on _____ and _____ .

3. French schools usually don't sponsor _____ .

4. _____ are organized to provide sports activities for French teens.

5. A youth center is called a _____ .

À Vous

1. Write an ad for a French discotheque.

2. Watch a French movie and write a critical review of it.

La Chasse au trésor

http://

Using your best Internet search skills, find an MJC site. List the activities in which you can participate at that particular MJC.

C'est authentique!

Qu'est-ce qu'on ne trouve pas dans ce musée? _____

1. des sculptures
2. le tombeau de Napoléon

3. des pistolets
4. des canons

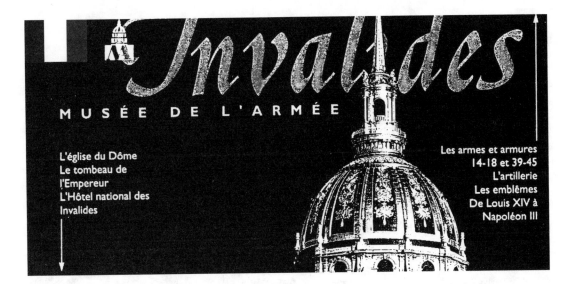

MUSÉE DE L'ARMÉE

L'église du Dôme
Le tombeau de l'Empereur
L'Hôtel national des Invalides

Les armes et armures
14-18 et 39-45
L'artillerie
Les emblêmes
De Louis XIV à
Napoléon III

MOTS NÉCESSAIRES

NOUNS
la boum party
le cirque circus
la discothèque discotheque
le divertissement amusement
le jardin garden
le jardin zoologique, zoo zoo
le match match
le musée museum
la piscine swimming pool

la plage beach
le stade stadium

VERBS
je vois I see
tu vois you see
il voit he sees
elle voit she sees
nous voyons we see
vous voyez you see
ils / elles voient they see

PRONOUNS
moi I, me
toi you
lui *m.* he, him
elle *f.* she, her
nous we, us
vous you
eux *m.* they, them
elles *f.* they, them

24
Projets d'été

*Using the Verb **recevoir**; Expressing Actions in the Past: Using the **Passé composé***

Vocabulaire

aller dans une colo(nie)
(de vacances)

faire une excursion

faire un voyage

aller à la campagne

aller à la montagne

faire une randonnée

faire du camping

aller à la mer

400

travailler à la maison

visiter un pays étranger

Activités

A. Listen to your teacher describe various activities and match them with the places listed below.

a. _____ Je travaille à la maison.

b. _____ Je vais à la montagne.

c. _____ Je visite un pays étranger.

d. _____ Je vais à la mer.

e. _____ Je vais dans une colo.

f. _____ Je fais du camping à la campagne.

B. Express how each person is spending a summer day.

1.

Vous _____

_____

2.

Nous _____

3.

Je _____

_____

4.

Tu _____

_____

5.

Les filles _____

_____

6.

Ils _____

7.

Robert _____

_____

8.

Je _____

9.

Tu _____

_____

10.

Elle _____

_____

Prononciation

- **c** and **g** may represent hard or soft sounds. When followed by *a, o, u,* or a consonant they have a hard sound: **c** sounds like *k* and **g** sounds like the *g* in *good*.

carte	court	document	classe	comment	cadeau	scolaire
gris	goûter	légume	glace	anglais	regarder	gros

La classe goûte la glace.

- When **c** or **g** is followed by *e, i,* or *y,* or when **ç** occurs, they have a soft sound: *c* and *ç* sound like *s* and *g* sounds like the *s* in *treasure.*

ce	ici	bicyclette	reçois	leçon	reçu	sciences
âge	rouge	gymnase	Gisèle	orangeade	garçon	argent

Ce garçon a reçu de l'orangeade dans le gymnase.

The verb **recevoir** is an important irregular verb because everybody likes to receive something, for example, a letter or a gift. Read this short narrative and try to find all the forms of the verb **recevoir** (*to receive.*)

L'anniversaire

C'est aujourd'hui le vingt-deux avril, l'anniversaire de Michel. Pour célébrer ce jour important, Michel apporte des gâteaux en classe. Le professeur dit:

— Merci, Michel! Parlons des anniversaires. Comment fêtez-vous votre anniversaire? Qu'est-ce que **vous recevez** d'habitude comme cadeau d'anniversaire?

fêter to celebrate

MICHEL: **Je reçois** des vêtements formidables et des jeux vidéo.

CHANTAL ET NICOLE: **Nous recevons** des vêtements, nous aussi. Claude, qu'est-ce que **tu reçois?**

CLAUDE: Moi, **je reçois** de l'argent.

SYLVIE: **Il reçoit** de l'argent! Quel veinard! **Mes frères**, eux aussi, **reçoivent** de l'argent. Moi, **je reçois** des CD.

quel veinard! how lucky he is!

LE PROFESSEUR: Moi aussi, **je reçois** un cadeau. Les membres de ma famille font tout mon travail pour moi!

Activité

C. Match the person with the gift. Write the matching letter(s) in the space provided.

1. Sylvie   _____
2. Claude   _____
3. Michel   _____
4. le professeur   _____
5. Chantal et Nicole _____

a. Il ne travaille pas.
b. des jeux vidéo
c. des vêtements
d. des CD
e. de l'argent

 Did you find the forms of the verb **recevoir**? Fill them in for all the subjects.

je _____   nous _____

tu _____   vous _____

il / elle _____   ils / elles _____

Activités

D. Match the descriptions with the pictures.

Nous recevons beaucoup de
    journaux.
Les enfants reçoivent des jouets. (*toys*)
Ma mère reçoit un bracelet.
Je reçois une bonne note en
    français.

Est-ce que tu reçois des fleurs
    pour ton anniversaire?
Lui, il reçoit une bicyclette.
Vous recevez des félicitations.
Bertrand et Marc reçoivent
    de l'argent.

1. _____ .

2. _____ .

3. _____ .

4. _____ .

5. _____ .

6. _____ .

7. _____ .

8. _____ .

E. What do these people get for their birthdays?

> EXAMPLE: Paul / de l'argent
> **Paul reçoit de l'argent.**

1. Chantal et Véronique / des cartes d'anniversaire

    _____

2. Vous / des CD

    _____

3. Julien / un ordinateur

    _____

4. Tu / des jeux vidéo

    _____

5. Nous / des vêtements

    _____

 Your school year is finally coming to an end. It is time to take a quick look back before making your summer plans.

Up to now, you have learned to talk about things happening **maintenant** (*now*), **aujourd'hui** (*today*), and even **demain** (*tomorrow*). Now you will learn to talk about things that happened **hier** (*yesterday*), **hier soir** (*last night*), **la semaine passée** (*last week*), **le mois passé** (*last month*), or **l'année passée** (*last year*). Of course, you need to use verbs in the past tense. One such tense in French is the **passé composé**. The **passé composé** is used to express actions or events that started and were completed in the past at a specific time.

 Read this story about an interesting report card. Pay attention to the verbs in bold type. They are in the **passé composé**, the past tense.

Le Bulletin scolaire

Hier, enfin, **les classes ont fini.** Gérard n'a pas de travail pendant l'été. Il peut passer les mois de juillet et d'août à se promener dans le parc ou à aller à plage. **Il a** beaucoup **travaillé** l'année passée et maintenant il peut s'amuser.

se promener to take a walk

Chez lui, **Gérard a trouvé** un document. Il **a dit** à son père: — Regarde ce document important!

Son père a regardé le papier. **Il a crié:** — Mais c'est ton bulletin scolaire final. Quelles notes horribles! **Tu as eu** 65 en maths, en sciences et en anglais. **Tu as reçu** 70 en histoire et en français. **Tu n'as pas** assez **étudié. Tu as trop regardé** la télévision. **Tu as** trop **écouté** la radio. **Tu as** trop **joué** avec tes amis. **Tu n'as pas bien travaillé** et je suis très déçu. Tu vas être puni.

crier to scream
le bulletin scolaire report card   as eu had
as reçu received
assez enough
trop too many
déçu disappointed
puni punished

Alors **Gérard a commencé** à rire. **Il a dit:** — **Tu n'as pas** bien **regardé** ce bulletin, Papa. **Tu as oublié** de regarder la date. Ce bulletin n'est pas à moi. C'est ton bulletin. **Je l'ai trouvé** parmi tes papiers au sous-sol.

rire to laugh
oublier to forget
parmi among

Son père a regardé le papier encore une fois et **il a rougi. Il a trouvé** la date: 1970. Alors **Gérard a montré** son propre bulletin à son père:

rougir to blush
propre own

Anglais	90
Sciences	95
Mathématiques	95
Histoire	85
Français	95
Éducation physique	90
Sciences sociales	90

Pas mal, n'est-ce pas?

pas mal not bad

Activité

F. Complétez les phrases.

1. Hier, enfin, les classes _____ .

2. Gérard _____ l'année passée.

3. Le père de Gérard a regardé _____ .

4. Il _____ "Mais, c'est ton bulletin scolaire final"!

5. Les notes de Gérard sont _____ .

6. Il a eu 65 en _____ , en _____ et en _____ .

7. Il a eu 70 en _____ et en _____ .

8. Le père de Gérard n'a pas regardé la _____ .

9. Gérard a trouvé le bulletin au _____ .

10. En réalité le bulletin de Gérard est _____ .

In the story you have just read there appear many examples of the **passé composé.** This past tense consists of two parts: a conjugated form of the helping verb **avoir** (*to have*) plus the past participle of the main verb. Here are some examples.

> **j'ai trouvé** *I (have) found*
> **il a travaillé** *he (has) worked*

Do you remember how to conjugate the verb **avoir**? Fill in the correct forms for all subjects.

j' _____ nous _____

tu _____ vous _____

il / elle _____ ils / elles _____

Now fill in all the negative forms of **avoir.**

je _____ nous _____

tu _____ vous _____

il / elle _____ ils / elles _____

Finally, provide all the question forms of **avoir** using inversion.

_____ _____

_____ _____

_____ _____

5 Now that we have all the forms of the helping verb **avoir,** you have completed the first part of the **passé composé.** The next step is to form the past participle of the main verb that is to be in the past tense. Look carefully at the table below so that you can complete the rule about forming the past participle.

INFINITIVE	PAST PARTICIPLE
écout*er*	écouté
jou*er*	joué
regard*er*	regardé
travaill*er*	travaillé
trouv*er*	trouvé

All the verbs in the left column belong to which verb family? _____

To form the past participle, drop _____ from the infinitive and add _____ .

What are the English meanings of these past participles?

écouté _____

joué _____

regardé _____

travaillé _____

trouvé _____

The **passé composé** combines the helping verb and the past participle.

	CONJUGATED	
SUBJECT	HELPING VERB	PAST PARTICIPLE
il	**a**	**trouvé**

The **passé composé** has two meanings.

il a trouvé   *he found / he has found*

NOTE: The verb **aller** is special and does not use the helping verb **avoir** in the passé composé.

Activités

G. Change these infinitives to past participles.

1. chanter _____
2. aimer _____
3. demander _____
4. chercher _____
5. inviter _____

6. danser _____
7. habiter _____
8. garder _____
9. oublier _____
10. visiter _____

H. Work with a partner. Take turns saying what you did in school this year.

EXAMPLE: You: **J'ai beaucoup travaillé cette année.**
Partner: **J'ai étudié le français.**

I. Here are some of the things you and your friends did yesterday. Complete the sentences with the correct form of the verb in parentheses.

1. (travailler)   Charles _____ du matin au soir.
2. (étudier)   Tu _____ pour un examen de français.
3. (visiter)   Hélène _____ un musée.
4. (parler)   Mes sœurs _____ au téléphone.
5. (chanter)   Vous _____ à la radio.
6. (danser)   Marc et Chantal _____ à la boum.
7. (écouter)   Moi, j' _____ de la musique.
8. (jouer)   Les enfants _____ avec leurs jouets.

J. Change what these people did from the present to the past.

1. Le professeur demande «pourquoi».

   _____

2. Les élèves goûtent la mousse au chocolat.

   _____

3. Nous écoutons des CD formidables.

   _____

4. Maman prépare un dîner excellent.

   _____

5. Marie donne son livre à Paul.

   _____

6. Je cherche un mot dans le dictionnaire.

   _____

7. Tu gagnes le match.

   _____

8. Mes amis dansent pendant (_for_) des heures.

   _____

6 To make a sentence negative in the **passé composé**, look again at the second table in section 4 and then add the past participle.

elle _n'_a _pas_ trouvé

Activité

K. Say what these people did not do last weekend.

EXAMPLE   je / jouer au golf
           Je n'ai pas joué au golf.

1. Michel / regarder le nouveau film français.

   _____

2. nous / jouer au tennis

   _____

3. Claire et Denise / préparer le dessert

   _____

4. vous / goûter la mousse au chocolat

   _____

5. les Anglais / gagner le match

_____

6. tu / écouter la radio

_____

7. François / chanter devant la classe

_____

8. je / parler italien

_____

If you want to ask a question in the **passé composé**, follow this pattern.

A-t-il trouvé le dictionnaire?

What are the two meanings of the question?

_____

_____

Of course you can also ask a question with **est-ce que** or with intonation.

Est-ce qu'il a trouvé le dictionnaire?
Il a trouvé le dictionnaire?

Activité

L. You are curious to find out what everyone did last Saturday. Ask some questions.

EXAMPLE: Vous / écouter la radio
Avez-vous écouté la radio?

1. tu / marcher dans le parc

_____

2. ils / jouer au tennis

_____

3. il / parler au téléphone

_____

4. elles / écouter des CD

_____

5. vous / aider votre mère à préparer le dîner

_____

6. elle / travailler au supermarché

_____

Now that you know the **passé composé** of regular -ER verbs, let's learn the **passé composé** of -IR and -RE verbs. First look carefully at the formation of the past participle of -IR verbs.

INFINITIVE	PAST PARTICIPLE
applaud*ir*	applaud*i*
chois*ir*	chois*i*
fin*ir*	fin*i*

> To form the past participle of -IR verbs, drop _____ from the infinitive and add the letter _____ .

Activité

M. Change these infinitives to past participles.

1. punir _____
2. saisir _____
3. maigrir _____
4. guérir (*to cure*) _____

5. remplir _____
6. obéir _____
7. grossir _____
8. désobéir _____

 Now look carefully at the formation of the past participle of -RE verbs:

INFINITIVE	PAST PARTICIPLE
attend*re*	attend*u*
entend*re*	entend*u*
répond*re*	répond*u*

> To form the past participle of -RE verbs, drop _____ from the infinitive and add the letter _____ .

Activité

N. Change these infinitives to past participles.

1. vendre _____
2. descendre _____
3. défendre (*to defend*) _____

4. perdre _____
5. rendre (*to give back, return*) _____
6. pendre (*to hang*) _____

The **passé composé** of **-IR** and **-RE** verbs follows the pattern of **-ER** verbs.

J'ai fini les devoirs.
Je n'ai pas fini mon petit déjeuner.
As-tu fini ton travail?

Nous avons perdu le match.
Nous n'avons pas perdu les stylos.
Avez-vous perdu votre petit chien?

Activités

O. Your friend is talking about the past, the present, and the future. Check the appropriate time frame for each statement he/she makes.

	PRÉSENT	PASSÉ	FUTUR		PRÉSENT	PASSÉ	FUTUR
1.	_____	_____	_____	**5.**	_____	_____	_____
2.	_____	_____	_____	**6.**	_____	_____	_____
3.	_____	_____	_____	**7.**	_____	_____	_____
4.	_____	_____	_____	**8.**	_____	_____	_____

P. You were out late on Saturday night and you slept late on Sunday. What did everyone do on Sunday morning?

1. tu / choisir de dormir jusqu'à midi

_____

2. maman / finir son travail à la maison

_____

3. Jean-Louis / vendre sa bicyclette

_____

4. nous / perdre un match de tennis

_____

5. mes frères / attendre leurs amis

_____

6. papa / punir mes petits frères

_____

7. vous / répondre au téléphone

_____

8. mes cousins / rendre leurs livres à la bibliothèque

_____

Q. Make a chart of what you did during the school year and what you plan to do over the summer. Label the columns:

PENDANT L'ANNÉE SCOLAIRE   PENDANT L'ÉTÉ

_____   _____

_____   _____

_____   _____

_____   _____

_____   _____

CONVERSATION

Vocabulaire

pendant for
épatante splendid
chuchoter to whisper

le rêve the dream
embrasser to kiss

vrai real
la joue the cheek

Parlons français

Work with a partner. Take turns talking about your summer plans.

EXAMPLE   You: **Qu'est-ce que tu vas faire pendant l'été?**
Partner: **Je vais rester à la maison. Et toi?**
You: **Moi, je vais aller dans une colonie de vacances.**
Partner: **Qu'est-ce que tu fais à la colo?**
You: **Je fais du sport. Je joue au foot.**

Page culturelle

Vivent les vacances!

Most French students have a demanding schedule and a heavy work load. A typical program for the ninth grade (**classe de troisième**) would include French, math, Latin and one or two foreign languages, history, geography, economics, physics, chemistry, natural science, and two hours of gym a week. In general, French students have four or five major subjects per day. They often study several foreign languages, a good thing since four foreign countries, England, Germany, Italy, and Spain, are neighbors of France.

During the school day there is a 1 to 1½ hour lunch break and there may be **"une heure de permanence,"** a study hour.

Report cards are distributed three times a year, at the end of each **trimestre** (3 months). Grades range from 0 to 20, with 10 being the passing grade. Sometimes letters A to E are also used to indicate how satisfactory the work of the student is: a 12 can easily be a B, and a 15 is a very good grade, usually an A. Teachers and parents may write notes, information, questions, and comments to each other in the **"carnet de correspondance,"** which they send to each other.

School vacations are frequent and students (and teachers) eagerly await them. They take place every 6 to 7 weeks. The exact dates for the winter and the spring vacations depend on the region in France. All other dates are the same for the entire country. The summer vacation lasts two months, July and August.

Rappel

1. French students study several foreign languages because _____

_____

2. French students may study or do some homework during _____

_____

3. Report cards are given out every _____ .

4. Grades range in number from _____ to _____ with _____ as the passing grade.

5. Parents and teachers may write notes to each other in a student's _____

_____ .

À Vous

1. Write your school schedule in French.

2. Prepare a 3-column report card for yourself. Label the columns: MATIÈRE (Subject), NOTE (Grade), COMMENTAIRE DU PROFESSEUR (Teacher's Comments).

3. Find a French-speaking country other than France where you would like to go on vacation, and write a travel brochure for that country.

La Chasse au trésor

http://

Using your best Internet search skills, find the answer to the following question:
What would you go to see in :

a. Québec?
b. Provence, France?
c. the Swiss Alps?

d. Saint Martin?
e. Tahiti?

C'est authentique!

Here are typical dates for school vacations in France.

VACANCES SCOLAIRES

RENTRÉE	TOUSSAINT	NOËL	HIVER	PRINTEMPS	PENTECÔTE	ÉTÉ
mardi 2 septembre *au matin* pour les élèves du primaire et les collégiens mercredi 10 septembre *au matin* pour les lycéens	du vendredi 24 octobre *après la classe* au mardi 4 novembre *au matin*	du samedi 20 décembre *après la classe* au mardi 7 janvier *au matin*	du mercredi 19 février *après la classe* au mercredi 5 mars *au matin*	du samedi 12 avril *après la classe* au lundi 28 avril *au matin*	du vendredi 16 mai *après la classe* au mercredi 21 mai *au matin*	samedi 28 juin

Which day would you expect a French student to be in school? _____

1. le 1ᵉʳ septembre

2. le 31 octobre

3. le 27 novembre

4. le 18 mai

M O T S   N É C E S S A I R E S

VACANCES
la **campagne** countryside
le **camping** camping
la **colonie (colo) de**
  vacances summer camp
l'**excursion** f. excursion
la **mer** sea
la **montagne** mountain
le **pays** country
le **projet** plan
la **randonnée** hike

le **voyage** trip
étranger (étrangère) foreign

VERBS
recevoir to receive
je reçois I receive
tu reçois you receive
il reçoit he receives
elle reçoit she receives
nous recevons we receive
vous recevez you receive
ils / elles reçoivent they
  receive

WORDS OF TIME
aujourd'hui today
demain tomorrow
hier yesterday
hier soir last night
l'**année** f. **passée** last year
maintenant now

Révision VI
(LEÇONS 21 – 24)

Leçon 21

a. To say TO or IN a country, use:

> **en** before a feminine singular country;
> **au** before a masculine singular country;
> **aux** before a plural country.

NOTE: When referring to small islands, use **à**, **à la**, or **aux**.

b. To say FROM a country, use:

> **de (d')** before a feminine singular country;
> **du** before a masculine singular country;
> **des** before a plural country.

c. Most adjectives of nationality form the feminine and plural like other regular adjectives. If a masculine adjective ends in **-ien**, the feminine form of the adjective ends in **-ienne**. Add **s** to form the plural of the masculine or feminine form of the adjective.

Leçon 22

The verb **prendre** *(to take)* is irregular. Memorize all its forms.

je prends	**nous prenons**
tu prends	**vous prenez**
il / elle prend	**ils / elles prennent**

apprendre *(to learn)* and **comprendre** *(to understand)* are conjugated like **prendre**.

Leçon 23

a. The verb **voir** *(to see)* is irregular. Memorize all its forms.

je vois	**nous voyons**
tu vois	**vous voyez**
il / elle voit	**ils /elles voient**

b. The stress pronouns are:

moi	*I, me*	**nous**	*we, us*
toi	*you* (familiar)	**vous**	*you* (formal)
lui	*he, him*	**eux**	*they, them (m.)*
elle	*she, her*	**elles**	*they, them (f.)*

Stress pronouns are used:

(1) to emphasize the subject pronoun;

(2) after prepositions;

(3) when the pronoun stands alone;

(4) in compound subjects or objects.

Leçon 24

a. The verb **recevoir** (*to receive*) is irregular. Memorize all its forms.

je reçois	nous recevons
tu reçois	vous recevez
il / elle reçoit	ils / elles reçoivent

b. To form the past tense (**passé composé**) in French, use these formulas.

REGULAR SENTENCE

subject + form of **avoir** + past participle

il	a	cherché
tu	as	choisi
ils	ont	répondu

NEGATIVE SENTENCE

subject + **ne** + form of **avoir** + **pas** + past participle

il	n'a pas	cherché
tu	n'as pas	choisi
ils	n'ont pas	répondu

INVERTED QUESTION

form of **avoir** + subject + past participle

a-t-il	cherché?
as-tu	choisi?
ont-ils	repondu?

The verb **aller** is an exception to this rule because it does not use the helping verb *avoir* to form the passé composé.

c. Past participles of regular verbs:

	INFINITIVE	PAST PARTICIPLE
-ER Verbs:	cherch*er*	cherch*é*
-IR Verbs:	chois*ir*	chois*i*
-RE Verbs:	répon*dre*	répon*du*

Activités

A. **Qu'est-ce que Robert veut pour son anniversaire?** Fill in these French words, then read down the boxed column to see what Robert wants for his birthday.

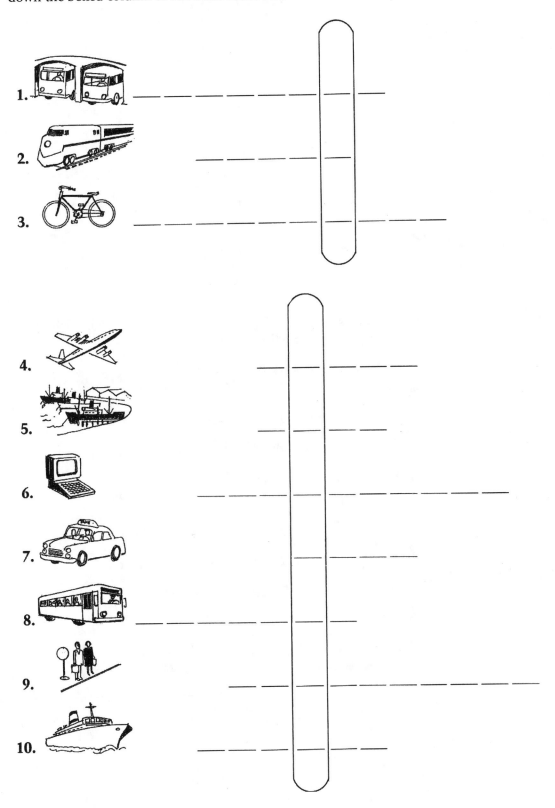

1. _ _ _ _ _ _ _ _

2. _ _ _ _ _ _

3. _ _ _ _ _ _ _ _

4. _ _ _ _ _ _

5. _ _ _ _ _

6. _ _ _ _ _ _ _ _

7. _ _ _ _ _ _

8. _ _ _ _ _ _ _

9. _ _ _ _ _ _ _ _ _

10. _ _ _ _ _ _

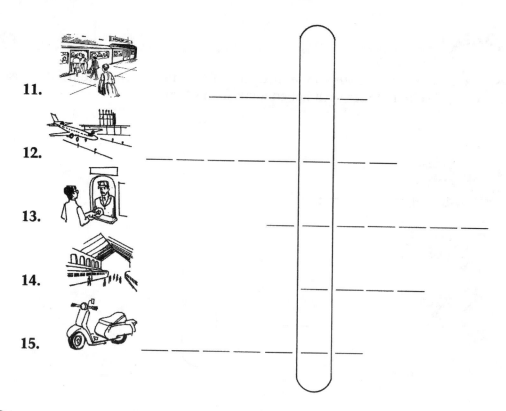

11. ___ ___ ___ ___ ___

12. ___ ___ ___ ___ ___

13. ___ ___ ___ ___ ___ ___ ___

14. ___ ___ ___ ___

15. ___ ___ ___ ___ ___ ___

B. Find the names of 10 countries in the puzzle. Circle them from left to right, right to left, up or down, or diagonally. Then write them down.

A	S	G	J	A	P	O	N	R	A
E	N	E	P	J	L	R	E	S	I
E	N	G	A	M	E	L	L	A	T
C	F	S	L	G	M	E	F	E	Ï
A	R	U	F	E	I	L	E	I	A
N	E	I	R	L	T	N	U	S	H
A	J	A	A	S	I	E	O	S	I
D	N	T	N	H	B	H	R	U	A
A	I	H	C	J	O	L	M	R	E
C	A	N	E	N	G	A	P	S	E

_____ _____ _____

_____ _____ _____

_____

C. Où vont-ils? Identify the amusement places. Then write the letters indicated in the boxes below to reveal where Philippe took Marie-Hélène to impress her.

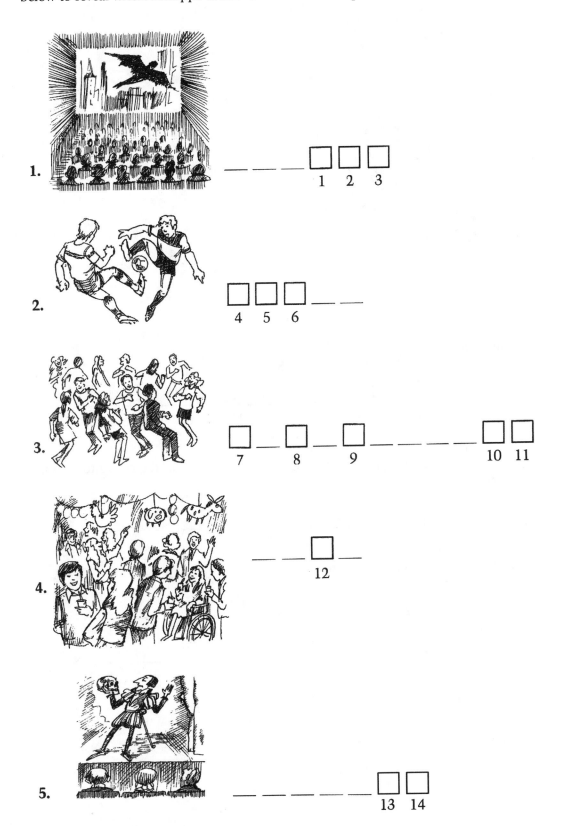

1. _ _ _ _ _ □ □ □
              1 2 3

2. □ □ □ _ _ _
   4 5 6

3. □ _ □ _ □ _ _ _ _ □ □
   7   8   9   10 11

4. _ _ □ _
        12

5. _ _ _ _ _ □ □
               13 14

6. _ _ _ _ □
15

7. _ _ □□□□
16 17 18

Solution: □□ □□□□□
3 10 2 12 8 1 11

□ □□□ □□□□□□□
7 5 13 6 4 9 17 14 16 18 15

D. JUMBLE. Unscramble the words. Then unscramble the letters in the circles to complete the message.

ONSUCXRIE _ _ _ ○ _ ○ _ _ _

GENANTOM ○ _ _ ○ _ _ _ _

ANDÉERONN _ _ ○ _ _ ○ _ _ _

AAMENGCP _ _ ○ _ _ _ _ ○

GVAOYE _ ○ _ _ _ _

Roger va passer ses vacances d'été à visiter des _____ .

E. Mots croisés:

HORIZONTALEMENT

1. (comprendre) nous _____
6. waitress
9. (to) you
10. this
11. factory
13. (dire) elle _____
14. where
15. your
16. (apprendre) il _____
19. (être) elle _____
21. art
22. (voir) il _____
25. one
26. (recevoir) vous _____
29. harbor
31. to see
33. his/her
34. one
35. far
36. (être) tu _____
37. this
40. in
41. (avoir) j' _____
42. one (pronoun)
43. him
44. and
45. dinner
46. cups
48. park
50. salt
52. (être) tu _____
53. without

55. dresses
57. **(voir) il** _____
59. restaurant

62. (to) you
64. **(danser) vous** _____
65. my

66. museum
67. in

VERTICALEMENT

1. knife
2. me
3. and
4. _____ **pas**
5. science
6. stadium
7. **(voir) je** _____
8. scooters
12. his / her
17. with
18. circus
20. napkin

21. **(apprendre) tu** _____
23. (to) you
24. this
27. at the house of
28. cars
30. cab
32. one *(pronoun)*
35. the *(m.)*
37. **(comprendre) tu**
    _____
38. in
39. your

41. plates
43. the
47. on
49. chosen
51. the *(f.)*
52. and
54. under
56. **(avoir) elles** _____
58. menu
60. tea
61. no
63. **(être) tu** _____

The Cognate Connection

Write the meanings of the following French and English words.

FRENCH		ENGLISH COGNATE	
1. apprendre	_____	apprentice	_____
2. arrêt	_____	arrest	_____
3. avion	_____	aviation	_____
4. vélo	_____	velocity	_____
5. comprendre	_____	comprehension	_____

Glossary of Grammatical Terms

adjective A word that modifies a noun or a pronoun.

adverb A word that modifies a verb, an adjective, or another adverb.

articles Words that precede nouns and usually indicate the number and the gender of the nouns.

auxiliary verb Also called a **helping verb**. One of two elements needed to form a compound tense, such as the *passé composé*. *Avoir* and *être* are the auxiliary verbs in French.

cardinal numbers The numbers we use for counting.

cognates Words that are the same or similar in both French and English.

conjugation The action of changing the ending of the verb so that it agrees with the subject noun or pronoun performing the task.

definite article (*the*) An article that indicates a specific person or thing: *the house*.

demonstrative adjective An adjective that precedes nouns to indicate or point out the person, place, or thing referred to: *this*, *that*, *these*, or *those*.

exclamation A word or phrase used to show surprise, delight, incredulity, emphasis, or other strong emotion.

false friends Words that are spelled the same or almost the same in both languages but have very different meanings and can be different parts of speech.

gender Indicates whether a word is masculine or feminine.

idiom A particular word or expression whose meaning cannot be readily understood by either its grammar or the words used.

imperative A verb form used to give commands or make requests.

indefinite article (*a, an*) It refers to persons and objects not specifically identified: *a house*.

indicative A verb mood that states a fact.

infinitive The basic "*to*" form of the verb.

intonation A way of asking a question by inserting a rising inflection at the end of the statement.

inversion A way of asking a question by reversing the word order of the subject pronoun and the conjugated verb within the sentence.

noun A word used to name a person, place, thing, idea, or quality.

partitive An article indicating an indefinite quantity or part of a whole: *some* or *any*.

passé composé A tense that expresses an action or event completed at a specific time in the past.

past participle A verbal form which, when combined with a helping verb, expresses an action or a condition that has occurred in the past.

preposition A word used to relate elements in a sentence: noun to noun, verb to verb, or verb to noun/pronoun.

present tense A tense that expresses what is happening now.

pronoun A word that is used to replace a noun (a person, place, thing, idea, or quality).

stress pronoun A pronoun used to emphasize and to highlight or to replace nouns or pronouns.

subject The noun or pronoun performing the action of the verb.

verb A word that shows an action or state of being.

French-English Vocabulary

à at, to; **à bientôt** see you soon; **à côté de** next to
aboyer to bark
acheter to buy
acheteur *m.* buyer
acteur *m.* actor
actrice *f.* actress
addition *f.* check
aéroport *m.* airport
affreux (*f.* affreuse) awful
afin de in order to
agent de police *m./f.* police officer
agir to act
agréable nice
aimable friendly
aimer to like, love
aliment *m.* food
Allemagne *f.* Germany
allemand German
aller to go; **aller bien/mal** to be well/not well
américain American
ami *m.* friend
amuser to amuse; **s'amuser** to have fun, to have a good time
âne *m.* donkey
anglais English
Angleterre *f.* England
animal *m.* animal; **animal domestique** *m.* pet
animé animated
année *f.* year; **l'année passée** last year
anniversaire *m.* birthday, anniversary
annoncer to announce
août *m.* August
appareil *m.* **photo (numérique)** (digital) camera
appeler to call; **s'appeler** to be named
applaudir to applaud, clap
apporter to bring
apprendre to learn
après after
après-midi *m./f.* afternoon
arbre *m.* tree
argent *m.* money
armoire *f.* wardrobe
arrêt *m.* stop
artiste *m./f.* artist
assez enough

assiette *f.* plate
associé *m.* associate
attendre to wait (for)
au to the
aujourd'hui today
au moins at least
au revoir good-bye
aussi also
autobus, bus *m.* bus
automne *m.* autumn
autour (de) around
autre other
aux to the
avant before
avec with
avion *m.* plane
avocat *m.(f.* **avocate)** lawyer
avoir to have; **avoir __ ans** to be __ years old; **avoir chaud** to be warm; **avoir faim** to be hungry; **avoir froid** to be cold; **avoir peur** to be afraid; **avoir raison** to be right; **avoir soif** to be thirsty; **avoir sommeil** to be sleepy; **avoir tort** to be wrong
avril *m.* April

baladeur *m.* walkman
balle *f.* ball (*baseball, tennis, golf*)
ballon *m.* ball (*soccer, basketball, football*)
baskets *f. pl.* basketball shoes
bateau *m.* boat
bâton de craie *m.* piece of chalk
batte *f.* bat
beau (*f.* belle) beautiful
beaucoup (de) many, much, a lot of
bébé *m.* baby
bêtise *f.* foolishness
beurre *m.* butter
bibliothèque *f.* library
bicyclette *f.* bicycle
bien well
bifteck *m.* steak
blaguer to joke
blanc white
bleu blue
boire to drink
boisson *f.* drink
bon (*f.* bonne) good
bonjour hello

bonsoir good evening
bonne *f.* maid
bouche *f.* mouth
boucherie *f.* butcher shop
bouillabaisse *f.* fish soup
boulangerie *f.* bakery
boum *f.* party
boutique *f.* store
bras *m.* arm
bruit *m.* noise
brun brown
bulletin scolaire *m.* report card
bureau *m.* office; desk

c'est it is
ça this, it
ça va fine, OK; **Ça va?** How's it going?
cacahouète *f.* peanut
cadeau *m.* gift
cadet(te) younger
café *m.* café, coffee
cahier *m.* notebook
calculateur solaire *m.* solar calculator
calme-toi calm down
caméscope *m.* camcorder
campagne *f.* countryside
camping *m.* camping
canadien(ne) Canadian
canapé *m.* sofa
canard *m.* duck
carte postale *f.* post card
casque *m.* helmet
ce *m.* this, that
ceinture *f.* belt
célèbre famous
cellulaire *m.* cell phone (*Canada*)
cent one hundred
centime *m.* cent
cerise *f.* cherry
certainement certainly
ces *m./f.* these, those
cet *m.* this, that
cette *f.* this, that
chaise *f.* chair
chambre *f.* bedroom
chance *f.* luck
chanter to sing
chapeau *m.* hat
chaque each
charmant charming

chat *m.* cat
chauffeur *m.* driver
chaussettes *f. pl.* socks
chaussures *f. pl.* shoes
chef *m.* chef, chief, boss
chemise *f.* shirt
chemisier *m.* shirt (*woman*)
cher (*f.* chère) expensive
chercher to look for
cheval *m.* horse
cheveux *m. pl.* hair
chèvre *f.* goat
chez at (the house) of
chic fashionable
chien *m.* dog
Chine *f.* China
chinois Chinese
choisir to choose
chose *f.* thing
chouette great
ciel *m.* sky
cinéma *m.* movies
cinq five
cinquante fifty
cirque *m.* circus
classeur *m.* looseleaf notebook
cochon *m.* pig
cœur *m.* heart
colonie *f.* de vacances summer camp
combien (de) how many, how much
combinaison *f.* combination
comme like
commencer (à) to begin
comment how; Comment allez-vous? How are you? ; Comment ça va? How are you? ; Comment vas-tu? How are you? ; Comment t'appelles-tu? What's your name?
comprendre to understand
compter to count
confortable comfortable
console de jeux *m.* game station
content happy
continuer to continue
convenable suitable
corps *m.* body
corriger to correct
cou *m.* neck
courant *m.* current
courir to run
cours *m.* course
court short
cousin (*f.* cousine) cousin
couteau *m.* knife
coûter to cost
couvert *m.* table setting

couverture *f.* blanket
craie *f.* chalk
cravate *f.* tie
crayon *m.* pencil
créer to create
crème *f.* cream
criard loud
crier to scream
criminel *m.* criminal
crosse *f.* hockey stick
cruel(le) cruel
cuiller *f.* spoon
cuisine *f.* kitchen
cyclisme *m.* cycling

d'abord first
dans in
danser to dance
de of, about, from; some/any; de plus furthermore
décembre *m.* December
découverte *f.* discovery
déçu disappointed
(se) défendre to defend oneself
déjeuner *m.* lunch
délicieux delicious
demain tomorrow; à demain until tomorrow
demander to ask
demi half; demi-heure *f.* half hour
démodé out of style
demoiselle *f.* young lady
dent *f.* tooth
dépenser to spend money
dernier (-ière) last
derrière behind
des of, about, from the; some
désastre *m.* disaster
descendre to go down
désirer to desire, want
détester to hate
deux two
devant in front (of)
devoirs *m. pl.* homework
dictionnaire *m.* dictionary
Dieu God
difficulté *f.* difficulty
dimanche *m.* Sunday
dîner *m.* dinner
dire to say, tell; à vrai dire to tell the truth
directeur *m.* principal
discuter to discuss
dispute *f.* argument
disque compact, CD *m.* CD
divan *m.* sofa-bed
divertissement *m.* amusement
divisé par divided by

dix ten
dix-huit eighteen
dix-neuf nineteen
dix-sept seventeen
docteur *m.* doctor
doigt *m.* finger
domestique domesticated
dommage *m.* damage; c'est dommage it is a pity
donner to give
douze twelve
drapeau *m.* flag
drôle funny
du of, about, from the; some
dur hard

eau *f.* water; eau minérale mineral water
échapper to escape
école *f.* school
écouter to listen
écran *m.* screen
écrire to write
éducation physique *f.* gym, physical education
église *f.* church
égoïste selfish
élève *m./f.* student
elle *f.* she, it; her
elles *f.* they, them
employer to use
en in; to; en avoir assez to have enough (of); en face (de) facing, opposite; en retard late
enfant *m./f.* child
ennuyeux (-euse) boring
énorme enormous
entendre to hear
entrée *f.* entrance
entrer to enter
envers towards
envoyer to send
épicerie *f.* grocery store
épinards *m. pl.* spinach
équipe *f.* team
erreur *f.* error, mistake
escalier *m.* stairs
Espagne *f.* Spain
espagnol Spanish
essayer to try to
estomac *m.* stomach
et and, plus
étage *m.* floor, story
étagère *f.* bookcase
États-Unis *m. pl.* United States
été *m.* summer
étrange strange
étranger (-ère) foreign

être to be; être à to belong to; être
  d'accord to agree
étroit narrow
étudiant *m.* (*f.* étudiante) student
étudier to study
eux *m.* they, them
examen *m.* test
excès *m.* excess
excité excited
exercice *m.* exercise
expliquer to explain

facteur *m.*, factrice *f.* mail carrier
faire to make, do; faire attention
  pay attention; faire beau to be
  nice weather; faire chaud to be
  hot weather; faire du soleil to
  be sunny; faire du vent to be
  windy; faire froid to be cold;
  faire le ménage to do the
  housework; faire les devoirs to
  do one's homework; faire
  mauvais to be bad weather; faire
  un pique-nique to go on a
  picnic; faire une partie de to
  play a game of; faire une
  promenade to go for a walk
famille *f.* family
fanfare *f.* band
femme *f.* woman; wife; femme
  d'affaires *f.* businesswoman
fenêtre *f.* window
ferme *f.* farm
fermer to close
féroce ferocious
fête *f.* holiday, feast; party
fêter to celebrate
feu d'artifice *m.* fireworks
feuille *f.* leaf; sheet; feuille de
  papier sheet, piece of paper
février *m.* February
figure *f.* face
fille *f.* girl, daughter
fils *m.* son
finalement finally
finir to finish
fleur *f.* flower
flocon *m.* flake
flotter to float
fois *f.* time
football *m.* soccer; football
  américain *m.* football
formidable terrific, great
fort strong
fou (*f.* folle) crazy
four à micro-ondes *m.* microwave
  oven
fourchette *f.* fork
français *m.* French

frère *m.* brother
frites *f. pl.* French fries
fromage *m.* cheese

gagner to win, earn
gants *m. pl.* gloves; gant de base-
  ball *m.* mitt
garçon *m.* boy; (*obs*) waiter
gare *f.* train station
gaspiller to waste
gâteau *m.* cake
généralement generally
généreux (-euse) generous
gens *m. pl.* people
gentil(le) nice
glace *f.* ice cream; mirror
goûter to taste
grâce à thanks to
gracieux (-euse) graceful
grand big; grand magasin *m.*
  department store
grand-mère *f.* grandmother
grand-père *m.* grandfather
grenier *m.* attic
grillé grilled
gris gray
gros(se) fat
guichet *m.* ticket window
gymnastique *f.* gymnastics

habiter to live (in)
haïtien(ne) Haitian
haricots verts *m. pl.* string beans
hélas alas
herbe *f.* grass
heure *f.* hour, o'clock; à quelle
  heure? at what time?
hier yesterday; hier soir last night
histoire *f.* history
hiver *m.* winter
homme *m.* man
hôpital *m.* hospital
hors de service out of order
huit eight
hypnotiseur *m.* hypnotist

idée *f.* idea
il he; it
il y a there is / there are
ils *m.* they
immeuble *m.* apartment building
imprimante *f.* printer
incroyable unbelievable
individuel *m.* individual
infirmier *m.* nurse
infirmière *f.* nurse
informatique *f.* computer science
inquiéter to worry; s'inquiéter to
  worry

insupportable unbearable
intéressant interesting
Italie *f.* Italy
italien(ne) Italian

jambe *f.* leg
jambon *m.* ham
janvier *m.* January
Japon *m.* Japan
japonais Japanese
jardin *m.* garden; jardin
  zoologique, zoo *m.* zoo
jaune yellow
je I
jean *m.* jeans
jeter to throw
jeudi *m.* Thursday
jeune young
joli pretty
jouer to play
jouet *m.* toy
jour *m.* day; jour férié *m.* legal
  holiday, day off
journal *m.* newspaper, journal
journée *f.* day
juillet *m.* July
juin *m.* June
jupe *f.* skirt
jus *m.* juice
jusqu'à up to, until

la *f.* the
laid ugly
laine *f.* wool
laisser to leave
lait *m.* milk
laitue *f.* lettuce
lampadaire *m.* floor lamp
lancer to throw
langue *f.* language; tongue
lapin *m.* rabbit
laver to wash
le *m.* the
leçon *f.* lesson
lecteur *m.* reader; player
lecteur de DVD *m.* DVD player
légume *m.* vegetable
lendemain *m.* next day
les *pl.* the
leur their
leurs their
lever to raise; se lever to stand up,
  get up
lèvre *f.* lip
librairie *f.* bookstore
lieu *m.* place
limonade *f.* lemon soda
lire to read
lit *m.* bed

living *m.* living room
livre *m.* book
loin (de) far (from)
long (longue) long
loup *m.* wolf
lui he, (to) him/her
lundi *m.* Monday
lycée *m.* high school

ma *f.* my
machine à écrire électrique *f.*
  electric typewriter
machine à traitement de texte *f.*
  word processor
magasin *m.* store
magnétoscope *m.* VCR
magnifique magnificent
mai *m.* May
maillot de bain *m.* bathing suit
main *f.* hand
maintenant now
maïs *m.* corn
mais but
maison *f.* house
maître *m.* master
maître-nageur *m.* lifeguard
maman *f.* mom, mother
manger to eat
manteau *m.* coat
marché *m.* market
marcher to walk; to work
  (*machine*)
mardi *m.* Tuesday
mars *m.* March
matériel scolaire *m.* school
  supplies
mathématiques *f. pl.* mathematics
matin *m.* morning
mauve purple
me (to) me
médecin *m.* doctor
meilleur best
mer *f.* sea
merci thank you, thanks
mercredi *m.* Wednesday
mère *f.* mother
mes *m./f.* my
métro *m.* subway
mettre to put
mexicain Mexican
Mexique *m.* Mexico
midi *m.* noon; Midi South (of
  France)
mille one thousand
mince thin
minuit *m.* midnight
miroir *m.* mirror
Mme (madame) Mrs.
mobile *m.* cell phone

moche awful
mode *f.* fashion; à la mode
  fashionable
moi I, me
moins minus
mois *m.* month
mon *m.* my
monde *m.* world
monstre *m.* monster
montagne *f.* mountain
montre *f.* watch
moteur *m.* motor
moto, motocyclette *f.* motorcycle

Nations Unies (*f. pl.*) United
  Nations
naturellement naturally
ne . . ni . . ni . . . neither . . nor . .
  nor
nécessaire necessary
nerveux (-euse) nervous
neuf nine
nez *m.* nose
noir black
non no
nos our
note *f.* grade
notre our
nous we, us; nous deux the two
  of us
nouveauté *f.* novelty, new item
novembre *m.* November
nuit *f.* night
numéro *m.* number

obliger to oblige
occasion *f.* opportunity
octobre *m.* October
œil *m.* eye
œuf *m.* egg; œuf dur hard-boiled egg
œuvre *f.* work
officiel official
oiseau *m.* bird
on one, you, we
oncle *m.* uncle
onze even
orangeade *f.* orange soda
ordinaire ordinary
ordinateur *m.* computer ; ___ de
  poche pocket ___ ;
  ___ portable laptop
oreille *f.* ear
où? where?
oublier to forget
oui yes
ouvrir to open

pain *m.* bread; pain grillé toast
panier *m.* basket

pantalon *m.* pants
papier *m.* paper
Pâques Easter
parc *m.* parc
parce que because
par-dessus above
paresseux (-euse) lazy
parfait perfect
parler to speak
parmi among
partie *f.* part
partout everywhere
passer to spend (*time*)
passé past
patin *m.* skate
patinage *m.* skating
pâtisserie *f.* pastry shop
pauvre poor
payer to pay
pays *m.* country
pendant during, for
penser to think
père *f.* father
perfectionné perfected
petit déjeuner *m.* breakfast
petit small
petits pois *m. pl.* peas
peu little
peut-être perhaps
pharmacie *f.* drugstore
phrase *f.* sentence
pièce *f.* room
pied *m.* foot
pique-nique *m.* picnic
piscine *f.* swimming pool
plage *f.* beach
plat *m.* dish
plat (e) flat
poils *f. pl.* body hair
poire *f.* pear
poisson *m.* fish
poitrine *f.* chest
poivre *m.* pepper
pomme *f.* apple; pomme de terre
  f. potato
pompier *m.* firefighter
populaire popular
porc *m.* pork
portable *m.* laptop
portatif portable
porte *f.* door
porter to wear
poule *f.* hen
poulet *m.* chicken
pour for, in order to
pourquoi why
pourtant still
pouvoir can, to be able to
pratiquer to practice

pratique practical
précis exact
préféré favorite
premier (f. **première**) first
prendre to take
préparer to prepare
près de near
prestigieux (-euse) prestigious
printemps m. spring
professeur m./f. teacher, professor
projet m. plan
(se) **protéger** to protect (oneself)
prune f. plum
punir to punish
pur pure

quand when
quarante forty
quart m. quarter
quartorze fourteen
quatre four
quatre-vingt-dix ninety
quatre-vingts eighty
quatre-vingt-un eighty-one
que that; what? **qu'est-ce que?**
   what? **Qu'est-ce que c'est?** What
   is it?
quel(le) what, which
quelqu'un someone
quelque chose something
quelquefois sometimes
quelques a few
qui who; whom
quinze fifteen
quoi? what?
quotidien daily

radis m. radish
raisin m. grapes
ramasser to gather up
randonnée f. hike
ranger to straighten
rapidement quickly, fast
raquette f. racket
rayon m. ray
recevoir to receive
recherche f. research
rédacteur (f. **rédactrice**) editor
regarder, to look at; to watch
règle f. ruler
remplir to fill (out)
renard m. fox
rendez-vous m. date, meeting
rentrée f. back-to-school day
renvoyer to send back
repas m. meal
répéter to repeat
répondre to answer
réponse f. answer

responsabilité f. responsibility
rester remain, stay
rideau m. curtain
rien nothing
rire to laugh
robe f. dress
rosbif m. roast beef
rose pink
rouge red
rougir to blush
rue f. street
russe Russian
Russie f. Russia

sa f. his, her, its
sac m. pocketbook; **sac à dos** m.
   backpack
sait see savoir
saisir to grab, seize
saison f. season
sale dirty
salle à manger f. dining room
salle de bains f. bathroom
salle de classe f. classroom
salon m. living room
saluer to greet
salut hi, bye
samedi m. Saturday
sans without; **sans doute** without
   a doubt
saucisse f. sausage
sauter to jump
sauvage wild
savant m. scientist
savoir to know
secrétaire m./f. secretary
seize sixteen
séjour m. living room, great
   room
sel m. salt
selon according to
sept seven
septembre m. September
serveur m. waiter
serveuse f. waitress
servir to serve; **se servir de** to use
serviette f. napkin
ses his, her, its
seul only
si so
s'il te plaît, s'il vous plaît please
singe m. monkey
six six
société f. company
sœur f. sister
soir m. evening
soixante et onze seventy-one
soixante sixty
soixante-dix seventy

soixante-douze seventy-two
son m. her, his, its
sorte f. type
sortir to go out
sou m. penny
sous-sol m. basement
spécialité f. specialty
spectateur m. spectator
stade m. stadium
stylo m. pen
sucre m. sugar
super great
supermarché m. supermarket
sur on
surpris surprised
surtout especially
survêtement m. jogging suit
sympathique nice

ta f. your
tableau m. picture; **tableau (noir)**
   m. chalkboard, blackboard
tailleur m. woman's suit
tant de so much
tante f. aunt
tas m. heap, pile
tasse f. cup
technicien m. technician
téléphone sans fil m. cordless
   phone
télévision à grand écran f. large
   screen TV
terminus m. terminal
terre f. earth
tes m./f. your
tête f. head
thon m. tunafish
tiens well, hey
toi you
toilettes f. pl. restroom
tomate f. tomato
ton m. your
tour f. tower
tous all
tout all; everything; **tout à coup** all
   of a sudden; **tout d'un coup**
   suddenly; **tout le monde**
   everybody; **tout le temps** all the
   time
travail m. work
travailler to work
traverser to cross
treize thirteen
trente thirty
très very
triste sad
trois three
trop too much/ many
trouver to find

tu you
typique typical

un, une a, an, one
usine *f.* factory
utile useful
utiliser to use

vacances *f. pl.* vacation
vache *f.* cow

vanille *f.* vanilla
vaut: *see* **valoir** to be worth
veille *f.* eve
vélo *m.* bicycle
vendeur *m.* salesman
vendre to sell
vendredi *m.* Friday
verre *m.* glass
vert green
veste *f.* jacket

vêtements *m. pl.* clothing
vol *m.* flight
vos, votre your
vouloir to wish, to want
vous you
vrai true
vraiment really

yeux *m. pl.* eyes

English-French Vocabulary

a, an un, une
able: be able pouvoir
according to selon
acquaint: be acquainted with
    connaître
activity activité f.
actor acteur m.
actress actrice f.
adore adorer
afraid: be afraid avoir peur
African africain
after après
afternoon après-midi m./f.
again encore une fois
age âge m.
agreement accord m.
air-conditioned climatisé
airplane avion m.
airport aéroport m.
algebra algèbre f.
all tout, toute, tous, toutes; all the
    time tout le temps
alone seul
already déjà
also aussi
always toujours
ambassador ambassadeur m.
American américain
among parmi
amuse amuser
and et
animated animé
another un/une autre
answer répondre; réponse f.
apartment appartement m.
apartment house immeuble m.
applaud applaudir
apple pomme f.
April avril m.
argument dispute f.
arm bras m.
around autour de
arrange arranger
arrive arriver
artist artiste m./f.
ask demander
aspirin aspirine f.
associate associé
at a
August août m.
aunt tante f.
author auteur m.

autumn automne m.
avoid éviter

baby bébé m.
bad mauvais
bag sac m.
bakery boulangerie f.
banana banane f.
band: brass band fanfare f.
bank banque f.
bark aboyer
basement sous-sol m.
basket corbeille f., panier m.
bathing suit maillot de bain m.
bathroom salle de bains f.
be être; be able pouvoir; be ill
    aller mal; be well aller bien
beach plage f.
because parce que ; because of à
    cause de
bed lit m.
beef bœuf m.
before avant
begin (to) commencer (à)
behind derrière
belong to être à
belt ceinture f.
beside à côté de
best meilleur
bicycle bicyclette f.; vélo m.
big grand
bird oiseau m.
birthday anniversaire m.
black noir
blanket couverture f.
blond blond
blouse chemisier m.
blue bleu
blush rougir
board tableau m.
boat bateau m.
body corps m.
book livre m.
boot botte f.
boss patron m.
bottle bouteille f.
boy garçon m.
bread pain m.
breakfast petit déjeuner m.
bring apporter
brother frère m.
brown brun

brunette brune
building édifice m.; immeuble m.
bus autobus m.
bus stop arrêt de bus m.
busy occupé
but mais
butcher shop boucherie f.
butter beurre m.
buy acheter
by par

café café m.
cake gâteau m.
calculator calculateur m.
call appeler; be called s'appeler
camcorder caméscope m.
camera (digital) appareil m. photo
    (numérique)
can pouvoir
Canadian canadien(ne)
car automobile f., voiture f.
card carte f.; postcard carte
    postale
careful! be careful! attention!
carrot carotte f.
castle château m.
cat chat m.
cathedral cathédrale f.
cell phone (téléphone) cellulaire
    m. (Canada); mobile m. (France)
cent centime m.
central central
cereal céréales f. pl.
certain certain
certainly certainement
chair chaise f.
chalk craie f.
chalk board tableau m.
character personnage m.
charming charmant
check addition f.
cheese fromage m.
chemistry chimie f.
cherry cerise f.
chicken poulet m., poule f.
child enfant m./f.
China Chine f.
Chinese chinois
chocolate chocolat m.
choose choisir
Christmas Noël m.
church église f.

circus cirque *m.*
city ville *f.*; **in the city** en ville
class classe *f.*
close fermer
clothes vêtements *m. pl.*
coat manteau *m.*
coffee café *m.*
cold froid; **be cold** avoir froid; **be cold** (*weather*) faire froid
combination combinaison *f.*
comfortable confortable
computer ordinateur *m.*
confused confus
congratulations félicitations *f. pl.*
content content
contest concours *m.*
contrary: **on the contrary** au contraire
convenient commode
cook cuisinier *m.* cuisinière *f.*
cord fil *m.*
cordless sans fil
corn maïs *m.*
cornflakes flocons de maïs *m. pl.*
cost coûter
costume costume *m.*
count compter
country pays *m.*; campagne *f.*
course cours *m.*
cousin cousin *m.*, cousine *f.*
cover couverture *f.*
cow vache *f.*
crazy fou (*f.* folle)
cream crème *f.*
create créer
criminal criminel *m.*
cross traverser
cruel cruel (*f.* cruelle)
cup tasse *f.*
current courant *m.*
cycling cyclisme *m.*

daily quotidien(ne)
dance danser; danse *f.*
darling chéri *m.*, chérie *f.*
daughter fille *f.*
day jour *m.*; journée *f.*, **the next day** le lendemain
dear cher (*f.* chère)
December décembre *m.*
decide décider
defend défendre; **defend oneself** se défendre
delicatessen charcuterie *f.*
delicious délicieux (-euse)
dentist dentiste *m./f.*
design dessin *m.*
desk bureau *m.*
dessert dessert *m.*

dictionary dictionnaire *m.*
different différent
difficult difficile
dine dîner
dining room salle à manger *f.*
dinner dîner *m.*
dirty sale
disappointed déçu
disaster désastre *m.*
discuss discuter
disguised déguisé
dish plat *m.*
divide diviser
doctor docteur *m.*, médecin *m.*
dog chien *m.*
dollar dollar *m.*
door porte *f.*
down: **go down** descendre
dozen douzaine *f.*
dress robe *f.*
drink boire
driver chauffeur *m.*
during pendant
DVD player lecteur *m.* de DVD
dynamic dynamique

each chaque
ear oreille *f.*
earn gagner
earth terre *f.*
Easter Pâques *f. pl.*
easy facile
eat manger
editor rédacteur *m.*, rédactrice *f.*
egg œuf *m.*; **hard-boiled egg** œuf dur
eight huit
eighteen dix-huit
eighty quatre-vingts
electricity électricité *f.*
elegant élégant
elephant éléphant *m.*
eleven onze
enemy ennemi *m.*
England Angleterre *f.*
English anglais
enormous énorme
enough assez (de)
enter entrer
escape échapper
especially surtout
evening soir *m.*; **good evening** bonsoir
event événement *m.*
ever jamais
every tout, toute, tous, toutes; **everybody** tout le monde; **everything** tout; **everywhere** partout

exact précis
example exemple *m.*; **for example** par exemple
exceptional exceptionnel(le)
excite exciter
excuse me pardon!
exercise exercice *m.*
expensive cher (*f.* chère)
explain expliquer
extraordinary extraordinaire
eye œil *m.* (*pl.* yeux)

face figure *f.*
factory usine *f.*
false faux (*f.* fausse)
family famille *f.*
famous célèbre
far loin; **far from** loin de
farm ferme *f.*
fat gros (*f.* grosse)
father père *m.*
favorite préféré
February février *m.*
feel sentir
ferocious féroce
few peu *m.*
fifteen quinze
fifty cinquante
fill remplir
film film *m.*
finally enfin, finalement
find trouver
finger doigt *m.*
finish finir
fire feu *m.*; **fireworks** feu d'artifice
fireman pompier *m.*
first premier; **at first** d'abord
fish poisson *m.*
fish store poissonnerie *f.*
five cinq
flake flocon *m.*
flat plat
float flotter
floor étage *m.*
flower fleur *f.*
flu grippe *f.*
fly voler
food aliments *m. pl.*
foolishness bêtise *f.*
foot pied *m.*
for pour; **for example** par exemple
forget oublier
fork fourchette *f.*
forty quarante
four quatre
fourteen quatorze
fox renard *m.*
France France *f.*

frankfurter saucisse *f.*, hot-dog *m.*
free libre
French français
Friday vendredi *m.*
friend ami *m.*, amie *f.*: copain *m.*, copine *f.*
from de
front: in front of devant
fruit fruit *m.*
funny drôle

game jeu *m.*, partie *f.*, match *m.*
game station console *f.* de jeux vidéo
garden jardin *m.*
gas essence *f.*; **gas station** station-service *f.*
generally généralement
German allemand
Germany Allemagne *f.*
gift cadeau *m.*
girl (jeune) fille *f.*
give donner
glass verre *m.*
glove gant *m.*
go aller
goal but *m.*
goat chèvre *f.*
God Dieu *m.*
good bon (*f.* bonne)
good-bye au revoir
gorilla gorille *m.*
gracious gracieux (*f.* gracieuse)
grade note *f.*
grandfather grand-père *m.*
grandmother grand-mère *f.*
grandchildren petits-enfants *m. pl.*
grass herbe *f.*
ground floor rez-de-chaussée *m.*
gray gris
great superbe
green vert
greet saluer
grilled grillé
grocery store épicerie *f.*
group groupe *m.*
guitar guitare *f.*

hair cheveux *m. pl.*; *(body)* poils *m. pl.*
Haiti Haïti *f.*
Haitian haïtien (*f.* haïtienne)
half demi; **a half hour** une demi-heure
ham jambon *m.*
hand main *f.*
handsome beau (*f.* belle)
happiness bonheur *m.*
happy content

hard dur
hat chapeau *m.*
hate détester
have avoir
he il
head tête *f.*
hear entendre
heart cœur *m.*
heat chaleur *f.*
hello bonjour
help aider
her son, sa, ses; elle; la; lui
here ici; **here is, here are** voici
hi salut
him le, lui
his son, sa, ses
history histoire *f.*
holiday fête *f.*
homework devoirs *m. pl.*
horse cheval *m.*
hospital hôpital *m.*
hot chaud; **to be hot** avoir chaud; **to be hot** *(weather)* faire chaud
hotel hôtel *m.*
hour heure *f.*
house maison *f.*; **at the house of** chez
housework ménage *m.*; **do the housework** faire le ménage
how comment; **how are you** comment allez-vous; comment vas-tu?; **how's it going?** ça va? **how many, much** combien de
hundred cent
hunger faim *f.*
hungry: be hungry avoir faim
husband mari *m.*
hypnotist hypnotiseur *m.*

I je, moi
ice cream glace *f.*
idea idée *f.*
identify identifier
immediately tout de suite
important important
impossible impossible
in en, dans; **in order to** pour
intelligent intelligent
interesting intéressant
invite inviter
island île *f.*
isn't that so? n'est-ce pas?
it il, elle, le, la; **it is** c'est
Italian italien (*f.* italienne)
Italy Italie *f.*
its son, sa, ses

jacket veste *f.*
January janvier *m.*

Japan Japon *m.*
Japanese japonais
joke blaguer
juice jus *m.*
July juillet *m.*
jump sauter
June juin *m.*

key clef *f.*
kiss embrasser
kitchen cuisine *f.*
knife couteau *m.*
know savoir, connaître

lamp lampe *f.*
language langue *f.*
laptop (ordinateur) portable *m.*
late tard, en retard
laugh rire
lawyer avocat *m.*, avocate *f.*
lazy paresseux (-euse)
learn apprendre
least: at least au moins
leave laisser
left gauche; **on/to the left** à gauche
leg jambe *f.*
lesson leçon *f.*
letter lettre *f.*
lettuce laitue *f.*
library bibliothèque *f.*
life vie *f.*
likable aimable
like comme; *(verb)* aimer
lion lion *m.*
lip lèvre *f.*
list liste *f.*
listen écouter
little petit; peu
live vivre; *(reside in)* habiter
long long (*f.* longue)
look at regarder
look for chercher
love aimer; amour *m.*
low bas
luck chance *f.*
lucky: to be lucky avoir de la chance
lunch déjeuner *m.*

magazine magazine *m.*
magnificent magnifique
mail carrier facteur *m.*, factrice *f.*
make faire
man homme *m.*
many beaucoup
March mars *m.*
market marché *m.*
mask masque *m.*
master maître *m.*

match match *m.*
mathematics mathématiques (maths) *f. pl.*
matter: no matter n'importe; it doesn't matter cela ne fait rien
May mai *m.*
me moi
meal repas *m.*
means moyen *m.*
meat viande *f.*
medicine médecine *f.*; médicament *m.*
meeting rendez-vous *m.*
member membre *m.*
menu menu *m.*, carte *f.*
merchant marchand
midnight minuit *f.*
milk lait *m.*
million million *m.*
minus moins
minute minute *f.*
miss mademoiselle *f.*
mister monsieur *m.*
modern moderne
moment moment *m.*
Monday lundi *m.*
money argent *m.*
monkey singe *m.*
monster monstre *m.*
monstrous monstrueux (*f.* -euse)
month mois *m.*
monument monument *m.*
more plus; more than plus de
morning matin *m.*
mother mère *f.*, maman *f.*
motor moteur *m.*
motorcycle motocyclette *f.*
mouse souris *f.*
mouth bouche *f.*
movie film *m.*
movies cinéma *m.*
Mr. monsieur
Mrs. madame, Mme
much: so much tant
muscle muscle *m.*
museum musée *m.*
music musique *f.*
mustard moutarde *f.*
my mon, ma, mes

name nom *m.*; what is your name? comment vous appelez-vous?, comment t'appelles-tu?, my name is je m'appelle
napkin serviette *f.*
nation nation *f.*
naturally naturellement
near près; near to près de
necessary nécessaire

neck cou *m.*
need avoir besoin de
neither . . . nor ne . . . ni . . . ni
never ne . . . jamais
new nouveau (*f.* nouvelle)
newspaper journal *m.*
next prochain
nice sympathique, gentil (*f.* gentille), aimable
night nuit *f.*
nine neuf
nineteen dix-neuf
ninety quatre-vingt-dix
no non
noise bruit *m.*
noon midi *m.*
nose nez *m.*
not ne . . . pas
notebook cahier *m.*
nothing ne . . . rien
notice apercevoir
November novembre *m.*
now maintenant
number numéro *m.*
nurse infirmier *m.*, infirmière *f.*

obey obéir
observe observer
ocean océan *m.*
October octobre *m.*
of de; of course bien sûr
offer offrir
official officiel(le)
O.K. d'accord, ça va
old âgé, vieux (*f.* vieille)
omelet omelette *f.*
on sur
one un: (*a person*) on,
only seulement, seul
open ouvrir; opened ouvert
operator téléphoniste *m./f.*
opinion opinion *f.*
or ou
orange orange *f.*
orangeade orangeade *f.*
order: in order to pour
ordinary ordinaire
organization organisation *f.*
other autre
our notre, nos
out of hors; out of service hors de service
oven four *m.*; microwave oven four à micro-ondes
owner propriétaire *m.*

pair paire *f.*
palm tree palmier *m.*
pants pantalon *m.*

paper papier *m.* ; piece, sheet of paper feuille *f.* de papier
parade défilé *m.*
parent parent *m.*
park parc *m.*
part part *f.*, partie *f.*
party fête *f.*, boum *f.*
pastry shop pâtisserie *f.*
pay payer
peanut cacahouète *f.*
pear poire *f.*
peas petits pois *m. pl.*
pen stylo *m.*
pencil crayon *m.*
people gens *m. pl.*
pepper poivre *m.*
perfect parfait
perhaps peut-être
person personne *f.*
pharmacy pharmacie *f.*
photograph photographie *f.*
physics physique *f.*
picnic pique-nique *m.*
picture tableau *m.*, photo *f.*
pig cochon *m.*
pile tas *m.*
pink rose
pity: it's a pity c'est dommage
place lieu *m.*, endroit *m.*
plate assiette *f.*
play jouer
player lecteur *m.*; (DVD) player lecteur de DVD
please s'il te plaît, s'il vous plaît
pleasure plaisir *m.*
pocket poche *f.*
pocketbook sac *m.*
poem poème *m.*
police officer agent de police *m./f.*
pool piscine *f.*
poor pauvre
popular populaire
pork porc *m.*
portable portable, portatif *adj*; portable *m.*
possible possible
postcard carte postale *f.*
potato pomme de terre *f.*
practical pratique
practice pratiquer
prepare préparer
president président *m.*
pretty joli
price prix *m.*
private privé
prize prix *m.*
program programme *m.*
protect protéger
provoke provoquer

pullover pull-over *m.*
punish punir
purple mauve
put mettre; **put on** mettre

quarter quart *m.*
quickly vite, rapidement

rabbit lapin *m.*
radio radio *f.*
radish radis *m.*
rain pluie *f.;* **it's raining** il pleut
raise lever
rapidly rapidement, vite
read lire
reason raison *f.*
red rouge
repair réparer
report card bulletin scolaire *m.*
research recherche *f., (verb)*
    rechercher
rest reste *m.*
restaurant restaurant *m.*
return rentrée *f.*
rice riz *m.*
rich riche
right droit; **on/to the right** à droite
right: be right avoir raison
roast(ed) rôti
room chambre *f.,* pièce *f.*
rule règle *f.*
ruler règle *f.*
run courir
Russia Russie *f.*
Russian russe

sad triste
salad salade *f.*
salt sel *m.*
same même
sandwich sandwich *m.*
Saturday samedi *m.*
sausage saucisse *f.*
savage sauvage
say dire
school école *f.;* **high school**
    lycée *m.*
scientific scientifique
scientist savant *m.,* savante *f.*
screen écran *m.*
sea mer *f.*
season saison *f.*
secretary secrétaire *m./f.*
see voir; **see you later** à tout à
    l'heure
selfish égoïste
sell vendre
seller vendeur *(f.* vendeuse*)*
send envoyer

September septembre *m.*
serious sérieux *(f.* sérieuse*)*
serve servir
set the table mettre le couvert
setting lieu *m.*
seven sept
seventeen dix-sept
seventy soixante-dix
several plusieurs
share part *f.*
she elle
sheep mouton *m.*
shirt chemise *f.,* chemisier *m.*
shoe chaussure *f.*
short court
shy timide
sick malade
side: at the side of au bord de
sing chanter
singer chanteur *m.*
sir monsieur
sister sœur *f.*
six six
sixteen seize
sixty soixante
skate patin *m.*
skinny mince
skirt jupe *f.*
sky ciel *m.*
sleep sommeil *m.;* **to be sleepy**
    avoir sommeil
small petit
snow neige *f.;* **it's snowing** il neige
so alors; **so so** comme ci
    comme ça
soap opera feuilleton *m.*
sociable sociable
sock chaussette *f.*
sofa divan *m.,* canapé *m.*
some quelques, un peu de
someone quelqu'un
something quelque chose
son fils *m.*
song chanson *f.*
soon bientôt; **see you soon** à
    bientôt; **as soon as** dès que
soup soupe *f.*
south sud *m.*
Spain Espagne *f.*
Spanish espagnol
speak parler
specialty spécialité *f.*
spend *(time)* passer; *(money)*
    dépenser
spice épice *f.*
spinach épinards *m. pl.*
splendid splendide, épatant
spoon cuiller *f.*
sport sport *m.*

sporty sportif
spring printemps *m.*
stadium stade *m.*
stairs escalier *m.*
station gare *f.*
stay rester
steak bifteck *m.*
steal voler
still encore
stocking bas *m.*
stomach estomac *m.*
stop arrêt *m.;* **bus stop** arrêt de
    bus; **subway stop** station de
    métro
store magasin *m.,* boutique *f.*
story histoire *f.*
strange étrange
street rue *f.*
string bean haricot vert *m.*
strong fort
student élève *m./f.* étudiant(e)
study étudier; étude *f.*
stupid stupide
style mode *f.*
stylish à la mode, chic
subject sujet *m.;* matière *f.*
subway métro *m.*
such as tel que
suddenly tout à coup
sugar sucre *m.*
suit costume *m.,* tailleur *m.*
suitable convenable
summer été *m.*
sun soleil *m.;* **to be sunny** faire du
    soleil
Sunday dimanche *m.*
supermarket supermarché *m.*
sure sûr
surprise surprise *f.;* **surprise party**
    surprise-partie *f.*
surprised surpris
swear jurer
swim nager
swimming natation *f.*
Switzerland Suisse *f.*

table table *f.*
take prendre
taste goûter
taxi taxi *m.*
teacher professeur *m.,* maître *m.*
team équipe *f.*
telephone téléphone *m.*
television télévision *f.*
ten dix
terminal terminus *m.*
terrible terrible, affreux *(f.*
    affreuse*)*
terrific formidable

terror terreur *f.*
test examen *m.*
text texte *m.*
thanks to grâce à
thank you merci
that ce, cela, cet, cette; que
the le, la, les
theater théâtre *m.*
their leur, leurs
there là; **there is, there are** voilà, il y a
these ces
they ils, elles
thief voleur *m.*
thing chose *f.*
think penser
thirst soif *f.;* **to be thirsty** avoir soif
thirteen treize
thirty trente
this ce, cet, cette; **this is** c'est
thousand mille
three trois
throw jeter
Thursday jeudi *m.*
ticket window guichet *m.*
tie cravate *f.*
tiger tigre *m.*
time temps *m.;* **have a good time** s'amuser
times fois
timid timide
title titre *m.*
to à
toasted grillé
today aujourd'hui
tomato tomate *f.*
tomorrow demain
too aussi; trop; **too much** trop de
tooth dent *f.*
toward vers, envers
tower tour *f.*
train train *m.*
transportation transport *m.*
tree arbre *m.*

trip voyage *m.;* **take a trip** faire un voyage
true vrai
Tuesday mardi *m.*
tunafish thon *m.*
turnip navet *m.*
twelve douze
twenty vingt
two deux; **the two of us** nous deux
type sorte *f.*
typewriter machine à écrire *f.*
typical typique

ugly laid
uncle oncle *m.*
under sous
unforgettable inoubliable
United Nations Nations Unies *f. pl.*
United States États-Unis *m. pl.*
university université *f.*
use employer, utiliser, se servir de
useful utile

vacation vacances *f. pl.*
vanilla vanille *f.*
vegetable légume *m.;* **raw vegetable** crudité *f.*
very très
video cassette recorder (VCR) magnétoscope *m.*
view vue *f.*
village village *m.*
visit visiter

wait (for) attendre
waiter serveur *m.*, garçon *m. (obs.)*
waitress serveuse *f.*
walk marcher; promenade *f.;* **take a walk** faire une promenade
walkman baladeur *m.*
want désirer, vouloir
warm chaud; **to be warm** avoir chaud; **to be warm** *(weather)* faire chaud
watch regarder; montre *f.*
water eau *f.*

we nous
wear porter
weather temps *m.;* **what is the weather?** quel temps fait-il?
Wednesday mercredi *m.*
week semaine *f.*
welcome bienvenu; **you are welcome!** de rien!
well bien
what que, quel(le)
when quand
where où
white blanc (*f.* blanche)
who qui
why pourquoi
wife femme *f.*
win gagner
wind vent *m.;* **be windy** faire du vent
window fenêtre *f.*
wine vin *m.*
winter hiver *m.*
wise sage
wish vouloir, désirer
with avec
without sans
wolf loup *m.*
woman femme *f.*
wool laine *f.*
word mot *m.*
work travailler, marcher; travail *m.*
world monde *m.*
worth: **it is worth** il vaut
write écrire

year an *m.*, année *f.*
yellow jaune
yes oui
yesterday hier
yet encore
you tu, vous, toi
young jeune
your votre, vos, ton, ta, tes

zero zéro
zoo zoo *m.*, jardin zoologique *m.*

Grammatical Index

Topical Index